CONSCIENCE AND COMMAND
A Motive Theory of Law

SCHOLARS PRESS
Studies in the Humanities

CONSCIENCE AND COMMAND
A Motive Theory of Law

by

Dale Segrest

Scholars Press
Atlanta, Georgia

CONSCIENCE AND COMMAND
A Motive Theory of Law

by

Dale Segrest

©1994
Scholars Press

The author acknowledges the use of extracts from the following sources:

Approximately 1500 Words from *Motivation and Personality,* 3rd Ed. by Abraham H. Maslow. Revised by Robert Frager, James Fadiman, Cynthia McReynolds, and Ruth Cox. Copyright 1954, © 1987 by Harper & Row, Publishers, Inc. Copyright © 1970 by Abraham H. Maslow. Reprinted by permission of HarperCollins Publishers, Inc.

Campbell, Joseph; *Hero With a Thousand Faces.* Copyright © 1949 (renewed) by Princeton University Press. Reprinted by permission of Princeton University Press.

"Law Like Love", from *Collected Poems* by W. H. Auden. Copyright © 1940 and renewed 1968 by W. H. Auden. Reprinted by permission of Random House, Inc.

Extracts reprinted with the permission of the Free Press, a Division of Macmillan, Inc. from *The Elementary Forms of the Religious Life* by Émile Durkheim, translated by Joseph Ward Swain. Copyright © George Allen & Unvin, Ltd.; Free Press Paperback Edition 1965.

Library of Congress Cataloging in Publication Data
Segrest, Dale, 1942-
    Conscience and command : a motive theory of law / by Dale Segrest ; edited by Harry W. Gilmer.
       p.   cm. — (Scholars Press studies in the humanities ; 18)
    Includes bibliographical references.
    ISBN 1-55540-970-9 (acid-free paper). — ISBN 1-55540-971-7 (acid-free paper)
    1. Law—Philosophy. 2. Faith and reason. 3. Conscience.
I. Gilmer, Harry W. (Harry Wesley) II. Title. III. Series:
Scholars Press studies in the humanities series ; 18.
K240.S44   1994
340'.1—dc20   94-12526
                                         CIP

Printed in the United States of America
on acid-free paper

To Betty, Philip and Mike

Contents

Preface

So many have assisted in preparing this volume that I can hardly write adequate acknowledgements. Even when I ignore friends, colleagues, teachers, students, and other acquaintances who have discussed these ideas with me, without actually looking at the manuscript, the list remains embarrassingly long. At least forty persons have read and commented on the manuscript at some stage of its evolution. I heard their comments and took them to heart. Suggestions from readers materially affected the final product.

By mentioning names, I intend simply to express deep gratitude for helpfulness and kindness; I certainly do not imply endorsement of the ideas set forth in this volume. I don't know if any reader agreed totally with every idea expressed here. Without blaming these ideas on anyone other than myself, I hope that listing the names and general background of persons who examined all or part of the manuscript in some way reflects my sincere desire for accuracy and authenticity in the argument presented.

I cannot possibly assign priority to the importance of comments received from readers. Every review was valuable and made a unique contribution. W. C. Bryant, a librarian at Tallassee Public Library, read and edited more than one edition of the manuscript. Dr. Paul Pruitt, historian and legal librarian, compiled an excellent bibliography of jurisprudence for my use, in addition to reading and commenting on a draft of the manuscript. Robin Foster and her colleagues at Dadeville Public Library and Horseshoe Bend Regional Library made available, via Alabama's Inter-Library Loan Service, many volumes that would otherwise have been inaccessible to a busy rural trial judge. Robin also read the manuscript and discussed ideas.

Craig Williams, M.D., psychiatrist, generously read and commented on various editions of the manuscript and made suggestions for further study. Without his encouragement, I probably could not have completed the project. Psychiatrist James Hooper, M.D., made valuable comments. From the field of psychology, Dr. Kathy Ronan, Mr. Jimmy McCain, and Dr. Marvin Grunzke, read and discussed various drafts. A number of members of the clergy also made helpful reviews: Dr. Larry Davis, Bishop C. W. Hancock, Dr. John Trobaugh, and Rev. Dan Morris. I am indebted to Dr. Trobaugh for suggesting Right-Writer software program for text editing!

A number of persons from the academic world took time to read and comment: Dr. Curtis Coleman, Chair of the Department of Religion and Philosophy at Athens College; Dr. Mark Ledbetter, Chair of the Department of Religion and Philosophy at Huntingdon College; Dean Nate Hansford, University of Alabama Law School; Ms. Susan Randall, University of Alabama Law School; Mr. Mark Miller, Emory University Law School; Jack and Olivia Solomon, authors and retired teachers of literature and folklore; and Dr. Elaine Hughes, English Professor at the University of Montevallo.

Several attorneys read and discussed the manuscript: Delores Boyd, Fred Gray, Sr., E. Paul Jones, Blaine Stephens, Larkin Radney, June Lynn, Clay Hornsby, Larry Morris and Tom Radney. People from several law related vocations helped: Probation Officer Ted Box; Frank Gregory, Director of the Alabama Judicial College; Tom Gilkerson, corrections research director; and social worker Lu Tosch. Secretaries Violet Burke and Teresa Huff typed portions of the manuscript, and they also read and commented. Even with their capable assistance and patience, I would never have accomplished the numerous revisions without WordPerfect in the home computer!

Then there were those who read, mainly to assure me that the book was readable: Suanne Chapman, Shelley Collinsworth, Debbie Gordon, Martha Simplinski. And finally, this manuscript and these ideas have been the basis for endless conversation for many years with my son, Philip, who grew up with the project and probably should be listed as co-author.

A concerted effort has been made to acknowledge the work of all writers on whose works I have relied. Their ideas, and where appropriate, permissions, are deeply appreciated. I hope that my effort here will stir greater interest in their works. I have borrowed ideas from many writers and thinkers. If I fail to acknowledge another's idea, the oversight is unintentional. I have made a concerted effort to give proper credit to other writers. Authenticity of my work depends on the credibility of source material which comes from those writers. However, I am responsible for the synthesis of ideas and accept personal blame for any errors.

The book contains extensive quotes from both original and secondary sources. Quotes give credit where credit is due. They make references and sources clear. Quotes present short, scholarly summaries of large, comprehensive ideas from experts in various fields. Thus, they authenticate concepts borrowed from fields of study other than my own. Since the material is quoted, the reader can judge whether I have misconstrued.

The connection between law and faith is intimate. I hope that the labyrinthine course that I have followed in my argument does not obscure that intimacy. Choosing an outline for the ideas was perhaps the most formidable obstacle. All the ideas are intimately connected and any chapter could have been the first chapter. The book will read best from front to back, not because of the way the ideas are connected internally, but because of the way I have presented them.

I should also note a significant difficulty in discovery or creation of a vocabulary for these ideas. The entire work attempts to create a new paradigm that relates law and faith. It draws on a number of disciplines, and terminology is borrowed liberally from the disciplines of psychology, sociology, philosophy, jurisprudence, anthropology and mythology. Often as I explored these disciplines, I found overlapping terminology. Words such as archetype, collective representation, open instinct and *a priori* ideas all seem to stand for quite similar concepts, for instance. One difficulty of a cross-disciplinary study such as the present one is lack of a common vocabulary. Clearly, all four of these ideas have much in common, but each social scientist has assigned different words. Perhaps differences in the concepts justify the different terminologies, but the differences make it difficult to see the remarkable similarities. Also, to express certain ideas, it was necessary to assign new or expanded meaning to words. Examples of words and phrases assigned special or expanded meaning include *mythos, motive, authentication, church, ecology, faith, archetype, age of reason, articulation* and *environment*. The special or expanded meaning of these words and others will unfold in the context in which the words are used, and it would be ineffective to attempt definitions here. The only word that requires special discussion here is *motive*. It is used both as an adjective and a noun. Often it means motivation or motivational, but if these terms were substituted, then phrases such as motivation theory, which already has specific meaning, would begin to appear and confuse. Besides, *motive* is a good short word that actually fits.

I divided the work into sections that are somewhat complete in themselves: an overview that describes the problem under consideration; a discussion of psychological components of law; a discussion of mythos; a discussion of territoriality that demonstrates the motive theory of law; a discussion of applications of the theory; and a culminating discussion of faith. The effort to make these sections understandable when read independently of other sections causes repetition. The tremendous interrelatedness of all the ideas makes repetition unavoidable. Throughout the text, I frequently summarize, review, recapitulate and preview. For some, this approach may be tedious. However, relationships between and among all these ideas can scarcely be captured in any other way. Each repetition restates an idea in order to add something to it.

As mentioned earlier, the ideas discussed in this volume draw on a wide range of disciplines and experience. They did not occur to me in the order in which I present them. For example, I had contemplated Jungian archetypes and reflective existence for several years before I zeroed in on *conscience* as a basis for law. I cannot explain why I was so slow in realizing the importance of the contribution of conscience to law. Although I had been familiar with the Freudian *super-ego* for many years, I simply did not make the connection. The ideas are presented here in the order that seems to me to make the clearest presentation of the material. The existential idea of *reflective existence* came into focus for me during the 1970s. Of course, it was not original with me, but I applied it to law and moral formation. We develop our self-concept by seeing how others react to us. This was one of the first ideas that occurred to me. I eventually realized that I was re-inventing the wheel. I was *rediscovering* processes of conscience formation that Sigmund Freud described long ago. I had started to put my ideas into words before I realized the importance of basic human needs or drives as described by Maslow. Basic needs explain much about human motive. They are a vital link in explaining what makes law happen.

Unfortunately, ignorance has no way of plumbing its own depths. I continued struggling with these ideas for several years. However, I finally realized there is a connection between and among all of them. The idea of *mythos* helped me to pull it all together. Then I discovered Joseph Campbell and Emile Durkheim. Everything cleared up. Mythology and psychology are the twin towers of law, relating individuals to society.

I am a reader. Much of my reading material has been different from that of most people in the general reading public and the legal community. It has been an interesting journey. Along the way I became familiar with C. G. Jung, Joseph Campbell, Emile Durkheim, Abraham Maslow, Robert Ardrey, Mircea Eliade, Erik Erikson, James Fowler, William James, Carl Menninger, Rachel Carson, Will Durant and many others. Assembly of the ideas has been an arduous and time-consuming task, but it has been a labor of love.

My research method has been unorthodox. I have allowed interest to lead me from one writer to another. Often, discussion of ideas has sparked suggestions from friends. Once an idea dawns and begins to grow, it is exciting to find a writer who has had similar thoughts and made similar associations. In some instances, discovery of such writers is purely *synchronistic*. Synchronism is a term used by C. G. Jung to convey the interrelatedness of all things. It explains the connection between events that have no apparent causal connection. Jung sometimes described it as an "acausal connecting principle." After realizing that a certain point exists and is important, I have often *accidentally* found confirming literature within a matter of days. My hunger for knowledge in areas such as psychology and philosophy may exceed my digestion of the subject matter. Nevertheless, ideas emerged as a result of reading in diverse fields that otherwise would not have occurred to me.

The reading, writing, and discussing have been great fun. To all those who have participated in this effort, accept my gratitude. It has been a special pleasure to work with Harry Gilmer and his associates at Scholars Press in the production of this work. I hope that publication will simply bring this dialogue to a new level of intensity.

Introduction

L aw quietly directs the activities of organized society. Efforts to define it—to capture its essence in words—have proved notably unsuccessful, although many have tried. Its gripping force to motivate human behavior remains an enigma. My earliest recollection about law centers on conversations in which adults said, *"It's against the law."* These words placed off limits the proscribed activity. The very word *law* evokes a deep response and reaction within most of us.

Beneath the dry, uninteresting exterior of law is an intriguing panorama of forces. Psychology, sociology, theology, and mythology describe forces that cause law to happen. Mythology receives serious study in the social science called anthropology. We cannot separate law from forces described in these sciences. The motive for law involves the subject matter of these disciplines. Law also relates closely to other studies such as history, political science, ethology, and religion. We need to understand in a new way the relationship of these disciplines to law.

We are sometimes cynical of our courts and legislative bodies. We comment unfavorably on their effectiveness. Nevertheless, we have innate faith in *law* and *justice.* We believe there is a legal solution to our controversies. We believe that correct answers exist and that we can find them. Do we forget that mere mortals run our courts? Our certainty that law will solve our conflicts is essential to effective operation of the legal system. Should that certainty disappear, society could not enforce law. We could not hire enough officers to do the job, if everyone chose to ignore law. Loss of our innate, often unconscious, faith in law would be disastrous. Such loss of faith would lead to chaos and anarchy. If we understand law's power source, we can promote the necessary faith in law and the values which support it.

Society must maintain profound respect for law. This is especially true for those of us who bear the sacred trust of personifying, embodying, teaching and pronouncing law. This book seeks a better understanding of forces that move the machinery of law. Perhaps it will help those who teach, make, interpret and enforce law to understand law's power sources more completely. This book calls for deeper understanding between the legal community and other disciplines.

Anyone who has not attended law school may assume that law schools deal with the matters discussed here. They do not. Law school courses in legal philosophy are usually elective. Law schools do not usually require students to take courses in philosophy, ethics, political science, psychology, sociology, anthropology, religion, or theology. I am not criticizing the training provided in law schools. Law schools prepare law students to deal with the existing legal system. They do not have time to cover all the background material discussed here.

Time constraints are not the only reason for not including this material in the curriculum. Legal philosophy has not accurately identified the true nature of law. Our philosophers do not see law as a *dynamic process*. Therefore, the approach which I advocate has not been available to law schools. Professionals in the legal field relate concepts discussed in this volume solely to disciplines other than law. Lawyers and judges generally do not understand that we cannot separate motive forces of law from the dynamics of psychology, sociology and other social sciences. However, without knowledge available from these sources, we cannot begin to understand the motive force of law. Our knowledge is divided along disciplinary lines.

One result of the complexity of civilization is specialization. Our division of knowledge into specialized fields of study is often artificial. We divide knowledge into fields although reality may be indivisible. As a result, the right hand often doesn't know what the left hand is doing. Lawyers and judges often have little understanding of psychology and sociology. This book discusses principles from several different disciplines. It is a new approach, in which I describe law's basis in human motive force.

Law is an integral part of a larger, holistic system of social control. Unless we understand that law's force comes from society and the individuals that compose it, we see law as a *rational* system, complete within itself. Such an approach is both dangerous and inadequate. Today we are realizing the interdependency of ecological systems. Law is such a system. Nature relates humans to each other and to their larger environment, and law arises from the resulting relationships.

This book is not written as a law school text, nor is it directed solely to a legal audience, although I sincerely hope that law schools will soon integrate these ideas into the curriculum. The book is intended for a general audience. If my analysis is sound, solutions to many problems facing the legal system lie beyond the legal establishment. The writing style is deliberately suitable for non-lawyers. Professionals from other disciplines, together with the general reading public, can cause the legal community to take a close look at itself. The examination is needed.

In describing motive for law, I have delved into other areas of knowledge quite extensively. I have spent more time weaving canvas than I have spent painting the picture. This makes the image more intelligible. Non-specific references to psychology, sociology, and mythology are meaningless. For the motive for law to be clear, principles borrowed from disciplines that describe motive forces must also be clear.

This book is about human activities that we call law. It is about motive forces for those activities. Development of these ideas occurred to me gradually over many years. Law has vitally affected me and the communities of which I am a part. A bit of personal background will make the ideas more understandable.

My Territory

The Creek Indian Nation ceded the area that is now Macon County, Alabama, to the United States in 1832. At the ruthless insistence of President Andrew Jackson, Indians were force marched to Oklahoma. In 1813, Jackson and his troops had defeated the Indians at Horseshoe Bend, which lies within the circuit which I serve as judge. While Jackson himself reportedly behaved honorably as a soldier, there was barbaric mutilation of Indians and unnecessary killing by some of his men.[1] Names and relics are all that remain of the Indians who occupied this land a mere 150 years ago.

A 1934 Alabama history book gives the following account:

> The Indians left with sad hearts; some were full of malice and hate, others surprisingly kind and magnanimous. Touching sentiments and charity were expressed by Chief Eufaula in a farewell address to the Alabama legislature, while a body of Creeks were assembled at Tuscaloosa awaiting shipment to the West. "I come, brothers," he said to his curious white auditors, "to see

---

[1] Halbert and Ball, *The Creek War of 1813 and 1814*, University of Alabama Press, 1969. The book was first published in 1895. The current edition is edited, with introduction and notes, by Frank L. Owsley, Jr.

the great house of Alabama and the men that make the laws, and say fare-well in brotherly kindness before I go to the far West where my people are now going. * * * We leave behind our good will to the people of Alabama, who build the great houses, and to the men who make the laws. This is all I have to say. I came to say farewell to the wise men who make the laws, and to wish them peace and happiness in the country which my forefathers owned, and which I now leave to go to other homes in the West. I leave the graves of my fathers, * * * but the Indian fires are going out, almost clean gone * * * and new fires are lighting there for us."[2]

Less than thirty years later, the "wise men who make the laws" for Alabama, in their wisdom, voted to secede from the Union. The institu-tional structure of the evil of slavery was broken in the carnage that followed. Between these two traumatic events, probably in the 1840s, my surname forbears arrived in Macon County, allegedly from the Orange-burg District in South Carolina. My family is not "old southern aristoc-racy." My forebears moved to Macon County shortly after Andy Jackson and the federal government took it from the Indians. They were among the early settlers of the county. However, they did not own large farms, plantation homes and many slaves. I descended from a long line of poor dirt farmers.

Sixteen years after the Civil War, in 1881, Dr. Booker T. Washington founded Tuskegee Institute (now Tuskegee University) at Tuskegee, the county seat of Macon County. Alabama's rolling black belt, a part of the upper gulf coastal plain, extends into the south end of Macon County. However, the biggest part of the county is sandy loam and red clay hills. It was in this sand and clay soil, wearied by unrelenting cotton farming, that Dr. George Washington Carver worked his magic with peanuts and other agricultural products and practices. *King Cotton* reigned until mid-twentieth century. There were a few well-to-do citizens, but for most Macon Countians, poverty was an accepted way of life. Most of the county's population was and is Black. Poverty was not limited to Blacks.

Before the 1950s, there were few paved roads. In summer, heat hung in the air, like the dust that passing vehicles stirred from clay gravel roads. The dust drifted through the screened windows of plain frame houses that dotted the countryside. Mule drawn dispensers blew toxaphene dust into cotton rows to poison boll weevils, and its odor joined with the dust. We did not know what all else it was killing.

---

[2] Moore, *History of Alabama*, p. 32.

As summer turned to fall, shreds of cotton, blown from wagons and trucks on their way to the cotton gin, whitened the roadsides. The faint but distinct aroma of cotton dampened by dew permeated the morning air. Fall relented to winter and hog killings and wood cutting. Every season had its own sounds, sights and odors. Winter's humid cold penetrated cracks and crevices of the homes of poverty, numbing feet, ears, noses, and fingers.

Spring's warming winds included the crisp scent of burning fields and woods. It gave notice that the time of planting was not far away. Regular burning cleared fields and woods. Farmers believed that burning helped to combat the boll weevil. For us, the boll weevil was the common enemy of humankind.

The Early Years

The circumstances of my life have deeply influenced the evolution of thoughts set forth in this work. I was born in Macon County on April 25, 1942. The United States was at war. The military effort engaged many close kindred and friends of my family. Unrelenting tension pervaded the entire population of the nation, and my family was no exception.

I suspect that world tension during the first three years of my life had a lasting impact. Anxiety, fear, and uncertainty of adults leaks through to children, and early years are the most formative ones. Those of us born during World War II had a strange date with destiny. The world-wide tension was unprecedented, and the effect of that tension may be an unexplored dimension of the sociology of war babies.

Perhaps the first after-shock came in the Sixties when we became adults. To say the least, my generation showed an unusual interest in the social scene at that time. Now we are mature. Perhaps it is mere coincidence that more than 10 percent of the circuit court judges in Alabama graduated with me from the University of Alabama Law School in 1967. However, it may also be a continuation of the sixties and our date with destiny.

I was born into a farming community of small family farms, in which cotton was the primary crop. Effects of the Great Depression were still quite clear. My first home was a two-room frame house constructed by my daddy and members of his family. Heat came from a fireplace. We cut firewood with an ax. There was no plumbing. We drew water from a well—after we dug a well. Before that, we brought water in buckets from a nearby spring, or from Uncle Earl's well a quarter of a mile away.

I remember our first electric lights and telephone. Daddy bought a used pickup truck—our first motorized means of transportation—when I was eleven or twelve years old. I had gone away to college when the family installed running water and indoor plumbing at home.

When I was very small, my chores included picking up wood chips for the fire place. Later, I would chop, hoe, and pick cotton, and feed chickens and pigs. The cotton allotment set by the federal government for our farm was about 11 acres. Daddy hired a few *hands* to do some of the chopping and picking. We all worked in the field together. I missed a few days of school to pick cotton, but not many.

The family was close-knit, and included our extended family of grandparents, aunts, uncles, and cousins. In the late 1940s and early 1950s, on Saturday night, Uncle R. V. sometimes loaded all the kids onto the back of a big truck and took us to the *white only* Macon Theatre in Tuskegee. We drank from the *white only* water fountain near the Confederate Memorial on the town square, which was owned by the United Daughters of the Confederacy. When the occasion arose, we went to the *white only* rest room in the Courthouse. All elected officials in Macon County and Alabama during my childhood were white. Few Blacks voted.

Growing Up Amid Change

Changes in my economic and social status over the years add to my vantage point. I have had the opportunity to see society from several different economic and social perspectives. Thomas Grey bade us not "disdain the short and simple annals of the poor."[3] We must experience certain feelings to appreciate them.

The 1954 decision in the *Brown*[4] school desegregation case did not hit its mark in 80-percent-Black Macon County (probably 90 percent by now) until 1963. By then, I was a senior at Huntingdon College. Integration of schools in Macon County produced significant changes in the community. I graduated from Shorter High School in 1960, and attended Huntingdon College from 1960 through 1964. My older brother, Wade, graduated from college in late 1960, and with the first fruits of his employment helped pay for indoor plumbing at home. It was a time of many strange and conflicting impressions for us.

---

[3] *Elegy Written in a Country Churchyard*
[4] *Brown v. Board of Education of Topeka*, 347 U.S. 483 (1954) and *Brown v. Board Education of Topeka*, 349 U.S. 294 (1955).

For six summers after completing high school I worked for the Macon County Agricultural Stabilization and Conservation Service (ASCS). I measured cotton land for the federal government's cotton allotment program. That is the same outfit that told us we could plant only 11 acres of cotton. If a farmer planted more than his allotment, the United States Department of Agriculture required him to destroy the excess. Our experience was not as vivid as that described by Steinbeck in *The Grapes of Wrath*, but it was similar.

Looking back, it was obvious that small cotton farms in Alabama would soon be history. The demise of small farms caused dramatic changes in the way people lived. Technology was making its mark. A way of life was passing. Local economic ties that had existed for generations melted away. The changes affected the way people related to each other. Division of labor into specialized occupations became more pronounced. The pace quickened, and the warmth of community fellowship subsided.

These changes were part of larger, national trends. During my lifetime the national economy has changed dramatically. Before World War II, emphasis was on capital. Scientific breakthroughs and advancement brought about during World War II led to the age of technology. While capital and technology are still important, emphasis now is on information and jobs. These shifts in economic emphases deeply affected the area where I grew up. These national and world-wide economic changes added to the turbulence of the times. Disruption of routine social patterns forces the mind to explore the meaning of social existence.

These national economic and social changes touched rural areas all over America—not just my own area. Nevertheless, they were significant in development of ideas presented in this work. They were a part of the environment that nurtured me. These same influences were factors leading to the Civil Rights Movement. Blacks were being displaced from farms of the rural south. Their need for alternative means of livelihood was intense.

I was a sideline spectator of Macon County during the 1960s while everything there was changing. During these years, I attended college and law school and began the practice of law. Although I did not live in Macon County, I was close enough to the events to feel the impact of the changes. Macon County was a focal point of change. The subculture of small cotton farms, tenant farms, cotton gins, and country stores crumbled. Local economic ties based on an agricultural economy evaporated.

Those who could find jobs in nearby towns did so. Blacks took their rightful place in political structures.

In this examination of the motive force of law, the Civil Rights Movement is a focal point that unifies the other economic, social and political events that have so deeply impacted on my life. Dr. Martin Luther King, Jr., sometimes called it the Negro Revolution, and its impact on law has been truly revolutionary. The Civil Rights Movement provides the background for my personal experience and illustrates many points that I will be making in this book.

The Civil Rights Movement

Tuskegee is the county seat of Macon County. As I mentioned earlier, it is the site of historic Tuskegee University. Many well-educated Black citizens in the county were not allowed to vote before the Civil Rights Movement. This inequity emphasizes the unfairness of the old political system.

The federal courts struck down segregation in Macon County public schools in the case of *Lee v. Macon*[5] in 1963. I was in college. Nineteen Sixty-Three and Sixty-Four were particularly eventful, bittersweet years. Shorter High School, where I had graduated, was one of the smallest in the State. There were less than 100 students, all white, in the 12-grade school. For years there had been pressure to consolidate it with Tuskegee High School. Both schools were all white. White residents of the Shorter community clung to the school, which was the focal point of the community. We were oblivious of far reaching changes that were imminent.

In 1963, I was elected president of the Student Government Association at Huntingdon, and feeling good about myself. Then President Kennedy's assassination shadowed the world. Governor George Wallace addressed the student body at Huntingdon that year, and I met him. He also sent State Troopers into Macon County to maintain order.

Wallace ordered State Superintendent of Education, Austin Meadows, to direct certain activities of the Macon County Board of Education. This, in turn, enabled United States District Court Judge Frank Johnson to rule that the State—not the county—controlled the Macon County school system. So Judge Johnson extended the effect of *Lee v. Macon* to the whole state. *Brown v. Topeka* had made its mark in Alabama.

I read in newspapers about the integration of the school and community in which I had grown up. Students were bussed from Tuskegee

---

5 *Lee v. Macon County Bd. Education*, 221 F.Supp. 297 (1963).

to Shorter. Then in early 1964, Shorter High School closed. Later, it reopened as a practically all Black junior high school. All of this was a lot of experience to absorb in one year. Macon Academy, a segregated private school, opened its doors in 1964. Many whites left the county to avoid integration. This kind of migration became known as *white flight*. Some whites stayed. My younger brother, Chan, completed his senior year of high school in 1964 at Macon Academy.

In the meantime, federal civil rights lawsuits abounded. Courts abolished segregation in restaurants. They desegregated rest rooms and water fountains. They integrated public parks and public transportation. They required businesses that serve the public not to discriminate. Control of governmental functions in Macon County passed from whites to Blacks. The effect of a different cultural influence was clear. It influenced government and affected the meaning of *law*. It created new impressions of the processes that make law. These massive changes, affecting daily life, resulted from legal decisions and threatened lawsuits.

The Alabama Legislature tried to maintain white control of government in Tuskegee. The *"wise men who make the laws"* excluded Tuskegee Institute (now Tuskegee University) from the Tuskegee city limits. This gave rise to the landmark case of *Gomillion v. Lightfoot*.[6] The United States Supreme Court made it clear that it would not allow such flagrant gerrymandering to exclude Black voters.

The federal courts reapportioned the Alabama Legislature. Reapportionment ended control of the Legislature by rural counties and created districts in which Blacks could elect representatives. The principle of *one man one vote* became law. Blacks registered to vote in large numbers.

During the second half of the 1950s, Ms. Rosa Parks refused to give up a seat in the front of a public bus in Montgomery. *Freedom riders* came to Montgomery while I was attending Huntingdon College in the early sixties. Freedom riders were people from other sections of the country who came into the South to challenge segregation laws. Civil rights advocates called them heroes. Conservative whites called them "outside agitators."

Huntingdon is four or five miles from the downtown area of Montgomery. There were riots in downtown Montgomery. Some of my college friends let curiosity overcome them and went downtown. As they drove into a parking space, a police dog greeted them. They estimated that he was so big he had to stoop down to look into the car. After book-

---

6   *Gomillion v. Lightfoot*, 364 U.S. 339 (1960).

ing, finger printing, and making mug shots, the *law* allowed the students to come back to campus. There was enough social pressure to prevent a repeat performance.

The *New York Times* printed ads about demonstrations and police activities in Montgomery. Montgomery's Police Commissioner, L. B. Sullivan, took exception to the ads, and filed suit for libel. A Montgomery County jury awarded him $500,000. The case found its way through appellate processes to the United States Supreme Court. In *Times v. Sullivan*7, the court discussed defamation of a public official in a landmark First Amendment case. It struck down the jury's verdict. The court ruled that laws of defamation as to public officials are subject to certain restrictions. It recognized that freedom of press, protected by the First Amendment, restricts traditional defamation suits in cases involving public officials.

The federal courts also changed the method of selection of prospective jurors. They made the process more inclusive. Probably the most prominent person in bringing about these many changes is attorney Fred Gray, Sr., who now practices law in Tuskegee, and regularly appears in my court. As a young Black lawyer, he was champion of the Civil Rights Movement. He was attorney for both Dr. King and Ms. Parks. He represented Vivian Malone in her quest for admission to the University of Alabama, which was successful, despite George Wallace's famous school door stand. He represented the plaintiff in the suit that opened Auburn University to Blacks. He was counsel in *Lee v. Macon* and *Gomillion v. Lightfoot*, and other cases too numerous to mention. He has had more impact on the history of Alabama during the past forty years, in my estimation, than any other one person.

In one significant case handled by Mr. Gray, state and local government was not the culprit. The United States government admitted wrongdoing in *Pollard v. United States*, CA-4126-N, in the United States District Court for the Middle District of Alabama. The government paid 9.5 million dollars to the plaintiffs. Approximately 600 black men participated in a human experiment known as the "Tuskegee Syphilis Study." The subjects were poor Black men of limited education who knew nothing of their role in the experiment.

After I graduated from Huntingdon in 1964, Betty and I married. We had started to school together in the first grade in the public school at Shorter. I attended law school from 1964 through 1967 at the University

---

7 *New York Times Co. v. Sullivan*, 376 U.S. 254 (1964).

of Alabama, with Betty working at various jobs to support us. In 1967, I began practicing law in Montgomery. We lived in Montgomery for a little over three years. My sons, Philip and Mike, were born during those three years. We moved back to Macon County early in 1971, searching for home. Many whites were still moving away because of increasing political dominance of Blacks in the County. When we moved back to Macon County, we moved in the opposite direction of the pattern of *white flight.*

I continued practicing law in Montgomery after moving back to Macon County, but there was more and more work for me in Macon County. In 1982, I was elected Circuit Judge in Alabama's Fifth Judicial Circuit, which includes Macon County. I defeated an incumbent for office in 1982, and was re-elected over opposition in 1988. Election campaigns added a new dimension to my understanding of democracy, government and law.

My experience on the bench, dealing with many cases and legal issues, added a new dimension to my interest in what makes law work. I searched for meaning in the stream of events which engulfed me, both on and off the bench. On the bench, the meaning of law became much more an existential problem than it had been before. This book results from an effort to understand events thundering around me.

In addition to Macon County, there are three other counties in the circuit: Tallapoosa, Chambers and Randolph. The Tallapoosa River meanders through the circuit, touching each county. The river, court system, and Indian heritage are the only elements shared by all four counties of the circuit. If circuits were given names in Alabama, mine should be called *Tallapoosa Circuit.*

The other three counties are all in the piedmont area. The piedmont is a plateau, probably the remnant of worn down mountains in the Southern Appalachian chain. Water power created by rivers descending from the piedmont to the Upper Gulf Coastal Plain, together with the cotton heritage, made the area a natural for the textile industry. There are several large textile plants in the circuit. The plight of the textile industry and employment concerns within the circuit promote an awareness of the emerging world-wide economic system. One of the two major textile firms was recently the subject of a hostile takeover. Even rural circuits in Alabama are now a part of national and world events. Concern in the textile industry about foreign competition confirms the point.

The Impact of Changing Laws

I have lived through an interesting period of local history. I have seen the passing of a way of life. It may not have been much of a way of life, according to present-day standards. It was rife with ignorance, poverty, and prejudice. Life in the Southern Appalachians further north has been romanticized in the ways of folklore. However, forces that create history did not choose a kind fate for the simple, earnest, poor country folks that I know.

One author, Robert J. Norrell, II, has devoted an entire volume, *Reaping the Whirlwind*, to events of this tumultuous time in Macon County. The whirlwind may not yet have completed its work. In the early eighties, Macon County was successful in passing legislation for a locally controlled greyhound racing track with legalized betting. It is phenomenally successful economically, and exerts huge political influence in the county, and throughout the state. Those persons actually in control of the operation are white. In 1985, the Macon County Courthouse was gutted by fire. Five years later it had not been restored or replaced, and court and county government were housed in temporary quarters.

Theodore Rosengarten's best seller, *All God's Dangers*, is an account of the life of Nate Shaw who was a sharecropper in Tallapoosa County. "Nate Shaw" was a pseudonym for Ned Cobb. Ironically, the Cobb family had to sue for their fair share of royalties from the book. Apparently there was at least one danger that the book failed to cover. The book portrays violence against Blacks who tried to form a union in the segregated society of the 1930s.

A picture of the Macon County Courthouse was on the cover of the American Bar Association Journal in the late 1960s or early '70s. The Journal recognized the historic significance of the Civil Rights Movement in Macon County. I saw the impact of those times on family and friends. *Law* required us to hammer out new relationships. A new culture is gradually emerging. This background has been fertile in producing some ideas about what makes law work. I have felt the impulses of my own soul. Against this background, psychology, sociology, religion and law take on special meaning.

The events and changes that I have described have literally swirled around me. Law has played a major role in these events. Early in my legal career, a good lawyer told me never to ask an adverse witness a *why* question. A *why* question offers the witness an opportunity to "unload on you," he explained. However, when I examine the role of law in these events the question that goes to the heart of law is *why* rather than *what.*

Let me avoid misapprehension. I am not questioning the wisdom or propriety of events that occurred. They were inevitable. Forces that produce law and cause it to function brought about these changes. My point is that the heart of law is its motive force. Most theories of law address the *what* question. Mine addresses the *why* question. Law's *what* is a *why.* Motive is the beginning of law, and motive is a *why.* My experience has brought me face to face with the *why* question about law time and again. Eventually, I realized that the reality of law lies in response to the question, "Why do we do it?"

Church has been an important part of my life, beginning with the small rural Methodist Church that I attended as a child. In 1985, I was elected Conference Lay Leader of the Alabama-West Florida Conference of the United Methodist Church. I served as lay leader for five years. The Conference includes over 700 local churches in the southern half of Alabama and the panhandle of Florida. This office brought me in contact with both clerical and lay leadership in the United Methodist Church from throughout the United States. Involvement in church has helped me understand the relationship between moral values and beliefs advanced by the Church and law adopted by the State.

The ideas expressed in these pages did not originate in some great center of learning, but I am not arguing superiority of practical experience. I often long for the opportunity for cool reflection and scholarly research. Such has not been my lot. I admire the scholarly works of academicians, and I have drawn heavily on them. But the ideas expressed here have a context. They came to mind amid tumultuous changes in law and government. They developed under pressures of a busy career as student, lawyer and judge. They grope for an understanding of the philosophy and psychology that caused these changes. Even as ideas emerged, I could hear children crying, because they were forgotten and neglected. I felt the anguish of victims who had lost loved ones to crime. I saw humanity coming to court, with great feeling, believing that answers exist and needs would be met. Somehow, I realized that both feeling and belief are vital parts of law itself.

The turbulence of the times has been a catalyst to thought about government. The essence of law and government is more clearly visible when law and government change than when they are constant. Adam saw the animals before he named them. I believe that I have seen the motive forces of law in action before applying words to them.

The system which I describe involves many points or ideas, all related to each other in one or more ways. In most instances, I have found writers who make some of the same connections that I make. However, I have found no one who fits all the points together to describe a system. The process is like putting a jigsaw puzzle together. The only trick is that you must first search for the pieces, but with all the pieces hidden in different places in a library.

1 | An Overview

The proper abbreviation for inch is in. It is not permissible to use ditto marks. That edict from a federal regulation applies to packaging and labelling merchandise. I discovered this interesting principle after practicing law for about four years. My mind rebelled. The proposition has no motive content. Many questions, only partly articulated, made a mockery of my meager understanding of the nature of law. Why does law deal with anything as unimportant as the abbreviation for inch? Where does such a rule come from? The legal answer is very simple. Congress delegated rule-making authority to a federal agency. The federal agency enacted the regulation. However, this simple answer did not silence the taunting questions. Can such a regulation really be *law*? The Bible reports that God delivered the law to Moses on a mountain. Clouds and deep mystery attended the event. The occasion was accented by thunder and lightning. There couldn't have been a clap of thunder in the distance when the flatland bureaucrats regulated the abbreviation for inch! No doubt, someone felt that the *in.* abbreviation would be easier for consumers to understand. Whether the abbreviation is easier to understand or not is beside the point. Did such a regulation make any difference at all in human behavior? If someone violates it, what *just* action will authorities take? Is it important enough to merit the attention of law?

I began to search for a deeper meaning in law. However, to realize the inadequacy of existing explanations of law is not to arrive at a plausible explanation. Does any principle that the legislature enacts become law, regardless of its content? Can a court or administrative agency simply *make* law? What material do they use to make it?

Today, acute problems mark the legal system's failures. The crime rate increases and prisons are overflowing. White collar crimes and crimes of violence abound. Rehabilitation of criminals seldom works. In the domestic arena, families break down. We see child abuse, custody disputes, child support problems, and juvenile delinquency. Civil verdicts skyrocket. Insurance companies, doctors and businessmen scream for reform of the civil justice system. Abuse of alcohol and other drugs permeates all these problems.

My rural circuit suffers all these afflictions. Often I impose sentences in criminal cases on a particular day that could cost tax payers many thousands of dollars. I once tried a civil case in which a jury awarded $400,000 for loss of a big toe. At least 80 percent of all matters which come before my court involve alcohol or drugs. In cases involving possession or sale of illegal drugs and driving under the influence of alcohol the involvement of alcohol and drugs is clear. However, robberies, murders, burglaries, rapes, divorces, child abuse cases and many others also involve alcohol and drugs.

Social problems are even more perplexing. Minorities look to law for civil rights. Why do we send more blacks than whites to the penitentiary? Why can't law deal effectively with the drug problem? Speaking bluntly, why is law breaking down? A theory of law based on motive provides new insights into these problems.

The Why Question

Why do most individuals respect law? If we want to know why law *doesn't* work in some instances, we must understand why it does work in other instances. Why does anyone bother to obey law? Is it purely fear of punishment? We stop at a red light, even late at night and with no traffic in sight. What strange inward compulsion causes us to stop? Most people do not steal, even when no one is watching. In many ways, every day, we choose patterns of behavior because of *law*. Why do some people feel no inward compulsion to obey law? Why does society compel compliance with its standards? What motive forces are at work? *What is the source of the standards that guide our conduct?* Why do we obey some laws, while practically ignoring others? Is there some exotic ingredient which law must contain to be successful? These nagging questions begin more often with *why* than with *what.* We will compress these questions into one and call it the *why* question.

The *why* question intruded in my thoughts after I discovered the "proper abbreviation for inch." Even the questions were not at all clear to me. Up to that point, I had believed that *if I learned enough about the law,* its ineffectiveness would disappear. I attributed the perceived ineffec- tiveness of law to my own lack of knowledge, experience and under- standing. Most lawyers probably feel that way. The legal community thinks that the legal system is autonomous. *They believe the answers lie somewhere in the system. Our job is merely to find them.* However, that is the problem. *The answers do not all lie within our legal system,* and, in fact, the legal system is not autonomous. We are simply unaware of and tend to ignore law's dependence on motive forces generated elsewhere in society.

Law School and the Case Method

Perhaps it will be helpful to ask how the legal community forms its attitudes. How do lawyers get the notion that the legal system is autonomous? Let me review my experience before I discovered the abbreviation for inch.

M. Leigh Harrison was dean of the University of Alabama Law School during the first two years that I attended. He was a man of few words. During my senior undergraduate year, I decided that I would like to attend law school. I wrote Dean Harrison a lengthy letter, explaining that I had majored in chemistry and that I wanted to discuss my chances of admission to law school. His response was a one-liner, "I will be happy to meet with you (on a certain day)."

Armed with a copy of my transcript from Huntingdon College, my older brother, Wade, and I drove one hundred miles from Montgomery to the University campus at Tuscaloosa. I handed the transcript to Dean Harrison and asked him if I could get into law school. He looked over the transcript and, without elaboration, said, "Yes." I asked if there were any courses that I should take during the remainder of my undergraduate work. He looked at my transcript again. "You might take a course in economics." The interview was over.

Dean Harrison was correct. Any course of study that sharpens analytical and linguistic skill is adequate preparation for law school. However, any academic major selected by an undergraduate omits much information involved in the functioning legal system. Law school does not and cannot supply the missing information. It was probably the shortest conversation for which I will ever drive a hundred miles. I took the course in economics, and the following August, started law school.

I soon became familiar with the *case method*. Appellate courts write opinions expressing reasons for their decisions in particular cases. As students, we read appellate court opinions to learn the reasons for decisions. From this study, a student derives the principle of law which brought about the decision. This is the case method. It is pragmatic and empirical. Law students also read statutes and treatises, but study of cases is the primary thrust of law school education.

Under the guidance of skillful professors for three tightly disciplined years, law students gain adequate knowledge of procedures and principles that make up our legal system. More importantly, they learn to *think like lawyers*. They learn enough about the legal system to recognize legal problems in a given factual situation. They learn how to research case law, statutes, and administrative regulations, to arrive at possible solutions to these problems.

During the first year of law school, we studied laws of real property, torts, contracts, criminal law, and legislation. In legal bibliography, we learned to find the written expressions of law. During the second and third years, we continued the study of substantive law, but also began to learn procedural aspects of the legal system. In the senior year, there were opportunities for a few electives, along with required courses in constitutional law and taxation.

We diligently pursued the case method. We read assigned cases and *briefed* them. Briefing entailed writing a brief synopsis of the facts and holding of the case. In class, professors called on students to recite. "Mr. Segrest, give me the *Palsgraf* case." I stood and recited the facts and holding of the case. Then the professor used the withering Socratic method of questioning for which law school is famous to develop our understanding of the case.

I remember a feeling of excitement during the second year, when I began to see the connectedness of the system. During the first year, we had learned quite a bit of law. Then, in the second year, we began to learn procedure: pleadings and evidence. We began to learn how a lawyer *uses* legal principles to solve his clients' problems. After reading hundreds of cases, it became clear that the separate parts work together as a system. "The law is a seamless web," we learned. The system is one big body and it all ties together. Contracts relate to torts, and torts to crime. Due process is due process wherever you find it, whether in civil or criminal law. The answers lie somewhere within the system. Law school drills these impressions into students. They are important parts of the legal discipline. The system makes it easy for students to assume that the legal system is autonomous and contains solutions to all of society's problems.

Law students learn that either the legislature enacts law or courts pronounce it. Once courts decide a case, it is *a precedent*. The doctrine of *stare decisis* then requires that courts rule consistently in future cases involving the same point. It's all very simple. With appropriate delegation of authority, governmental agencies can adopt regulations. That, law students learn, is how law comes into being. These are *formal* acts of law making. All these procedures are expressed or implied in a *constitution*, according to legal scholars, which is also a part of law's formalism. Much modern legal philosophy concerns itself with formalism, and it is important to grasp this meaning of the word *formal* as used in legal philosophy. These procedures give *form* to law. A word often used in conjunction with form is *substance*, which refers to content or meaning of the principle.

Is that actually the way law comes into being? Does law start in a decision by a court? If so, what was it and where was it before the court decided the case? Does a principle become *law* just because a legislature or regulatory agency says it is law? Is law merely the rational solution to a problem; the *rule of reason*? Is government simply a rational way to make rules that solve problems? Does law result from mere formality? Is that all there is to it? No, more than these activities is involved in the origin and enforcement of law, and that is what this book is all about.

The law student learns that the adversarial system, even with all its faults, is the best method of arriving at truth and justice. Each party to litigation hires a lawyer. Zealous preparation on both sides assures that the judge and jury will hear a well-balanced presentation of facts and law. We assume that truth and justice naturally emerge under those circumstances! The trial judge is merely a passive participant in the proceedings, comparable to a referee of a sporting event. Delicate problems of inadequate preparation, unequal ability or unequal influence of attorneys, and different economic and social standing of parties or attorneys, make no difference. We assume that these matters will not affect truth and justice.

Assume that this discussion fairly describes the education and training that occurs in law school. Does this somewhat formal approach to law explain why people alter their behavior, *without need for external compulsion*, when the legislature passes a law or courts decide a case? Does it explain why witnesses usually appear without further compulsion in response to a subpoena? What produces the fear or awe that most individuals experience when required to participate in legal proceedings? Does law school teach us the source of societal energy which compels compliance with law? Does it expose the sources of rules themselves? Unfortunately, answers to such questions are not readily available in the usual law school curriculum.

Fallacies of the Case Method

The case method has helped to create the illusion of autonomy in the legal system in the twentieth century. It blinds us to psychological and sociological motives involved in lawmaking process. The case method itself started at Harvard in the nineteenth century and quickly became the standard method of law school instruction. It is an empirical method of study. By studying specific phenomena, according to the scientific method, one reaches general conclusions. The greatest compliment for any system of learning today is to be called *scientific*. What better or more *scientific* way can there be to see law in action than to study actions of Courts? This is the argument for the case method. However, continual and necessary resort to courts to learn the meaning of law supports the illusion of an autonomous legal system. Such an approach leads to the conclusion that we must go to court to learn the principle of law.

The greatest weakness of the case method is that it ignores the many situations when law *actually works*. Law gets its desired results when people don't have to go to court. Most human activities occur in harmony with the requirements of law. Commuters find their own cars when the work day is over. They do not take someone else's car. Most shoppers do not stuff items that they want in their pockets without paying for them. *In fact, instances in which lawlessness occurs are a very small percentage of all instances of human activity.*

The case method focuses on instances in which people did not obey law. It is a study of lawlessness rather than a study of law. It focuses on what the *reasonably prudent person* should *not* do, rather than on what he or she actually does. We try to understand law solely by studying court cases in which law did not work. Our method is comparable to studying life in a beehive by dissecting the remains of a bee killed with a fly swatter on a screened porch. We have separated the event from its natural environment. As an empirical tool, the case method is inadequate because the phenomenon we think we are studying is not the one under the microscope.

The case method is a good tool for teaching the legal *system*, and even for teaching legal *thinking*. Nevertheless, it does not teach the *nature of law*. It may even blind us to the true nature of law. Members of the legal profession, trained in law schools, often have little or no educational exposure to the actual nature of law. The case method begs the question, if the question is "What is law?" The case method itself creates the false perception that law *arises* in the court. It causes us to forget that causes for decisions arise elsewhere. When we look for *the law*, we turn to court opinions. Therefore, we, along with the great legal positivist, John Austin, conclude that courts actually make law. The court's role in law making is bothersome. We will return to it repeatedly. One legal theorist, Lon L. Fuller, states that modern-day legal writers believe "(t)he reality of law is to be found in the decisions of courts, that is, in the actions they take concerning the controversies that are submitted to them for resolution."[8]

In twentieth century America, the legal community believes that *law is what a court decides it to be if the court has power to enforce its decision.* This, as we will see, is a facet of the theory of jurisprudence known as *legal positivism*, to the extent that the court is an official agency for making law. The statement is also quite compatible with teachings of legal realism. The case method itself reinforces the conclusion that law is what a court does, which misconceives the nature of law. Opinions themselves do not articulate such a philosophy. However, *we implicitly recognize that law is what a court says it is* when we use the case method. A child in an urban setting might reasonably assume that the grocer makes meat and vegetables. For a child to have such an idea is a good reason for a field trip to the farm. Maybe it is time that our legal community take a field trip to the farm where law and legal principles originate.

Without deeper understanding, the idea that law is what a court says it is assures an ever-increasing burden of litigation. If law is no more than what a court says it is, we can learn what law is only by getting a

---

[8] Fuller, *Anatomy of the Law*, p. 11. This book offers an excellent discussion of *made* law and *implicit* law and the court's role in making law.

court ruling. The standards by which one is to live should be available without going to court.

We assume that law has a rational basis, which we can discover by studying actions of courts. We tout law as the *rule of reason* and idealize that omni-present creature of law, the *reasonably prudent person*. We believe that we obey law because it is *reasonable* to do so. Is that really why we obey law? Perhaps the articulated principles of law are somewhat *rational*, and certainly, it is *reasonable* to obey law. However, anyone who has ever participated in a legal dispute knows that law involves something beyond mere rationality. Reason has its place in law, *but it is not the motive force for law.* The motive force for law, the force that makes it happen, is not its rational principles. The rational principle may be the *solution* to a legal problem, but it does not *make the solution happen.* The motive force for law has its origin elsewhere.

Looking back at the law school curriculum, it clearly did not satisfy the empty, uneasy feeling about law created by my experience with the abbreviation for inch. Something was clearly missing in that regulation. Something pushed me on in quest of the awesome forces that cause law to happen, but are not described in law school courses. The quest was for the thunder and lightning and mountains and clouds that attend appearance of real law. In this book, I will explore these mysterious forces and try to explain why law happens.

Existing Theories Ignore Motive

Dean Roscoe Pound was one of the most influential legal philosophers of this century. In his book, *An Introduction to the Philosophy of Law,* Dean Pound set out twelve ideas which he believed to encompass existing theories of law. Pound's list included (1) divinely ordained rule; (2) tradition; (3) recorded wisdom of the wise men of old; (4) philosophically discovered systems of principle; (5) a body of ascertainments and declarations of an eternal and immutable moral code; (6) a body of agreements; (7) reflections of the divine reason governing the universe; (8) a body of commands; (9) a system of precepts discovered by human experience; (10) a system of principles discovered philosophically and developed in detail by juristic writing and judicial decision, whereby the external life of man is measured by reason; (11) a body or system of rules imposed on men in society by a dominant class for the time being in furtherance, conscious or unconscious, of its own interest; and (12) the dictates of economic or social laws with respect to the men in society, discovered by observation.

Pound's summary is probably as adequate and comprehensive as any. However, none of the theories that he listed satisfactorily identifies the societal forces that cause law to happen. Although the theories he described all have validity or truth about them, they are not *dynamic* theories. They are static. They try to say what law *is*, without explaining why anyone feels compelled or motivated to do anything about it. They do not suggest motive. They do not explain why anyone follows legal principles voluntarily, or why society compels compliance.

The spirit of Mr. Pound's times discounted any theory that did not base law in rational principle. Pound and his contemporaries were seeking a *rational* basis for law. The difficulty with the rational approach is that rationality often depends upon cause and effect. Certain causes produce certain effects, and results are *predictable*. In law, the desired result does not flow from the rational legal principle. Something has to make the result happen, other than the rational principle. Law clearly involves something more than mere rationality. Rationally, two plus two equals four. The "two plus two" of law must cause someone to make four happen. Causal forces involved in law differ from those involved in physical laws of nature, such as the law of gravity. In any human system of laws, *somebody* must be motivated to *do something* for the system to work. Without motive force, law is motionless and meaningless.

Roscoe Pound, along with many others, realized that our legal philosophy is inadequate. Although he knew that we cannot return to metaphysical concepts of the Middle Ages, he offered nothing in their place. Pound tried to escape from *natural law* and *metaphysical jurisprudence* and to approach law more scientifically. His belief that natural law loses itself in unprovable metaphysical speculation has merit. However, the theories of law which he catalogued do not explain forces that *make law happen*. They ignore the motive for law. The legal positivism which Pound helped to champion loses itself in rationalism and formalism.

Any purported explanation of law that ignores its behavioral base is inadequate. Rules are inseparable from societal forces that bring them into existence and give them energy. A rule that fails to harness human energy is almost no rule at all. A rule that has no motive force has no energy. Nevertheless, Pound's brand of legal philosophy, with its emphasis on rationalism, has been fashionable throughout most of the twentieth century. It searches for law in rationality while ignoring motive forces that cause law to happen.

The search for law in rationality is not new. Scientific breakthrough launched the Age of Reason. Throughout the text, I will use the term *Age of Reason* to designate the modern era, commencing at the end of the Middle Ages. Early in the modern era scientists and mathematicians discovered rational laws of nature, based on cause and effect, that explained natural phenomena. Western society has continually tried to find a similar rational basis for laws of human conduct in society. However, law involves the entire range of human behavior, including emotions and unconscious impulses. Human rationality is only one cause of behavior and is not the basis of law. We will be exploring other causes of behavior as we proceed.

Prerequisites of Law

I have introduced several important suggestions in the preceding discussion. (1) Law must be based on human motive, involving more than mere rationality. It involves more than the *rule of reason*. (2) The case method, which concentrates on instances in which law did not work, cannot explain motive for law. (3) Existing theories of jurisprudence do not explain motive for law. (4) The formal origin of law in legislative act, judicial decree, or government regulation, does not explain motive for law. Formal origin and motive are separate and distinct matters.

What, then, are the actual prerequisites for law? First, the principle of law must be *articulated:* Law must be either spoken or written. To recognize a principle as law, we must state it in words. This is true even though the principle arises from underlying motive forces. Secondly, the *articulated* principle must be *authenticated*. There are different ways to authenticate legal principles. Early societies attributed legal principles to the gods, which accomplished authentication. Modern societies use other processes and rituals to authenticate law, which we will discuss later. Regardless of the method, public acceptance of a particular principle as law always requires some form of authentication. Naturally, in the modern era, the authentication process must meet the requirements of rationality, since rationality is the central motif for our authenticating myths.

Most of us who live in a country with a reasonably stable government have little difficulty with these two prerequisites. We accept the premise that government makes law. We rationalize the process by remembering that we elected the people who make law. Perhaps some of us are uncomfortable when we remember that we do not elect federal judges, and *they* occasionally make law. Further, selection processes, as well as the seldom-used power of impeachment provides some public control of the federal judiciary. In any event, we accept the idea that government makes law. We agree that whatever the legislature or court says *officially* is law. Later we will see that this approach is consistent with a theory of law known as *legal positivism*, which is widely accepted. Outwardly, we accept the authenticity of principles established by government. We accept the authority of government to make law, even though one authentic law may be more difficult to enforce than another. If all enacted law is equally genuine, why are some laws easier to enforce than others? This question leads inexorably to the third prerequisite.

For law to exist there must be human motive. This is not a proposition of law; it is a description of reality. It is not a *secondary rule* or rule of recognition that validates other rules, nor is it a principle of legality or part of the inner morality of law. All these concepts deal with authentication. What we are injecting here deals with the nature of law. Law deals with human behavior. Without motive force, an articulated, authenticated principle is just so many words. Again, I am not suggesting that motive is an authenticating legal principle for which courts should search in deciding whether law is authentic. Lack of force caused by lack of motive is self-executing.

Traditional treatment of legal philosophy in western civilization has limited itself largely to the first two requirements: articulation and authentication. We see these two as the source of law. No one asks what causes people actually to *do* the acts required by law. To understand what law is all about, we must explore in depth the motive forces that lie at its root.

Failure to Understand Motive

Lack of a comprehensive understanding of the motive force of law in existing legal theories has far-reaching implications. Legal scholars, judges, legislators, and even legal philosophers do not understand what makes law work. There is danger that judicial oligarchy will move into the emptiness created by lack of a comprehensive theory of law. Even worse, the system itself may break down.

Lack of common understanding impacts on other disciplines. I recently inspected the descriptive word index in a standard textbook on social interaction. The word *law* was not there! An understanding of the nature of law, shared by the legal profession, sociologists, psychologists, theologians, and others is essential. Lack of that common understanding weakens law's ability to accomplish its purposes. Also, we cannot understand these social sciences properly without understanding how they relate to law.

Lack of an interdisciplinary understanding of the nature of law has had unfortunate results. Psychotherapists (and pop-psychologists) have ignored the impact on society of their efforts to eliminate guilt feelings. There is a close relationship between law and morals. Since religions concern themselves with morals, a more adequate understanding of motive for law will benefit theological circles. Religious leaders need to be keenly aware that law depends on faith.

There is almost universal belief that justice *exists*. Even though law fails to solve a particular problem, we do not question the existence of *justice* itself. Members of all disciplines share this faith in law, even though they may not understand the precise nature of justice. We complain when law does not bring about a particular result we believe to be just, but never question the existence of justice. We assume that a just legal principle *exists*, but somehow the court has overlooked it, or failed to apply it, in a particular situation. I am not suggesting that we should discard our faith in the existence of justice. Indeed, I am suggesting that the natural origin of law itself depends on that faith. However, that faith, coupled with the idea that law arises in court decisions, places significant power in the hands of courts—particularly appellate courts. Careful analysis leads to the enigmatic and paradoxical conclusion that courts indeed make law through their decisions, and properly do so, as long as they are not intentionally making law rather than deciding a case.

The Usefulness of Nothingness

The Taoist philosopher, Laotse, posed this question: "What is useful about a spoon?"9 The question expands the mind, by showing the usefulness of nothingness. The answer to the question is that it is not the material of the spoon that is useful. The *hollow* portion—the nothingness—is the useful part. The nothingness was there all along, just like any other unoccupied space. The cupped out hollow holds the food or liquid.

Perhaps, to make certain that we have posed the entire problem, we should ask, "What is useful about law?" After all, law is not accessible to the senses. We don't know where it is, and we don't know precisely what it is. Intuitively, we know that it is useful, but precisely what is its

---

9 See *The Wisdom of Laotse*, Lin Yutang, editor, p. 87.

usefulness? Its usefulness may be in the "space" that it encloses, organizes, and protects, but does not occupy.

A Poetic Image

The dilemma of any attempt to define law is captured poetically by W. H. Auden:

Law, say the gardeners, is the sun,
Law is the one
All gardeners obey
To-morrow, yesterday, to-day.

Law is the wisdom of the old
The impotent grandfathers shrilly scold;
The grandchildren put out a treble tongue,
Law is the senses of the young.

Law, says the priest with a priestly look,
Expounding to an unpriestly people,
Law is the words in my priestly book,
Law is my pulpit and my steeple.

Law, says the judge as he looks down his nose,
Speaking clearly and most severely,
Law is as I've told you before,
Law is as you know I suppose,
Law is but let me explain it once more,
Law is The Law.

Yet law-abiding scholars write:
Law is neither wrong nor right,
Law is only crimes
Punished by places and by times,
Law is the clothes men wear
Anytime, anywhere,
Law is Good-morning and Good-night.

Others say, Law is our Fate;
Others say, Law is our State;
Others say, others say
Law is no more
Law has gone away.

And always the loud angry crowd
Very angry and very loud
Law is We,
And always the soft idiot softly Me.

If we, dear, know we know no more
Than they about the law,
If I no more than you
Know what we should and should not do
Except that all agree
Gladly or miserably
That the law is
And that all know this,
If therefore thinking it absurd
To identify Law with some other word,
Unlike so many men
I cannot say Law is again,
No more than they can we suppress
The universal wish to guess

Or slip out of our own position
Into an unconcerned condition.

Although I can at least confine
Your vanity and mine
To stating timidly
A timid similarity,
We shall boast anyway:
Like love I say.

Like love we don't know where or why
Like love we can't compel or fly
Like love we often weep
Like love we seldom keep.[10]

Auden was a serious poet; rest assured that his lines are much more than satire. He composed these lines in September, 1939. In November of the same year, Auden composed a poem to the memory of Sigmund Freud, who had died in September. Auden's interest in psychology gave him a poetic glimpse of law's connection to emotion that legal philosophers had missed.

In this chapter, I have posed several questions about our understanding, or misunderstanding, of law. We assign to law many problems that it cannot solve. In other instances, law provides quite adequate solutions. We expect much of law. The question that this chapter poses, stated succinctly, is, "Why does law fail to solve certain problems which we assign to it?" The answer is that we don't know what makes it work in the first place! What is the motive force of law? Why do people do it? The

---

[10]   Auden, *Selected Poems*, pp. 89-91.

essence of law, I suggest, is as much verb as noun. Lawyers, judges, and law enforcement officers are people who *law*. Criminals must be *lawed*. However, as Auden suggests, definitions of law fall short of the mark.

A Motive Theory of Law

Motive force lies at the heart of law, and I propose to describe a motive theory of law. Human motive is complex, and a theory of law based on motive will also be complex. Therefore, I will give a short, general description of the motive theory before embarking on a detailed explanation. This chapter contains a brief summary of the principle points discussed in the remainder of the book. This approach will enable readers to compare the motive theory of law to other theories.

Law is *dynamic*. It must have energy, or motive force. Law gets that energy from motive forces that govern human behavior. Nothing happens just because a rational principle exists, even if it is a *just* principle. There must be some motive force that causes something to happen for law to occur. Motive—the *why* question—is the central question of law. Why does each participant do what he does to make law happen? Law is also *holistic*. Society is not merely a collection of individuals. Society functions as one big organization or creature, and law is part of the connective tissue. Society has a life of its own, and law is an essential part of that life.

The motive "theory" that I describe is not technically a theory. It is a working hypothesis. It is speculative, but probably no more so than the theory of evolution. It is intended to spark discussion; not to present final conclusions. I find it easier to present such a hypothesis with direct assertions than to couch each suggestion in tentative, guarded language that reflects all necessary reservations. The hypothesis is stated *arguendo*.

The Psychology of Law[†]

Society acts directly only through individuals or groups of individuals. Energy for law comes from individual members of society. Intangible forces shape individuals into groups. The group exerts pressure, but energy for group pressure comes from individuals. The energy derives from the individual's efforts to satisfy his own basic

---

[†] This topic is treated in depth in Section 2.

needs. As individuals act to satisfy their own needs, they also satisfy needs of the group. For instance, the sex drive does not merely work toward selfish gratification; it brings about the next generation of society. In the process, sex can also produce feelings of self-esteem to participants. Channelled in wrong directions, the sex drive can produce feelings of guilt and loss of self-esteem. All this serves purposes of the group.

We do what we do to get what we need, and activities of law are no exception. We need security that law provides. There are also other intangible, psychological needs that only appropriate relations with other humans can satisfy. Strong desire to satisfy these needs propels us into relationships with others. For those relationships to be orderly there must be norms. Norms arise naturally, when individuals respond to each other in the processes of group formation. Groups satisfy individual needs and norms that organize the group provide structure in which need satisfaction can occur.

I have chosen the word *need* deliberately. It is synonymous with the word *drive*. Needs of society and needs of individuals are synergic—they support each other. Needs of every individual include survival, reproduction, achievement of full potential, socialization and search for meaning. Fulfilling these needs brings individuals into unavoidable relationships with others. Individual actions and opinions energize norms of the group. At the same time the individual's needs are being met, so are needs of the group.

Law does not operate as a result of cause and effect. Events that set processes of law in motion do not automatically produce certain results. Punishment does not automatically follow commission of a crime. For law to work, human motive forces must intervene. Causation in law is a part of a much larger system. That system is part of human ecology. People relate to each other through their motive forces.

The basic enforcement mechanism for norms of society is individual conscience. Conscience, with varying degrees of success, causes individuals to follow society's norms. The group *programs* its norms into individuals. Parents usually instill the group's values into their children. The process of acquiring a conscience is sometimes called *moral formation*. A core of conformity to norms of society results from moral formation. Freud, Piaget, Kohlberg and others have described the process. Kant and Jung suggest that we are born with a sense of duty, or at least a propensity toward it. Conscience serves purposes of society and is not merely an individual sense of right and wrong.

Much moral formation occurs during early years, but the process continues throughout life. The individual's microcosm, including the peer group, has greater input into moral formation than does society at large. As a person matures, the cognitive function plays an ever-increasing role in moral formation.

Feeling attaches to group norms. Individuals who have internalized norms expect everyone else to follow those norms. Therefore, norms that are helpful to the group perpetuate themselves. Individuals participate emotionally in norms. More than rational commitment is involved. Collective psychology occurs and forces compliance by a non-conformist in instances when conscience alone does not produce the necessary degree of conformity. Thus, society itself adds a new dimension to normative forces that reside in individuals. Norms arise naturally from group formation. In a sense, society is the source of norms through processes of collective psychology.

Psychological mechanisms operating within individuals produce social organization. Jung's description of energy-laden archetypes and symbols help to explain human relationships in society. The father, mother, wise old man, trickster, hero and other archetypes condition us for roles assigned by society. We all share them in a universal unconscious according to Jung. Archetypes occur genetically. Experience funds them with content specific to a particular culture.

Mythos[†]

I use the word *mythos* in a special sense. Mythos is part of the cultural environment. Mythos includes myths, legends, literature, and religious rites. It also includes ethos. Mythos stores the values of a particular culture and impresses those values on the individual members. It installs those values in each succeeding generation. Society formulates norms that reflect those values.

Both moral formation and mythos operate largely at an unconscious level. Thus, both norms and motive force for law derive from a non-rational source. Rationality is not the basis of law. Usually, we do not even know what causes moral formation to occur. Similarly, we are not usually aware of normative forces of mythology. It is strange that we describe something we don't even know about as *rational*.

Mechanics of mythos include archetypes, symbols, narratives, and collective representations. Each of these mechanics has counterparts in

---

† This topic is treated in depth in Section 3.

individual psychology. As mentioned above, C. G. Jung described the images of the hero, the wise old man, the father, the mother, the self, the trickster and others as *archetypes*. All these archetypes appear both in psychology and mythology. Mythos of the culture activates archetypes that are latent in individuals.

Mythos organizes ideals and images of law and channels individual energy to achieve purposes of society. Mythology is the social counterpart of individual psychology, perhaps because it is an art form in which individuals project their inward symbols and archetypes. However, mythology takes on a life of its own that is embedded in the social group. Mythology and psychology are poles of the force field of law. Values, ideals, taboos, and norms of a culture begin and perpetuate themselves in its mythos. Myths store values, ideals, taboos and norms, and transmit them from person to person and generation to generation. From mythos, values are available for introjection into individuals of each succeeding generation. Myths—belief systems—utilize archetypes to draw from individuals the force needed to enforce and perpetuate the group's values, ideals, taboos and norms.

Mythos is critically important in the motive forces of law. It contains and stabilizes the moral base. It stabilizes our beliefs. It sets up rituals by which we live, including those that authenticate and support law. Myths are stories truly exposing human nature. They instill their values into each succeeding generation of culture. They are like DNA strings that store the genetic code. Like DNA strings, they assure that the group's values will replicate themselves in each new generation.

Collective representations are images of a reality that a group shares. They are products of collective psychology and embody the ideals of society. French sociologist, Emile Durkheim described collective representations. They originate in society's myths. Myths keep collective representations alive within the group. Myths have normative force because of collective representations. A collective representation is an impression shared by the group that joins with other such impressions to create the total reality that the group can share. For that group, the shared impressions are reality. Durkheim believed that collective representations form the basis of conceptual thinking. Their role in the mental life of individuals makes them quite influential. They promote survival of society, which explains their durability. In this sense, Durkheim's theory, which I am endorsing, is quite Darwinian.

Mythos participates in all three conditions essential for law, which we identified earlier: (1) The impulse for law derives from human motive. Mythos organizes the ideals and images of law and channels individual energy to achieve its purposes; (2) We must state the principle in words before we can recognize it as law. Mythos is the connection between impulses that give rise to law and language that expresses it; (3) We must accept the principle as authentic law. Mythos maintains belief systems that confer authenticity on law.

Language and Articulation[†]

Since the *thingness* of law is abstract, its reflection in words is its most visible evidence. Language is its means of expression. Frequently, we do not look beyond words to underlying forces. We ignore unconscious urgings that words reflect. Mythos connects impulses that produce law with language that expresses it. Emile Durkheim shows us that collective representations are the bases of concepts. We express concepts in language.

Differences in language reinforce cultural differences in law. Territoriality preserves both differences in law and differences in language. Territoriality may even cause the differences. Differing environmental conditions present differing obstacles to survival.

In evolution of law, particular cultures eventually express their values in words. Mythos is the storehouse for these linguistic expressions and their psychological underpinnings. Mythos includes myths, folk stories, fairy tales, literature and sacred writings. It also includes songs, poems and all other written and spoken expressions of the culture. Mythos preserves those expressions, in memory, on paper, and in other ways. By preserving stories and themes, mythos also preserves values and ideals of the culture.

Concepts of law cannot extend beyond the limits of the capability of language to express. For law, if we can't say it, we can't do it. Anything that we cannot express in language cannot be accepted as law. This limitation has important practical applications. Any limitation on development of language limits development of law. There are societies whose language cannot receive all of the nuances of modern legal systems. A society without nuclear capability, for instance, would have great difficulty regulating use of atomic energy. Even so, when that capability does develop, the society must deal with the age old rule, "Thou shalt not kill."

[†] This topic is treated in depth in Chapter 3.2.

A necessary step in law's development is statement of the principle *as a proposition of law*. Someone must say "Thou shalt not steal" or "Use only the notation *in.* to abbreviate inch." Obviously, someone must express the principle in words before society can recognize it as law. I call expression of the principle *articulation*. Rationality has a place in articulation. Primordial urgings alone do not produce law as we know it. Our conception of law intertwines with language. The organizing principle of rationality must act upon primordial urgings and myths that shape them for there to be law.

Authentication[†]

Mere expression of a principle is not enough to bring about recognition of that particular principle as law. The next step is what I call *authentication*. Early in the history of law, lawgivers ascribed law to the gods. Religion and law were not separate means of social control, but were one and the same. The religious leader was also the lawgiver. Ritual reinforced authority of the lawgiver. Mythos maintains belief systems that confer authenticity on law. Our modern systems of beliefs lend authenticity to our law, just as belief systems of ancients did for theirs. We know that the ancients thought their gods were authors of law. Yet we are unaware of the source of authority for our own law. Rationality, which is morally neutral, cannot be the basis of authenticity in law. Values we collectively hold are the fabric from which law is made. Mythos provides and maintains those collective values.

Mythos has rituals of authentication. Ancients had their rituals, and we have ours. Our rituals include formalities of legislative procedures and court proceedings. Only when properly and formally recognized with appropriate pomp and circumstance can even the loftiest impulses and expressions be *law*.

Thus, formal authentication determines whether it is proper to use the word *law* to describe a particular principle. However, the real test of effectiveness of the principle comes when we try to enforce it. If the formally authenticated principle lacks backing of the moral base and mythos, its enforcement will be difficult. As used here, the term *moral base* refers to forces of individual and collective conscience described above, and the term *mythos* includes belief systems of society. Possibly, law guides moral conscience, as contended by Aquinas and modern-day social engineers. However, such guidance is the exception rather than the

---

[†] This topic is treated in depth in Chapter 3.3.

rule. More frequently, moral conscience guides the development of law. Law is dependent on the moral base, along with the socialization drive, for enforcement power. When law becomes a guide to conscience, as often happens, it has become a part of mythos, and is operating as part of the moral base. If a legal principle is sufficiently acceptable to the masses, it becomes a part of the moral base.

Faith[†]

The apex of the hierarchy of human needs is the search for meaning in human existence. The argument presented in this book moves step by step from traditional theories of jurisprudence, through a description of various motive forces, to the ultimate motive for law, which exists in the realm of faith. The search for meaning is the search for *reality* or the *ultimate environment*. I am indebted to James Fowler for the term *ultimate environment*. His book, *The Stages of Faith*, describes the concept. The ultimate environment is as much mental as physical. It is our very best perception of what *is*. It is the cosmos. The search for the ultimate environment involves the desire to transcend finite human existence and relate to the infinite and eternal. We want to believe that we are significant. We sometimes try to find meaning in life by identifying with ephemeral, fleeting causes. Unless we identify our faith with our highest perception of the cosmos, however, it is likely to prove inadequate. Emptiness and lack of meaning result.

The search for meaning comes with the package of basic human needs. Survival is a useful but limited principle for explaining human behavior. We do not survive merely for the sake of survival and procreation. We seek meaning and purpose in life, and we usually survive as a result. The search for meaning is the fountainhead of all human activity, including law. Faith in eternal verities, eternal truth, and transcendent justice has been a historical mainstay for law. Transcendent justice means justice that is more than just someone's idea of right and wrong. Such justice extends beyond the individual and has a place in the scheme of things. This faith is alive and well among the general population today, although often stripped of motive advantages of belief in eternal reward and punishment.

Mythos has preserved our faith in *justice*. Along with Socrates, we believe that justice is *one*. Religious and irreligious alike appeal to justice as the basis of reasonableness for their positions on various issues. We

---

[†] This topic is treated in depth in Section 6.

believe that justice exists and that we can find it. Without such faith in justice, there would be no power in law. There would be no motive force.

If simple legends and myths have a strong impact on humans, then the power of the great religious traditions is obvious. Stories and rituals perpetuated by the great religions form the basis of weddings and funerals and other important events in the life of society. Each president of the United States has placed his hand on the Bible while pronouncing the oath of office. Without question, the Judeo-Christian heritage remains a major factor in the normative forces of western civilization. Its value system is the basis for authenticity of institutions, as well as for our perceptions of right and wrong. Other religious traditions, such as Islam and Buddhism, are equally influential in their areas of operation. Major problems often result from conflict between various systems of belief.

Only a Summary

This has been an all-too-terse summary of the motive theory of law for a broad-brush comparison with other theories. The theory that I am advancing will require all the remaining chapters to fully develop and explain.[11]

---

[11] A deeper understanding of this material will probably result from rereading this chapter as a summary after reading through the remainder of the book.

Chapter 1.3	Natural Law and Legal Positivism

What do lawyers think law is? Natural law and legal positivism are the two principal theories of jurisprudence that find support in today's legal community. Let me explain the meaning that I assign to the terms, since their usage is not always consistent. Natural law and legal positivism are categories into which practically all theories of jurisprudence fit. Natural law theories hold that law arises *naturally*, meaning that humans do not intentionally create it. Positivism holds that humans intentionally create law. The distinction proposed here is admittedly mine, but I submit that it is generally consistent with the writings of leading legal philosophers. H. L. A. Hart and Hans Kelsen are two leading proponents of positivism and Lon Fuller a leading proponent of natural law. Ronald Dworkin advocates a position somewhere between the poles of the dichotomy of natural law and positivism. These writers were active from the middle of this century into the seventies. Dworkin is part of a group who style themselves the new analytical school. More recently there has been a movement called the Critical Legal Studies Movement, led by writers such as Roberto Mangabeira Unger. Whatever the merits of these subsequent writings, they have not escaped the general classificatory scheme described here.

Please note that the natural law/positivism dichotomy largely omits the possibility of unintentional or unconscious origin of law in human sources. Many, if not most, writers appear somewhat aware of this possibility but choose not to deal with the matter in any depth. This possibility obviously poses a greater problem for positivists than for natural law advocates. The origin of Hart's rules of legitimation, Kelsen's *Grundnorms*, and Fuller's principles of legality are difficult to explain without consideration of this third possibility. Social and psychological motives are a necessary ingredient and prerequisite for existence of law and cannot be ignored or minimized. Natural law theorists sometimes recognize these motives, but because of their preoccupation with authentication and the role of reason, do not develop the point.

The distinction between natural law and positivism is a useful scheme of classification for dealing with the many existing theories. For instance, divine law is a natural law theory in the scheme of definition which I have suggested. Divine law holds that God created law. Since humans have nothing to do with its creation, divine law is more akin to natural law than to positive law created by humans. The classic description of positivism, by contrast, is that law is the *command of the sovereign*, which is clearly a human origin.

Social theories of law, holding that law arises from social aspects of human behavior, as opposed to intentional human conduct, are a species of natural law. All this terminology becomes very confusing, especially if the discussion involves whether law is of *human origin*. Law can be of human origin without being a creation of human intellect. There are two varieties of sociological theories of law. The more important, but less understood social theory, contends that law arises from the dynamics of society. According to this theory, laws, indeed courts and governments themselves, came into being as a result of social dynamics. The so-called historical school of jurisprudence that originated with Savigny in 19th century Germany with its emphsis on volksgeist, is social in nature. This viewpoint has a certain affinity with natural law theory and with the motive theory that I advocate. The second so-called social theory consists merely in admission of sociological facts into evidence in the trial of cases. The effect on resulting decisions introduces sociology into law. The second theory is more akin to positivism.

The moral order, key to Aquinas' natural law theory, is absent from pure sociological theories of law which see law arising purely at the level of society. Morality finds its way back into my theory, as *moral formation*. Individual conscience is the source of the moral base. Sources of societal forces are also in my theory: conscience, basic human needs, collective psychology, and group dynamics. My motive theory is compatible with social theories but explains origins of the motive for law in more psychological depth.

The idea of divine law is an important historical theory of law, but has few, if any, followers in today's community of legal scholars. The possibility of divine law, the direct mandate of law by God, is not given serious consideration in modern legal thinking. Scholars recognize historical importance of divine law as a theory. The earliest authentication of law was accomplished by attributing law to gods. Accounts of divine origin of law in the earliest history of law are now regarded by students of legal philosophy as *myth*. The possibility that law results from God's transcendence into our inward being, as opposed to transcendence into the external world, is not even considered.

The historical importance of divine law is not limited to an almost imperceptible ancient history, however. The *divine right of kings* was of major importance in legal theory in ousting power from the Church and vesting it in the state. It was popular at the time modern nation states began to emerge and break from authority of the Church. It was a convenient way to straddle the fence. The population was still tuned in to the idea of divine law. Advocates for the state contended that rather than making rules directly, God establishes kings to make law. In the Bible, St. Paul proclaimed that the powers that be are ordained of God. Legal positivism brought the other foot across the fence. It asserted that law is nothing more than a human contrivance. God has nothing to do with making law under this modern theory, not even by creating a moral order, and certainly not by creating a legislature or court! Nevertheless, it is likely that even to the beginning of the present century, the hope of eternal reward and fear of eternal punishment was a serious practical consideration underlying the legal-moral motive base of law.

It is one thing to hold that a god physically handed the law to a person; it is quite another to contend, as I do, that law is based, in part, on mythos of the culture. If religious impulse is understood as the human search for meaning, and myths as a natural human vehicle by which society interacts with individuals to provide that meaning, then "divine origin" of law becomes more interesting. In this connection, faith must be understood, at least in part, as the human perception of the ultimate environment, or the cosmos itself. Faith gives meaning to existence and forms the basis for our myths. Such faith involves the entire mental function, not merely the reasoning capacity.

Blaise Pascal observed:

> The last proceeding of reason is to recognize that there are an infinity of things which are beyond it.[12]

Ultimately, it is the search for meaning that gives rise to morals. The search for meaning justifies survival. We don't just eat to live and live to eat. All needs focus on the search for meaning. I am not advocating the divine origin of law as such. However, *belief* in the divine origin of law is

---

[12] Pascal, *Thoughts*, taken from *The European Philosophers from Descartes to Nietszche*, p. 122.

likely much more common than scholars admit, and divine law was a precursor of modern natural law theories.

The positivist idea that law is created by humans has also been around for a long time. Apparently the Greeks of Plato/Aristotle vintage were among the first to assert that humans can create law. In modern theories of legal positivism, creation of law by humans has come to be closely associated with the nation state. The motive theory does not displace or eliminate either natural law or positivism—it subsumes them, in much the same way that Einstein's theory of relativity subsumed the law of conservation of matter and the law of conservation of energy.

The Civil Rights Movement, which has so deeply affected the culture of which I am a part, provides interesting insights into both natural law theory and legal positivism. As we will see, Dr. King espoused natural law as a theory, but legal positivists can accurately claim that changes in law that resulted from the Civil Rights Movement were effected by court decisions and acts of Congress. The motive theory which I am advancing puts the Civil Rights Movement into a somewhat different and clearer perspective.

The Risk of Generalizations

Any general statement about legal positivism, natural law, or any theory of law is risky. There is no official spokesperson for any theory. Among individual legal philosophers, there is a tendency toward eclecticism. Various theories tend to overlap. Practicing lawyers adopt whatever approach is helpful to a client at the time. The present discussion relates my own understanding of the various theories. There are many books and articles which provide excellent discussions of natural law, positivism and all other theories. Therefore, I will not discuss these theories in detail. My purpose is only to provide enough insight into these theories to compare them to my motive theory. A huge amount of time and space would be required to produce a complete comparison, so I must limit myself to broad generalities.

The Natural Law Theory

Modern natural law traces its roots to St. Thomas Aquinas (c1224-1274) in the thirteenth century. This school of thought insists that law arises from the *moral order*. The human function is merely to discover the already existing principle. Any law that is not moral is just not law. The moral order is a part of God's creation. Recognition by the legislator is merely a formal step, to advise the public of the law's existence. Law, according to this theory, arises *naturally* from the moral order (as opposed to the physical order) of nature. The term *natural* is confusing. In its original usage, it applied to a metaphysical system of morality created by God and existing in nature, from which the legislator can extract legal principles. That description no longer agrees with our concept of nature. Please note, however, that natural law theory differs from a strict concept of divine origin in that the moral order (as opposed to law itself) was created by God, and laws are derived from it.

Today, natural law provides a way to explain *natural rights*. According to its advocates, individual rights are an inherent part of nature. This argument counters the contention often made by legal positivists that social utility, or the greatest good for the greatest number of people, is the justification for law. Legal positivists often, but do not always, attempt to justify law on utilitarian principles.

For the utilitarian, individual rights are subservient to the rights of the majority. Welfare of the group is more important than that of individuals. The utilitarian position is difficult to overcome without resort to some *higher order* to justify natural rights. To avoid the charge of resort to *metaphysics*, modern day natural rights advocates resort to humanism. Natural rights are difficult to explain without resorting to some abstraction such as *justice.* However, justice is a belief, and is as difficult to explain as rights themselves.

Immanuel Kant argued that morality has an independent universal existence. We are born with a sense of duty and can extract its principles through exercise of reason. According to Kant, the *categorical imperative* exists *a priori*. This approach is a natural law theory, in the sense that I use that term. It replaces Aquinas' moral order with a rational order. We can discover principles that undergird law and morality using *pure reason*, according to Kant.

Natural law theory was still very prevalent when the United States was founded, as is evident in historical documents. "We hold these truths to be self-evident, that all men are created equal, and that they are endowed by their creator with certain inalienable rights, that among these are life, liberty, and the pursuit of happiness. . . ." Legal positivism was only then being articulated as a theory by Bentham and Austin. Often, the U. S. Constitution is the hiding place for metaphysical rights of natural law. While Austin and Bentham were ascribing law to the sovereign, the French Revolution, in the name of democracy, was declaring the right of the majority to rule. A constitution was the only safe hiding place for the natural rights of individuals.

Natural Law Compared to Motive Law Theory

Motive theory agrees that law arises naturally and that the moral base is an important element in the natural derivation of law. However, it differs from historic and current descriptions of natural law in several ways. I contend that law and morals actually arise from a common source: individual conscience and its interaction with society. Law is a social, or corporate, response to basic human needs. Balancing of needs and goods is part of the role of law. Also, law differs from morals in that it exists only when *authenticated*. Authentication is formal enactment or pronouncement of law by the legislature or court.

To say, as some natural law advocates do, that law is "based on morals" is not a complete statement of the matter. In their origin, morals and law are practically *the same*. Only as the element of necessity comes into play do they begin to diverge. The split crystallizes in the enactment, or authentication, of law through accepted ritual.

The motive theory is dynamic (as opposed to static), in that it explains why law happens. Motive theory recognizes that motive force must be present for law to be effective. Natural law theory does not explain law as a dynamic process. Natural law advocates see law as a *set of principles* derived from the moral order. The approach focuses on the natural origin of law in the moral order as the basis of law's *authentication*. Modern varieties of the theory seem to base the natural origin of law on reason or logic, but this is more a shift in emphasis than in theory. What I mean is that logic and reason, as a basis for natural law, are seen as part of reality existing independently of human origin—as something that we find, rather than something we created. In this, logic and reason are merely modern day equivalents of Aquinas' moral order. They are Platonic and metaphysical.

Origin of law differs from authentication of law. Both are necessary for law to be effective. Traditional natural law theory ignores collective psychology, mythos, and the close relationship between law and language. I see those factors as integral parts of the reality of law. Without them, law does not *effectively exist.*

Natural law leaves the situs and origin of law unclear. When Aquinas wrote in the Middle Ages, the metaphysical origin of morals was quite acceptable. After all, the Church was right there, tangibly representing moral principles. My theory traces law to a fountainhead in the social nature of humans. To narrow the origin to motive forces in human nature leaves the origin appropriately mysterious. Yet it doesn't have us pulling law out of thin air. Even the rational aspects of law obviously begin in mental activity. The natural law appeal to an unexplained moral order is inconsistent with present day faith patterns, and confuses motive with authentication.

How can the motive theory that I am proposing overcome the argument that human nature and motive forces are too vague to form the basis of law? One starting point is that mathematical laws of probability stabilize the vagueness of human nature and its motive forces. These mathematical laws, dealing with the behavior of groups of things, as opposed to behavior of individuals composing the group, show that group behavior is predictable. For instance, actuarial tables are possible because of such mathematical laws of probability. More importantly, however, collective psychology and group dynamics transform individual energies into social forces. This adds to stability by inducing conformity.

Natural law, in some instances, does not have the same respect for the role of authentication which I recognize. Natural law reserves the right to disavow certain authenticated laws thought to be *immoral*. This is perhaps the toughest problem facing legal theory. Such a *right* cannot harmonize with legal theory. It is not a theory of law—it is a theory of *law not working*. A duly enacted law that is immoral is ineffective law, but law just the same. It does not gain the power of the culture—the power of mythos. The "right to disobey an immoral law" is a "right of revolution," and is inconsistent with any legal system. It is mythos reasserting itself when law has failed. It happens, and is natural, but it is not law. Nature apparently provides no means wholly separated from human agency for authenticating law. Our legal system has procedural rules for challenging established law. Paradoxically, those rules are themselves part of established law, and have their limits.

To criticize a properly declared law, which officialdom refuses to retract, we resort to a *higher justice*. Many writers refer to such justice. Yet who is author of such higher justice? To condemn law on moral grounds is to say, "I read mythos differently. My view is better than that of the legislature or court." If enough people follow the dissenters, then after a period of disorder, order reasserts itself and there is a new effort at law.

Nevertheless, law doesn't govern violent revolutions. *Effective* law is responsive to needs of people. It makes needed changes and thereby prevents revolutions. Law creates and protects rights as the mirror image of duty. One person's right is another's duty. Power for good or evil, for survival or dissolution, is natural.

Appeal to natural law is not a regression to the Middle Ages. During the Civil Rights Movement, Dr. Martin Luther King, Jr., in his famous *Letter from the Birmingham City Jail*, passionately appealed to natural law. He contended there is a *"moral responsibility to disobey unjust laws."* The following is from the text of the letter:

> One may well ask, "How can you advocate breaking some laws and obeying others?" The answer lies in the fact that there are two types of laws, just and unjust. One has a moral responsibility to disobey unjust laws. An unjust law is a human law that is not rooted in eternal law and natural law. Any law that uplifts human personality is just, any law that degrades human personality is unjust. An unjust law is a code that a numerical or power majority group compels a minority group to obey but does not make binding on itself. This is difference made legal.
>
> I do not advocate evading or defying the law, as would the rabid segregationist. That would lead to anarchy. One who breaks an unjust law must do so openly, lovingly, and with a willingness to accept the penalty. An individual who breaks a law that conscience tells him is unjust, and willingly accepts the penalty of imprisonment in order to arouse the conscience of the community over its injustice, is in reality expressing the highest respect for law.[13]

In a very real sense, Dr. King did not disobey *the law*, when he refused to follow segregation laws. He appealed not only to natural law, but also to federal courts. His mythos won out in the Civil Rights Movement. Did the Civil Rights Movement make new law, as positivists would contend, or did it invoke Dr. King's natural law? Or did laws that originated in the Civil Rights Movement arise from human motive forces, to address human needs? Were they discovered as a part of Dr. King's natural law, or did they arise from his archetypal activity, that drew on the deepest myths of our culture? After all, Dr. King was not primarily a legal theorist—he was a man of the cloth.

Legal Positivism

Legal positivism is a product of the modern era, appearing about six hundred years after Aquinas described his theory of natural law. The Age of Reason set its hold on the human intellect before Jeremy Bentham and John Austin first described legal positivism. The decline of the Church and ascendancy of the nation state were complete at the time legal positivism appeared. The mode of authentication of law had

---

[13] Dr. M. L. King, Jr., *Letter from the Birmingham City Jail*, 1965.

evolved to legislative processes, often in the framework of a representative democracy. The change from edicts of an absolute monarch to the enactments of a legislative body presented no problem to this new theory. The basic purpose of law is to provide the greatest good for the largest number of people. This is the utilitarian approach, typical of the Age of Reason. For the utilitarian, this was the justification for law. It is easy to see why this theory has had tremendous appeal in a world that seeks law in reason or rational principle. Utilitarianism is an alluring appeal to mathematical justification for law. The problem, of course is *who says* what is *good*, for the greatest number, or whomever.

Legal positivism is a product of its times. The motive forces that produce law settled a particular mode of *authentication*; i. e. legislative enactment or pronouncement by a court. Bentham and Austin seized upon that mode as the *origin* of law. After all, before enactment, a principle is not law; but afterwards, it is law. This approach gives rise to *formalism* which searches for legal authenticity in *formal* enactment or pronouncement. By the time legal positivism arrived on the scene, the nation state had triumphed over the Church and had sole control of the lawmaking function. The people *believed* in the nation state. Please notice the subtle authenticating role of faith.

The problem for jurisprudence, according to the legal positivist, is to trace the particular principle back to an *authentic source*. If a principle arises from such a source, then the principle is law. If a principle is a command of the sovereign, it's law. The sovereign is the authentic source. In modern parlance, the sovereign is established by H. L. A. Hart's rules of legitimation and Hans Kelsen's *Grundnorm*. Basically these are national constitutions, although both writers make an effort to explain away the effect of custom by incorporating it into their theories as part of the "constitution." Does the "adoption" of formal vehicles for making law, such as legislatures and courts, mean that any whim or caprice duly enacted by the legislature or pronounced by the court becomes law? Theoretically, the positivist is locked to that conclusion. Interestingly, Kelsen departs from the thrust of his own theory to say that if a law is totally ineffective, it is not valid. If the principle that ineffective law is not law is part of Kelson's *grundnorm*, (and custom also, as he admits elsewhere), one wonders what useful purpose a *grundnorm* serves. No more effective Scylla and Charibdis could be devised by fate for destruction of *grundnorms* than *custom* and *ineffectiveness*.

Legal positivists find the origin of their theory in Jeremy Bentham and his utilitarian theory. John Austin developed the positivist theory in a specific legal sense. Oliver Wendell Holmes adjusted the theory to twentieth century America. "Law is what a court does," according to Holmes. In this statement, Holmes recognized the court as at least part of *the sovereign*. He also set the stage for the overemphasis of the case method which we discussed earlier.

Holmes' statement that law is what a court does provides interesting material for analysis. If a law professor or senior law partner tells a student or young lawyer that law is what a court does, it is probably, in a metaphorical sense, sound practical advice. The statement conveys the message that the practitioner is bound by court rulings, and that court rulings are due great respect. However, taken literally and as a statement of absolute truth about the nature of law, the statement is absolutely frightening. As a judge, I am a trial court, but I certainly do not suffer from the delusion that what *I* do is law, although I try with all my ability to always rule consistently with law. Of course, my work is subject to review in state appellate courts and in some instances, in federal courts. So perhaps what Holmes was saying was that what the court of final review does is law, but that won't work either. In most matters, mine is the final ruling in the matter before me. Are we to assume that when a case arrives in the Supreme Court of the United States, the justices look at each other to see what they are doing so that they will know what the law is? Holmes' homespun metaphor breaks down completely when analyzed in this manner. It is frightening to think that Holmes has been taken literally and seriously. Perhaps my theory about involvement of human motive forces in law can help make sense of Holmes' statement. Perhaps if we look at motive forces acting on and within judges, including their devotion to ideals of our system of justice and their accountability to the public we see more of the true nature of law. Such forces and ideals arise within the depths of society. But forces and ideals must in some way precede the court's decision. Holmes probably knew all of this, but those who followed him did not. One might just as well say that ham is what a butcher does as to say that law is what a court does.

The positivist approach leads to the conclusion that the system of law is autonomous. Positivists assume that we can extend rationales of the legal system to solve any new problems that may arise. We do not have to leave the system. Extension of the system is a function of reason, according to positivists. Courts alone can do it all. Positivists hold that law is a proper tool for social engineering; that is, for mandating rational solutions to human problems.

An ever-increasing role of government in social control is a predictable result of legal positivism. The increasing role of government in social control is at the expense of moral development. It is at the expense of other valued institutions such as family, schools, churches, business organizations, and labor unions in a pluralistic society. Mythos and moral conscience are not believed essential in the system described by legal positivists. Ignoring mythos and moral conscience is a flaw in legal positivism.

The major problem with legal positivism is its inability to explain satisfactorily the existence of individual rights. This gives continuing vitality to natural law theory. Legal positivists have difficulty overcoming the argument that their theory favors powers of the state over the rights of individuals and naturally forming groups. Meeting needs of the greatest number achieves more good than satisfying the demands of an individual. Legal philosophy for most American courts and lawyers is a strange amalgamation of natural law and positivism. The conflict cannot be resolved without considering motive.

Legal Positivism Compared to Motive Theory

The motive theory affirms the need for formal authentication which is a central idea of legal positivism. However, motive theory insists that the force of law—the motive for law—arises from the social nature of humans. Authentication, as positivists contend, is important, and law doesn't exist without it. However, without backing of the moral base in human nature, law is weak and ineffective. Authentication alone does not make law effective. Moreover, legal positivism has no theoretical control for absolute power of the state. After all, the state is the source of law, according to this theory. How can the creature control the creator? My theory includes motive force and the requirement of survival as basic ingredients of law. Government *must* enact those laws necessary for survival, or else government loses authenticity. Individual rights are a part of the package. Otherwise, human motive that makes law work will not be available.

Motive theory explains how mythos and moral conscience control arbitrary exercise of immoral power by the state. These natural forces authenticate government and law and impose appropriate restraints on exercise of power. Legal positivists do not solve the problem of uncontrolled governmental power. They do not look beyond the authenticated *form* of government.

Without the support of conscience and mythos, law is ineffective and difficult to enforce. If enforced, it breeds revolution. A state that is so rigid that it cannot adjust to evolving realities of life will fail. It will either decline naturally or by revolution. The legislature and courts cannot adopt as law whatever whim or caprice may occur to them. Mythos, individual and social conscience, and basic human needs set the limits for effective law. The legislature and courts have a range of choices of principles which fall within these limits. However, they do not have absolute discretion to disregard the limits. They act always at the risk of impotency, if not revolution. I should mention specifically the risk of failure at the polls, for American political parties. Dissolution of the Soviet Union in the face of pressing need illustrates and magnifies the assertion of this paragraph, which was first written before disintegration of the Soviet Union became evident to the world.

Human intuition constantly replenishes the supply of workable legal principles. These new principles become part of mythos if society allows freedom of expression. Therefore, the lawmaker has many choices in establishing law. This illustrates how basic human rights are part of the power of law. Viability of a society depends on support and energy of individuals. Society *must* recognize basic human rights, if it is to survive. Legislative and judicial pronouncements which fall beyond the limitations of motivating power are *law*, but *ineffective* law.

The legal positivist is correct when he argues that law is traceable back to an authentic source. But where do authentic sources originate? What makes a source *authentic?* This is a real problem for positivists. I contend that this is more a matter of faith—of belief systems—than a matter of rationality. Further, not every law from an authentic source is a good law. There are differences in quality of law. Natural law advocates say that an immoral law is not authentic law. I say that it is not efficient law and that it is destined to fail. The moral quality of law is a part of its motive base. Merely tracing law to an authentic source assures neither its moral quality, nor its effectiveness.

Importance of Chronology

Every theory that tries to explain law reflects the belief systems, or world-view of its time and place. Chronology of the appearance of various legal theories is important. For instance, natural law appeared at the height of the Middle Ages, when Church and state were in competition for social control. At the time of Aquinas, the Church-state struggle for supremacy in social control was at its height. By the time of Bentham and

Austin, six centuries later, the state was firmly in control of the power that regulates social order. Legal positivism appeared only after the state was firmly in charge of the only recognized official means of ordering social control. Legal positivism is characteristic of the age of the nation state. Understanding thought processes and politics of their times is essential to understanding existing theories of law and their relationship to my theory. All existing theories, except possibly social theories and legal realism, appeared before Sigmund Freud, Jean Piaget, and others explained the dynamics of moral formation. The time has arrived for articulation of a new theory which more adequately reflects the world-view of our times. The theory must be survival oriented, so that it recognizes Darwinism. Neither natural law, positivism nor any combination of them adequately comprehends the demand for orderliness in the presently emerging world order.

The theory known to jurisprudence as legal realism appeared early in the twentieth century. The case method and the audacity of courts in pronouncement of law, naturally lead anyone who examines external appearances to conclude that law is what a court says it is, and nothing more. Legal realists see this state of affairs both as a problem, when judges are reluctant to advance social causes, and an opportunity for problem solving when judges are willing to be social engineers. The term "realism" as used to describe this school of thought has absolutely nothing to do with the historical concept of "realism" (as opposed to nominalism) in philosophy.

The legal realists saw that judges make decisions "subjectively." They thought they saw an *objective* reality consisting of *hard facts* with which law is or should be concerned. In a sense, legal realism is not a theory of law at all. It is a response to the overall problem of authentication that says, "Law is not real; only what judges decide in particular cases is real." Legal realism is a predictable response of skeptical minds to dogmas of legal positivism. It does not escape the fold of positivism. Its skepticism has led many to doubt the reality of legal principle, which has encouraged case by case dispute resolution without predictability. Lack of predictability in the legal system brought on by legal realist thinking possibly encouraged revitalization of natural law, with its appealing universals.

Modern legal philosophers have built on work of earlier legal philosophers without sufficient attention to the burgeoning social sciences. Legal theorists still appeal to rationalism as the basis of law. Sometimes they purport to embrace a social theory of law. However, as mentioned before, they usually merely embrace treatment of sociology in the law of evidence rather than a theory that law arises from inner workings of society. Words such as *nature* and *human nature* are very slippery. Words acquire meaning and content from their culture and place in history. Psychologists have only recently explored the workings of the unconscious. Earlier legal philosophers did not consider this information, or have it in mind when they used the words *human nature*. All presently existing theories appeared before Maslow described the hierarchy of needs that are the basis of human motive. The major theories appeared before the works of C. G. Jung and Emile Durkheim, which show the deep relationship between psychology and mythology. Thus even though earlier legal philosophers frequently referred to *human nature*, they did not have the in-depth understanding of human nature now available. Focusing on our new understanding of human nature and the workings of the unconscious will change our perception of law.

Both law and morals proceed from interaction of individual consciences with society. Any theory of law that does not recognize this elementary point is a hall of mirrors and echoes. Any point looks like the beginning. Cause and effect become hopelessly confused. Law and justice are merely shadows of operative principles which arise from the depths of the social nature of humans. The source may be beyond the depth that our rationality can penetrate.

Failure to understand these factors causes us to deal with mere appearances of various manifestations of law. Thus, naturalists see law arising from morals. Legal positivists see law as the command of the sovereign. Social theorists see law arising from social dynamics. Legal realists see law as merely a problem solving technique. This reminds us of the fable of the blind Indians examining an elephant! "He is like a wall (the side)." "No, he is like a snake (the tail)." "No, he is like a tree (his leg)." We can paint a better picture of an elephant than of law, but a common element underlies all these perceptions of law. There is merit in each theory, but each theory is only part of the picture. Each theory reflects the world-view of the culture and time in which it arose.

Natural Law and Legal Positivism

Natural law has roots into the age of faith. Legal positivism, the product of the Age of Reason, is a product of empiricism, typical of the scientific age. In all legal theories, authentication focuses on the basic philosophical questions: What is law? How does one determine whether a particular principle is or is not *law*? The different theoretical definitions of law focus on these questions. Positivists contend that law is the command of the sovereign—a product of human intellect. Identity of the sovereign is historically posited. Naturalists say that law arises naturally—from the moral order, for instance. I contend that the two positions are reconcilable and that motive theory confirms the truths of both positivism and natural law. The two converge at the point where public utility meets private rights. The two positions are parts of the natural dynamics of law, and there will always be tension between them. They are the dual poles of a single system. They both draw upon the motive forces that undergird law, but fail to articulate motive force as a necessary ingredient in law.

The question of what is to be law resolves itself to one of perceived need, or necessity. If a principle is essential to survival, we either adopt it or we do not survive. This limiting factor applies to both natural law and positivism. The difference between the two is one of *judgment* about what is necessary. The theories are consistent. This does not mean that the two sides should forsake their respective viewpoints. One task of law is to adjust the tension between needs of individuals and needs of society, which, after all, consists of other individuals. Tension is a necessary part of the dynamics. Divergent viewpoints are desirable in maintaining balance. The two viewpoints are part of a single system, like debits and credits in double entry accounting. The mistake of communism may have been its Hegelian attempt to synthesize. The needs of society and individuals are always in some ways antagonistic, but ultimately each depends on the other. When debits synthesize with credits the result is zero. Assets have been liquidated to pay debts.

The struggle between rights of individuals and rights of society do not always have clear solutions. Questions of consistent application of principles, equal treatment of parties, and distributive justice in a world of relative scarcity have their place. Reasonable people can disagree over questions of allocation of resources. The authenticating principle of need for survival is thickly overlaid with such questions. We must resolve such questions before we can judge what principles we *need* for survival of society. Sometimes it is unimportant which principle is chosen, but it is essential that one of the alternative principles is selected. For instance, it makes no difference whether law requires that we drive on the right or left side of the road, so long as we are all directed to drive on one side or the other. Necessity mandates a workable system, often leaving open the choice of specific principles.

We can consider basic rights as bench marks. They arise in our mythos. They represent our judgment about the amount of freedom an individual must have for society to function well. They have emanated from human nature in societal relationships and become defined in the same manner as other legal principles. They reinforce individual security necessary for mental health. They are, therefore, necessary. There is no theoretical difference between the point at which rights of individuals begin and the reach of society ends. Society will do what it must do to survive. After all, it is composed of individuals, all doing their best to survive! So there will be strong motive to enforce individual rights. Obviously, society is more likely to survive than are particular individuals, and survival of the population—the group—is important to individuals.

In these discussions I have frequently used the Civil Rights Movement as a background to help bring the discussions into focus. We have seen Dr. King's endorsement of natural law. Certainly legal positivists claim a major role in civil rights, especially in court-made law such as the *Brown* school desegregation case. Let me simply pose a question here to which I will return later: does either natural law or positivism provide an adequate explanation for the power of forces that brought about changes in law incidental to the Civil Rights Movement? Does either explain the continuing power of civil rights laws? In the next two chapters I will explain in more detail what I believe to be the motive forces of law. Consistently with his appeal to natural law, Dr. King frequently appealed to *conscience* in his writings and speeches. In the next chapter, we will explore conscience as a motive force. Then we will move on to a discussion of basic human needs as sources of motive. I invite readers to look carefully at the success of the Civil Rights Movement in light of these discussions.

2 Psychological Components

odern psychological theory describes forces that work at the deepest levels of law. Theories of motivation, moral formation, cognition, and personality structure help to explain why law happens. Theories about the unconscious explain much about the hidden force of law. Such explanations were not available before knowledge of modern psychology emerged, and have not been appropriately considered in legal philosophy.

Psychology claims to be a new science. The textbook for my college course in general psychology declared that psychology became a separate science in 1879, when Wilhelm Wundt set up a laboratory for study of conscious experience.[14] I am not so sure. There was much knowledge of psychology long before that time. Psychology has made tremendous progress since 1879, but in many ways psychology remains within the womb of philosophy. It is the modern counterpart of epistemology—the theory of knowledge —which is an integral part of philosophy.

Significant progress of psychology during the past century opens new vistas for legal philosophy. Progress in psychology does not rest upon its separation from other fields of knowledge. It is quite important, in fact, that we see psychology as an extension of western epistemology. Close relations between psychology of the West and philosophy of the East are emerging. These connections are important to legal philosophy. They provide new insight into the psychological structure of social order, and renew our understanding of the importance of belief systems.

Psychological theories that show how individuals relate to the social cosmos are critically important to understanding the force of law. Let me

---

14 Ruch, *Psychology and Life, Fifth Edition*, 1958, p. 28.

paint a big picture with a short sentence. *Metaphysical concepts, wandering nomads in the Age of Reason, find a home in unconscious mental processes.* Aquinas' *moral order*, the cornerstone of his theory of natural law, finds a counterpart in modern theories of moral formation. Once we grasp this important connection we can understand the central role of psychology in the natural motive for law. The vast arena of unconscious mental activities in which moral formation occurs provides a situs for Aquinas' *moral order*. We need no longer resort to metaphysics. We can understand the thrust of Aquinas' thinking with benefit of modern psychological concepts.

In this section we discuss psychological underpinnings of law. In the first chapter, we discuss psychology of moral formation, which describes the realm of moral order on which natural law relies. I realize, of course, that Aquinas did not consider modern concepts of moral formation as a part of his theory. However, morals are what they are, and modern theories of moral formation shed new light on his theory. In the second chapter we discuss basic human needs—psychological theory of motivation. Basic human needs help explain what motivates individuals to obey law, and they are quite utilitarian. What better way can there be to pursue happiness than to satisfy basic needs? Basic human needs also help show what motivates groups of individuals to compel compliance by non-conformists. Such compliance provides the greatest happiness for the greatest number. Examination of basic human needs shows how economic theories relate to human motives that produce law. Just as psychological concepts of moral formation undergird Aquinas' moral order and natural law, psychological concepts of motivation embraced in basic human needs undergird Bentham's utilitarian positivism.

The chapter on archetypes and symbols introduces Jungian principles important to the imagery of law. The chapter shows how basic individual needs act through genetically posited mental structures called archetypes to direct energies of individuals so that they also satisfy needs of the group. It also lays a predicate for discussion of connections between mythology and psychology.

The fourth chapter describes *collective psychology*, the force behind law. Collective psychology emerges from dynamics discussed in the first three chapters of this section. Collective psychology is a facet of sociology. Emile Durkheim introduces us to *collective representations*. In a sense, collective psychology is merely an extension of those earlier discussions, but takes us beyond psychological underpinnings of natural law and positivism, and indeed integrates the two.

Law arises from human ecology as a result of naturally occurring psychological and social forces. The forces are often unconscious. Law enables human beings to relate to each other and to the larger environment in a meaningful, orderly way.

Conscience

What is the origin of the force within us that requires us to obey law? What is the internal urge that we call *duty*? Why is conscience well-developed in some individuals, while almost absent in others? How do we induce individuals to obey law? We focus on these questions in the present chapter. In fact, we examine these questions throughout the book. You will recall these as the *why* questions mentioned earlier. *Why do people engage in activities that amount to law?*

Earlier, I argued that we should ask why most people obey law, to discover why certain persons do *not* obey law. I pointed out that the case method does not explain why people obey law. It neither teaches about forces that cause rules, nor explains why we enforce rules. The case method relies heavily on rational aspects of law. Rational aspects are only a small part of the psychology of law. By exploring mysterious forces that usually bring about compliance with law's requirements, we are likely to discover reasons for non-compliance. We also begin to see how society taps into the individual's motive energy to compel adherence to its rules, and we begin to uncover the origin of rules themselves.

The word *conscience* frequently appeared in writings and speeches of Dr. Martin Luther King, Jr. He appealed to the *conscience* of southern whites. He appealed to the *conscience* of the nation. He challenged laws which he believed unjust on the basis of *conscience*. His appeals to conscience were heard. The idea of conscience is a central concept of the Civil Rights Movement, and deserves careful attention. Dr. King's appeal to natural law was founded on conscience, and invoked the moral order which Aquinas made the basis of natural law. Just exactly what is this thing called conscience to which Dr. King made his appeal?

The Unconscious

The best explanation of the source of conscience, or the sense of duty, comes from modern psychology. Kant and others in the late eighteenth and early nineteenth centuries presented interesting theories suggesting *a priori* origin of the sense of duty. I will examine those theories later.

One searches in vain among ancients for an explanation of the *existence* of conscience. Development of conscience occurs mainly at *unconscious* mental levels rather than at a rational level.

Sigmund Freud recognized the importance of the *unconscious*. Other thinkers recognized the existence of unconscious mental operations long before Sigmund Freud acquainted the world with its *importance*. Freud's disciple, Dr. A. A. Brill, describes Freud's perception of consciousness and the unconscious as follows:

> Unlike those psychologists and philosophers who use such terms as conscious, co-conscious, and sub-conscious in a very loose and confused manner, Freud conceives *consciousness* simply as an organ of perception. One is conscious or aware of those mental processes which occupy one at any given time. In contrast to this, the unconscious is utterly unknown and cannot be voluntarily recalled. No person can bring to light anything from his unconscious unless he is made to recall it. . . . Midway between conscious and unconscious there is foreconscious or preconscious, which contains memories of which one is unaware, but which one can eventually recall with some effort.[15]

Freud focused attention on many mental processes of which we are unaware. Although we are unaware of them, unconscious mental processes vitally affect our behavior.

Many processes that are active in the poorly understood force of law occur unconsciously within individuals or between individuals. We do not *consciously* acquire our set of values and taboos. Values and taboos which we convey to or instill in our children are not always conveyed consciously. We consciously acquire some specific *contents* of conscience, and we consciously transmit some of those values. Nevertheless, this does not explain how those contents attach to our emotions so that we feel compelled to obey them. Conscience has an emotional foundation that compels or at least urges us to abide by the norms and values of our culture. Conscience is not specific norms or values themselves. It is one thing to know that one should not do a particular act. It is another to feel shame for having done that act, and yet another to feel anger when we see someone else doing the forbidden act. We do not consciously acquire the emotional basis for conscience. Conscience formation occurs mainly at an unconscious level of mental operation.

Understanding the role of the unconscious in human behavior is a pivotal point in understanding the theory of this book. I frequently refer

---

[15] *The Basic Writings of Sigmund Freud*, Introduction by A. A. Brill, p. 13.

to the unconscious throughout the book. Unconscious operations are basic in formation of conscience, or sense of duty. The individual's sense of duty translates into collective psychology that energizes law. All these processes and others that are important to operation of law occur, at least in part, unconsciously.

Basic human needs, the sources of motive, often operate unconsciously. Archetypes and symbols involve a special type of unconscious described by C. G. Jung. He argued there is a universal unconscious that all humanity shares, which he called the *collective unconscious*. While the role of the unconscious has been explored by psychology, its role in social matters is poorly understood.

Moral Formation: The Super-ego

Sigmund Freud labeled what we know as *conscience* as the *super-ego*. Conscience formation involves internalization of the parent's commands. It also entails internalization of the *image* of parents. Freud's daughter, Anna, described formation of the super-ego or conscience for a group of teachers:

> But this detachment of the child from the earliest and most important of his love objects [the parents] only succeeds on one very definite condition. It is as if the parents said: You can certainly go away, but you must take us with you. That is to say, the influence of the parents does not end with removal from them and not even with the abatement of feeling for them. Their influence simply changes from a direct to an indirect one. We know that the little child obeys his father's or mother's orders only when he is in their immediate environment and has to fear a direct reprimand from them or their personal interference. Left alone, he follows without scruple his own wishes. But after his second or third year his behavior alters. He is now well-aware, even when the person in authority has left the room, of what is permitted and what forbidden, and can regulate his actions accordingly. We say that besides the forces that influence him from without he has also developed an inner force which determines his behavior.

> Among psychoanalysts there exists no doubt as to the origin of this inner voice, or conscience, as it is generally designated. It is the continuation of the voice of the parents which is now operative from within instead of as formerly, from without. The child has absorbed, as it were, a part of his father or mother, or rather the orders and prohibitions which he has constantly received from them and made these an essential part of his being. In the course of growth this intensified parental part of him assumes ever more and more the role of the parents in the material world, demanding and forbidding certain things. It now continues from within the education of the

child who has already become independent of his actual parents. The child gives to this part of his being which has come originally from without a very special place of honor in his own ego, regards it as an ideal, and is prepared to submit to it, often indeed more slavishly, than in his younger days he had submitted to his actual parents.[16]

No doubt the intimate level of communication between parent and child is central to formation of the sense of duty. At that level there is non-verbal communication, as well as commands. Basic acceptance or rejection—often more felt than heard—is all important in this formative process. The super-ego has two functions. It *demands* and it *forbids*. The sense of duty involves both functions. They serve separate purposes. Forbidden activities are *taboos*. Incest is usually *taboo*. The term applies to any activity that the super-ego places off limits. Dr. A. A. Brill gives a more technical description of conscience, or super-ego:

> For just as the ego is a modified portion of the id as a result of contact with the outer world, the super-ego represents a modified part of the ego, formed through experiences absorbed from the parents, especially from the father. The super-ego is the highest mental evolution attainable by man and consists of a precipitate of all prohibitions and inhibitions, all the rules of conduct which are impressed on the child by his parents and by parental substitutes. The feeling of conscience depends altogether on the development of the super-ego.[17]

The super-ego also places its *demands* on individuals. This function gives rise to the *ego ideal*. In exaggerated form, the ego ideal can result in the individual placing unreasonable, perfectionist demands upon himself. More commonly, the ego ideal instigates a positive sense of duty and requires us to exact high standards of conduct for ourselves. Social psychologist Argyle describes the ego ideal:

> In addition to perceiving themselves more or less as they actually are at present, people build up in imagination an ideal self, which is what they would like to become. This is a future goal, to be striven for. It need not be unattainable; for some people it is just a little better than the actual self; when it is attained, the ideal self is then revised upwards a little. It may refer to positions and roles to be occupied, or to personality traits. [* * *] An important and curious feature of the ideal self is that when the desired standard is attained, people do not sit back enjoying their self-esteem, but

---

[16] Anna Freud, *Psycho-Analysis for Teachers and Parents*, pp. 86-88.

[17] *The Basic Writings of Sigmund Freud*, Edited and with Introduction by A. A. Brill, pp. 12-13.

re-set their goals. This does not appear to reduce self-esteem, and it seems that satisfaction is desired from accepting the new goal, which in some sense is part of the self-image. To travel hopefully is better than to arrive.[18]

Perhaps one way to distinguish these two functions is by content. Taboos are specific. They forbid particular activities. The ego ideal is a coercive model, by which individuals ask, "What do my parents (or my ideals) expect of me in this situation?" The ego ideal is the mechanism by which the sense of duty expands during maturation and cognitive development. The ego ideal is the emotional base to which new content attaches. It interacts with cognitive function and reason. Both specific taboos and the ego ideal motivate individuals to obey law.

Internalization

Some will no doubt protest that the Freudian super-ego is no longer in vogue. Many psychologists reject Freud's theory in its narrow, technical reliance on formation of conscience arising from resolution of the *Oedipus dilemma*. Oedipus was a character in Greek mythology who unwittingly killed his father and married his mother. The Oedipal dilemma arises from the young child's competition with the parent of the same sex for attention of the parent of the opposite sex. Fear of the parent of the same sex resolves itself into the superego. The child internalizes the powerful image of the parent of the same sex. He then obeys commands of the internalized parent. This description of conscience formation relates the process to sexuality. I do not depend on this narrow interpretation of Freudian principles. However, internalization of norms, and of powerful images, is clearly a part of the source of conscience. All theories of moral formation involve internalization of demands of society. Jean Piaget, one of the leading child psychologists of the twentieth century, supports the idea of internalization. Piaget left no doubt about the widespread acceptance of the notion of internalization in moral formation. Along with co-author Barbel Inhelder he wrote:

> Freud popularized the notion of the "superego," or the internalization of the affective image of the father or parents, which becomes a source of duties, coercive models, remorse, and sometimes even of self-punishment. But this conception is older than Freud: it can be found remarkably developed, in the work of Baldwin. This writer explained the formation of the self in terms of imitation (since imitation is necessary to provide first a complete image of the child's own body, then a comparison between the general reactions of

---

[18]   Argyle, *Social Interaction*, p. 359.

the other and the self). Further, Baldwin showed that beyond a certain point, which is reached because of conflicts of will and the superior general powers of the adults, the self of the parents can no longer be imitated immediately, and thus becomes an "ideal self" which is a source of coercive models and of moral conscience.[19]

Thus, without rejecting internalization, Piaget argues that formation of a sense of duty results from a combination of the child's affection and fear concerning the adult. He shows that relationships from which a child gets his values can be of two kinds. First, they can be unilateral, between a child and a superior. Secondly, they can result from mutual respect based on reciprocity, between equals. The second type is the relationship with the peer group. Respect for the parent includes both affection and fear. Both affection and fear enter into formation of the sense of duty.

Piaget holds that moral development is a continuing process, moving through definable stages as maturation occurs. Thus, according to Piaget, the process of moral formation continues throughout a lifetime. In later stages of moral development, rationality plays a larger role. Rule making in the peer group becomes a participatory activity. Boys playing marbles eventually start agreeing on their own rules. Piaget does not satisfactorily explain why boys feel compelled to play by the rules after they have made them. He also does not fully weigh the difference between marbles and murder. By this I mean that he does not deal with the difference in the emotional charge that attaches to various activities. Cognitive development teaches boys the relative importance of marbles to other matters, but does not fully replace the internalized monitor. Lawrence Kolberg attempted to further refine Piaget's stages of moral development in his cognitive developmental theory, to which we will refer later.

The psychological process of moral formation involves *internalization* of commands, wishes, taboos, and inhibitions of parents and significant others. Parents instill many important values in early childhood. Most children learn at an early age that they should not steal. Moral training goes beyond mere learning, however. Guilt feelings reinforce the taboo against stealing. The child later *learns* that theft of services, such as hooking up a T. V. cable without paying the cable company, is the same as stealing. Guilt emotion then attaches to that activity, so most people do not do it. Thus, cognitive development enables the maturing child to identify authority figures, authoritative norms, and, in general, to think

---

[19] Piaget and Inhelder, *The Psychology of the Child*, p. 122.

morally. Roles of authority figures are actually internalized. Rules learned later in life get motive force by attaching to a properly formed sense of duty.

Obedience to law is, at least in part, a function of conscience. If a conscientious person knows that something is against the *law*, then feelings that arise from the sense of duty attach to the principle. We *know* that it is *rational* to abide by a legal principle. Moreover, we *feel* that it is *wrong* to violate the principle. The cognitive element is important, but the emotional element is equally important. We must *learn* many of the principles that guide our conduct. However, images or ideals deeply embedded in unconscious processes and charged with emotional energy actually operate conscience. Education is not the sole answer to a moral crisis.

Conscience, or sense of duty comes from psychological dynamics. Some of the dynamics arise from maturation and cognitive development. Just as a child grows physically, he grows emotionally and morally. The sense of duty comes from continual interaction with parents and significant other persons. Experience gives meaning to specific images or ideals during maturation. The microcosm—the family and immediate circle of friends—is of inestimable importance in installing the child's sense of duty. It is the part of society that touches the developing child's life directly.

We can compare the child to a computer. The father and mother and significant others *program* the child with taboos and norms of the culture. Indeed, parents themselves are part of the *software* package. Their *image* becomes an *operating* part of the child's program of values. However, the program is not deterministic. Individuals have freedom and can choose. The program instills a basic inclination. It does not create an automaton. The image—the ego ideal—is flexible in normal development, allowing exercise of choice within certain limits.

No one can say where programming of the sense of duty begins or where it ends. Parents are not the only significant persons in a child's life. Grandparents, foster parents, baby-sitters, teachers, and even televisions, are quite significant in moral formation. Stories that we read and songs that we sing to the child are a part of the process. As the child grows older the peer group plays an increasingly important role.

Parents, or parent substitutes, in a particular culture are all affected by the same ideals and images. Parents get their values from the culture, including their own parents. If we assume that parents get their sense of duty from *their* parents, where did taboos and images start? I will return to this question in later chapters.

The personality structure described by Freud, which includes the id, the ego, the super-ego, and the Oedipal complex may be somewhat overstated. Nevertheless those images are helpful because they show how internalization can occur. Even a caricature is a useful image, with its overemphasis on prominent features. More recently, psychologist Sylvan Tompkins explored the vast array of *affects*, or emotions, and described their development. The panorama of affects, which include shame, guilt, humiliation, joy, and numerous others are far more complicated than Freud believed. They all play a part in socialization of individuals. Nevertheless, Freud's overstated imagery of the structures of personality and emotions opens the door to understanding vast complexities of unconscious structures of motive that relate individuals to the social world.

Law and Conscience

The idea that individual conscience has a direct relationship to law is not new. Greeks and Romans may not have known the cause or origin of conscience, since knowledge of modern psychology of moral formation was not available to them. However, they were aware of the existence of conscience and of its relationship to law. Cicero, the famed Roman jurist, eloquently described the existence and importance of conscience in enforcement of law.

> . . . There is really no expiation for the crimes against men or sacrilege against the gods. And so men pay the penalty, not so much through decision of the courts (for once there were no courts anywhere, and today there are none in many lands; and where they do exist, they often act unjustly after all); but guilty men are tormented and pursued by the furies, not with blazing torches, as in tragedies, but with the anguish of remorse and the torture of a guilty conscience.

> But if it were a penalty and not Nature that ought to keep men from injustice, what anxiety would there be to trouble the wicked when the danger of punishment was removed? But in fact there has never been a villain so brazen as not to deny that he had committed a crime, or else invent some story of just anger to excuse its commission, and seek justification for his crime in some natural principle of right. Now if even the wicked dare to appeal to such principles, how jealously should they be guarded by the good! But if it is a penalty, the fear of punishment, and not the wickedness itself, that is to keep men from a life of wrong doing and crime, then no one can be called unjust, and wicked men ought rather to be regarded as imprudent; furthermore, those of us who are not influenced by virtue itself to be

good men but by some consideration of utility and profit, are merely shrewd, not good. For to what lengths will that man go in the dark who fears nothing but a witness and a judge? What will he do if, in some desolate spot, he meets a helpless man, unattended, whom he can rob of a fortune?[20]

Conscience usually influences individuals to obey law. In a larger sense, however, as Dr. King realized and demonstrated, law follows conscience. The formation of legal principles involves conscience. How can mandates, taboos, and prohibitions of individual conscience become normative social principles with binding effect in the community? How can they become law? There are several ways to envision metamorphosis of mandates of individual conscience into legal principles.

One mechanism for transforming individual conscience into group norms is *common conscience*. Similar people, living in the same area, attending the same schools and churches, sharing common economic concerns are likely to develop similar individual value systems. What one person believes to be wrong, all are likely to believe wrong. What one believes to be right, all are likely to believe right. These common beliefs set standards of conduct expected of members of the community. Custom is part of the process. The common conscience approach is a common sense approach that provides insight into how conscience becomes the standard.

However, no two people have *exactly* the same moral views. In a close-knit group, this may not be a serious problem for the common conscience concept. A considerable amount of uniformity usually exists in such a group. Family or immediate circle of friends is usually the microcosm in which moral formation occurs. However, that small group is not the macrocosm in which standards become law. The macrocosm is the state or nation, and in the macrocosm of a heterogeneous society, there is great diversity of opinion. How, then, can dictates of conscience be the basis of law?

Mathematical rules of probability provide one theoretical basis for the proposal. Probability deals with behavior of groups. Scientists cannot predict the life of radioactive carbon. However, by studying behavior of many atoms, they can predict the *half life* of an atom. Actuaries cannot tell how long an individual will live. However, they can predict the *average* life expectancy for a *group* of people. Scientists cannot locate the exact position of the electron on a single hydrogen atom, or even say for sure that it has location. Nevertheless, when hydrogen atoms are studied as a

---

[20] *The Great Legal Philosophers*, p. 47.

group, scientists can predict the orbit of the electron with precision.[21] Thus, group functioning provides observable predictability, despite individual differences. *Law is a group function.* Therefore, all individuals do not have to be in complete agreement for there to be functional norms for a society. Mathematical rules of probability supply certainty.

The point made here has not escaped attention of legal philosophers. W. A. Robson writes:

> (P)hysicists, astronomers, and biologists frankly admit that the natural laws with which they are concerned relate mainly to the behaviour of crowds. Once we enter the domain of aggregates and averages, it becomes far easier to link up the knowledge we have of mankind drawn from the social sciences with our knowledge of the external world derived from the natural sciences. The jurist assumes the physical characteristics of human beings, wrote W. G. Miller in *The Data of Jurisprudence*, and also that they possess the power of controlling their actions by means of the will. "But while this is a fundamental assumption with regard to the individual man, it is also true that as a body men are subject to invariable laws like physical matter. Suicide is an act of the will on the part of each individual, and yet statistics show that a definite annual percentage of the population commit the act; it is induced by external circumstances, disease, famine, calamity, and even the weather." Human life, echoes Eddington, is proverbially uncertain, yet few things are more certain than the solvency of a life insurance company. The average law is so trustworthy that we can predict the expectation of life of the children now born with great accuracy. But that does not enable us to foretell the span of life of a particular child. "The eclipse of 1999 is as safe as the balance of a life insurance company; the next quantum jump of an atom is as uncertain as your life and mine."[22]

In certain major areas of law, common conscience combines with mathematical laws of probability to provide a very adequate explanation for workable norms. Criminologists assure us that major crimes such as murder, robbery, theft, and incest, receive almost universal condemnation. Practically no one in any society approves of these acts. Interestingly, factory pollution is also on the list.[23]

Motive theory does not rely solely on this mathematical explanation to explain how mandates of individual conscience become norms. The process of supplying motive force to rules is not merely a mechanical, mathematical operation. Psychological factors within the group intensify

---

[21] Leshan and Margenau, *Einstein's Space and Van Gogh's Sky*, pp. 111-112.

[22] Robson, *Civilisation and the Growth of Law*, pp. 332-333.

[23] Wilson & Herrnstein, *Crime and Human Nature*, p. 22.

norms. French sociologist, Emile Durkheim, argues that the group completely metamorphoses forces of individual conscience.[24]

Many writers of the natural law school have recognized that moral persuasion—indeed conscience itself—is necessary for law to work. However, they do not explain what makes *conscience* happen. Samuel Enoch Stumpf provided interesting insight into the relationship between morals and law.

> The reason, therefore, for the coalescence of the law and morals is that they both partake, not only of a similar type of internal experience, but frequently of the very same *internal motives*. The stimulus which affects one's moral sensibilities as he confronts his fellow man in society is the same stimulus which may lead him to deal with that occasion through the medium of the law. And the very question of the relationship of the individual to the law raises a very important question, for if there are no moral connotations to the law, then it must be held that the law must be obeyed only because it is "official," which is to say,. . . only because if one does not obey he will suffer pain. (Emphasis added)[25]

Stumpf did not explain the *internal motives* to which he referred.

Jerome Frank Disaster

A few twentieth century legal philosophers have recognized that law depends, to some extent, on psychology. However, no one has undertaken a complete exploration of the matter. Only one legal philosopher has seriously tried to deal at length with the psychology that I am developing here. Jerome Frank published his book, *Law and the Modern Mind,* in 1930. It helped set the tone for legal philosophy in twentieth century America. He had discovered the important concept of the *father image* in psychological literature. He analogized the authoritative role of courts to the *irrational father image* of psychology. He berated practically every legal philosopher who had ever written as being *childish* and looking upon law as the *displaced father.* Apparently, Frank based his opinions on the work of Piaget, and believed that all other legal philosophers operated on a Freudian model. He felt that law arises purely from consensual arrangements within the peer group as described by Piaget, and rejected Freud's ideas as the model for law. Frank's attempt to relate psychology to law was too superficial.

---

24 Durkheim, *Sociology and Philosophy,* pp. 24-25.
25 Stumpf, *Morality and the Law,* p. 80.

As we have seen, Jean Piaget, upon whom Frank relied, did not underestimate or misunderstand the importance of a healthy development of a sense of duty. Moreover, he did not dismiss the role of the father image in moral development as *irrational* or *childish*. He recognized it as an early stage of moral development. Certainly, Piaget's work did not come close to saying that judges had remained in this early stage of moral development, as Frank argued. Frank's attack was intemperate. He described the father image as a *myth*. Unfortunately, he showed no appreciation for the importance of myths, and used the term disparagingly. Frank's conclusions and contentions represent a serious misunderstanding of the relationship between important psychological principles and law.

Frank launched a vitriolic attack on leading legal philosophers of his day. He based his attack in part on his misinterpretation of psychology. His critics were many. Unfortunately, critics did not realize that Frank had misunderstood both the importance and the true nature of moral formation and its relationship to law. Therefore, they did not attack his mistaken view of the relationship between law and psychological principles. They simply *dismissed psychology* as an unproven science and attacked his theses on other grounds.

Jerome Frank and his school of *legal realism* have had considerable impact on twentieth century jurisprudence. Frank's mishandling of the importance of moral formation and its relationship to law was a tragedy. A correct analysis of this important relationship in 1930 may have prevented many problems that law has encountered since that time. Nevertheless, we must credit Jerome Frank with recognizing, early on, that a relationship exists between dynamics of law and the psychological development of conscience. He simply misunderstood that relationship.

Kant and Conscience

One important suggestion about the origin of conscience differs from the models suggested by Freud and Piaget. Immanuel Kant, an eighteenth century philosopher, suggested that the sense of duty is an *a priori* concept. In layman's terms, an *a priori* idea is something we are "born with." Kant called the innate sense of duty the *categorical imperative*. His categorical imperative does not depend on learning, or even conditioning, as does the super-ego. He acknowledged that our minds deal only with neural impulses derived from the outside world. The mind cannot deal with external objects directly. The mind does not act like a sponge, soaking up actual images from the outside world, or a blank chalkboard recording them. The mind is an active, organizing principle, and it takes an active part in sorting out and actually shaping sensory data internally.

According to Kant, we know about *time* and *space* when we are born.[26] We don't have to learn about them. They, like the sense of duty, are *a priori* concepts. Kant articulated the *categorical imperative.* "Act only on a maxim by which you can will that it, at the same time, should become a general law."[27]

Have Freud and his followers shown Kant to be wrong about conscience being innate? Actually, they have not completely displaced his idea. We can partially reconcile the super-ego with the *a priori* existence of conscience. The difference between the two approaches involves the popular debate between heredity and environment. Kant apparently overlooked the fact that parents program conscience—the sense of duty—with specific contents. Thus, he failed to account for the role of environment. Even more problematical was his belief that he could derive duty directly from *pure reason.*

Nevertheless, there may be a *genetically produced inclination toward development of a sense of duty.* We may have innate mental structures that unfold during development that enable us to learn requirements of our society quickly and easily. Consistently with Darwin's theory, such an ability would aid in survival of the human race. Such a precoded inclination would enable individuals to gain more quickly a sense of duty through internalization. Although Kant's theory does not square completely with modern ideas about moral formation, his ideas about conscience have considerable merit. We will pick up this theme again when we discuss archetypes.

Insufficiency of Reason

At this point, I need to point out that *reason* does not give rise to the sense of duty. Intense faith in reason may have been Kant's greatest shortcoming. If the problem of enforcing law were merely one of cognition, or knowing what is right, then education would answer every law enforcement problem. Such is not the case. The popular idea that equates law with *reason* is not correct. Nevertheless, we refer to law as the *rule of reason,* and since the time of the Greek philosophers, we have looked to

---

[26] Kant, *Critique of Pure Reason,* from *The European Philosophers from Descartes to Nietzsche,* p. 388.

[27] Ibid, p. 473.

reason, or rationality, as the foundation of law, while disparaging the affective side of our human nature. Frederick Copleston says of Plato:

> To the idea that virtue is knowledge and that virtue is teachable, Plato seems to have clung, as also to the idea that no one does evil knowingly and willingly. When a man chooses that which is *de facto* evil, he chooses it *sub Specie Boni*: he desires something which he imagines to be good, but which is, as a matter of fact, evil.[28]

This argument has its adherents today. Lawrence Kohlberg, in his cognitive developmental theory, embraces this argument in its entirety. Even Aquinas, the father of modern natural law, argued that law could be discerned in the moral order by the use of "right reason."

All modern theories of jurisprudence rely heavily on rationality as the source of law. Most thinkers feel that *rationality* is the key to solving all problems, including problems assigned to law. We must adopt rational laws, and deal with people rationally, they contend. If we do, we are sure to get a rational response, the argument runs. Solution of all problems is only a matter of education, or becoming more rational. Our faith in reason is a very strong force. It shapes our thoughts. In fact, I suspect that our faith in reason has more impact on our thoughts than does our use of reason. We must become aware that we do not apply reason as often as we assert reason as the basis of our arguments.

People simply do not always do what they know to be right. This problem has long perplexed philosophers and theologians. St. Paul complained, "For the good that I would, I do not: but the evil which I would not, that I do." Then he adds a disclaimer. "Now if I do that I would not, it is no more I that do it, but sin that dwelleth in me." Comedian Flip Wilson immortalized the thought by saying, "The devil made me do it." Indeed, there are times when forces other than rational judgment control our lives, both for good and evil. We like to identify ourselves with the element of rational control, and have even pretentiously given ourselves the scientific name *homo sapiens*.

But rational judgment is not always saintly. Roman Jurist, Cicero, realized, ". . . [M]an can use his reason to devise means of satisfying his lusts and evil passions. . . ."[29] Reason, in modern times, has devised means of destroying the entire human race. Reason is the basis for neither virtue nor law. Law and righteousness do not necessarily result

---

[28] Copleston, *A History of Philosophy, Vol. I*, p. 219.
[29] *The Great Legal Philosophers*, p. 71.

from reason, and in fact, evil can, and often does, result from reason. The *non-rational* element of human nature known as conscience or duty motivates the choice between good and evil conduct. Likewise, the feeling that we must obey law arises from the sense of duty, or conscience. Rationality is a tool of adaptation. At best it *mediates* mandates of duty, which arise from another source.

Rationality and cognitive function are not the same. Rationality is, in layman's terms, *problem solving* ability while cognitive function is the ability to know, or to perceive. Clearly, there is a cognitive element in moral development. However, we cannot agree with Plato and Lawrence Kolberg that if one knows what is right one will do what is right. Lawrence Kohlberg advanced a *cognitive developmental theory* of moral formation. His theory grew out of the work of Jean Piaget. The cognitive element is important, but in his original formulations of the theory, Kolberg probably placed too much reliance on rational factors. The importance of the cognitive element is that, if we do *not* know what is right, we are not likely to do what is right. Therefore, education, including moral education, is an important part of moral formation. However, there are deeper motive factors in the psychology of moral formation, and they are more important than the cognitive element. I rely more closely on psychosocial theories of Sigmund Freud and Erik Erikson than on cognitive developmental theories of Piaget and Kohlberg.

Conflict Between Conscience and Law

Many argue that one should disobey law if it conflicts with conscience. Dr. King took precisely this position in his *Letter from the Birmingham City Jail*. Superficially, the possibility of such a conflict appears inconsistent with my theory that conscience is part of law's basis. No doubt there are instances when a person should *disobey* law as a matter of conscience. But there are many points of ethics on which conscientious persons can disagree. Instances in which conscience supports law far outnumber instances when the two are in conflict. Unquestionably, Dr. King and the Civil Rights Movement were on the right track in making a strong appeal to conscience. Conscience not only attacked unjust laws—it provided the motive for new laws.

Nevertheless, as the Civil Rights Movement demonstrates, law and virtue are not the same. Dean Lon Fuller has pointed out the distinction between morality of aspiration and morality of duty. This distinction supports the thesis I am developing. Motive force is the basis of law, and relates closely to morality of duty. Morality of aspiration is available to criticize law. Often the two coalesce. Virtue can be a source of motive. Conscience is a motive force. However, when a person decides to disobey law as a matter of conscience, he must, as Dr. King acknowledged, accept results. He may be wrong in the final judgment of law. Other consciences may differ, and prevail. Whenever conscience and law appear to conflict, conscience is not saying that law should not exist. It is simply saying that law should be different. Hence, it is engaging in the law*making* function. The lawmaking function was the crowning role of conscience in the Civil Rights Movement.

Protection of the right of dissent is a legal proposition. It can extend only so far, if law is to survive. For instance, we cannot allow religious cults to test laws against murder, contending that human sacrifice is a tenet of religious belief.

Conscience, Law and Literature

Literature reflects the role of conscience in law. In *Crime and Punishment* and *The Brothers Karamozov*, Dostoyevsky shows deep psychological insight into the role of conscience in law. The guilty conscience in each story is the central theme. In the first, the guilty conscience brings the culprit to justice. The second is an interesting study of how conscience can, in fact, misconceive and appearances mislead. Edgar Allan Poe's *The Tell-Tale Heart* is another poignant example of conscience trapping the culprit. The role of conscience figured prominently in Shakespeare's *Macbeth*. Examples are many and often are discussed in law and literature courses. Repeated inclusion of this theme in literature is no accident. Literature provides operative models which perpetuate the cultural role of conscience. It captures and maintains themes which perpetuate our ideals and images of right and wrong. This observation anticipates the in-depth treatment that I will give to mythology in Section 3. Our literary heritage is part of our mythos.

Conscience and Civilization

Law intimately involves the motivation of conscience. Freud himself was aware of this fact. He saw that an ever increasing burden of guilt accompanies the advance of civilization. In *Civilization and Its Discontents*, he wrote:

> So long as the community assumes no other form than that of the family, the conflict is bound to express itself in the Oedipus complex, to establish the conscience and to create the first sense of guilt. When an attempt is made to widen the community, the same conflict is continued in forms which are

dependent on the past; and it is strengthened and results in a further intensification of the sense of guilt. Since civilization obeys an internal erotic impulsion which causes human beings to unite in a closely-knit group, it can only achieve this aim through an ever-increasing reinforcement of the sense of guilt. What began in relation to the father is completed in relation to the group. If civilization is a necessary course of development from the family to humanity as a whole, then—as a result of the inborn conflict arising from ambivalence, of the eternal struggle between the trends of love and death—there is inextricably bound up with it an increase of the sense of guilt, which will perhaps reach heights that the individual finds hard to tolerate.

* * *

. . . This [discussion of the sense of guilt] corresponds faithfully to my intention to represent the sense of guilt as the most important problem in the development of civilization and to show that the price we pay for our advance in civilization is a loss of happiness through the heightening of the sense of guilt.[30]

Two things are clear from this passage. First, Freud understood that conscience is the vehicle that advances civilization. Second, he worried that individuals might not be able to handle the increasing burden of guilt that necessarily attends the advance of civilization.

Conscience and consequent guilt are necessary ingredients in the formula for civilization, just as Freud suggested. However, Freud's concern that the load of guilt will become ever more burdensome and possibly unbearable is not justified. Specialization spreads the burden, and there are more people to share it. Each person does not have to acquire all the morals for every activity of society, since everybody does not engage in every essential activity of society. However, if we lack a universalizing, all-encompassing moral base, there is indeed a great danger. Without a unifying mythos, civilization will incur the curse of the Tower of Babel.

---

[30] Freud, *Civilization and Its Discontents*, pp. 80-81.

We do what we do to get what we need, and activities of law are no exception to that general principle. We need security. The strong desire to satisfy basic needs, including the need for security, propels us into relationships with others. For those relationships to be orderly there must be norms. Norms arise naturally. Motive arising from needs relates to Bentham's utilitarianism, in the same way that moral formation relates to Aquinas' Moral Order. Like conscience, forces that satisfy basic human needs often operate unconsciously, which adds to the argument that the force of law does not arise from rationality.

Before launching into specifics, we need to describe the larger framework of motive. In this chapter we will continue probing the *why* question which we posed earlier. Our specific interest now will be sources of energy for law. What motivates people to engage in activities that we know as law? From a very broad view, we can see that a basic restlessness stirs humans to activity. Restlessness is inherent in human nature. Maslow's theories show how that restless energy moves us to satisfy basic needs. I will try to place Maslow's findings into a larger philosophical context.

Conscience, which we discussed in the previous chapter, does not fully explain the motive for law. Standing alone, conscience does not answer the *why* question. However, it couples with other motive forces to give rise to impulses that produce law. In this chapter, we explore these other motive forces, which we call *drives* or *needs*. Conscience is a part of a larger set of psychological elements that enable humans to live together as a group. We will be dealing now with basic concepts of human motivation. Abraham Maslow is a renowned leader in this area of study.

Conscience, together with fear of punishment, explains why most people obey law voluntarily. We should note that both conscience and fear of punishment involve emotions, and not merely rational processes. Conscience partially explains the motive force of law, in that individuals give energy to dictates of conscience. *Feelings* back dictates of conscience.

Violation of taboos and prohibitions written on the conscience creates a state of uneasiness in individuals. Violation of taboos and mandates of society by others also creates *feelings* of disapproval, indignation or anger toward violators. Feelings are deeply involved in establishment and maintenance of norms. In certain ways, conscience is a specialized product of basic human needs, whose proper functioning brings orderliness to the group, while satisfying esteem needs of the individual. It is a tool of the socialization drive. A person living alone on an island would need no conscience.

What are the sources of energy for the force which society brings to bear on an individual who disobeys law? What causes individuals to fear the results of acting illegally? What is the source of energy to deal with non-conformists? Why do persons such as judges, lawyers and policemen, who are not personally involved in a particular dispute, insist that parties in dispute submit to law? Why do friends and family usually stand by and allow law to take its course?

The commonly expressed belief that enforcement of law arises from fear of punishment begs the *why* question. It assumes that certain individuals within society want to inflict punishment on offenders but does not explain why those individuals have such a desire. Fear of punishment certainly plays a part in causing individuals to follow rules of society. The use or threat of physical force or restraint is necessary for enforcing law. Economic sanctions also have their place. However, the question of motive remains. Why do certain persons in authority use, or threaten to use, force or economic sanctions? What motivates them? Motive is necessary for law to work.

As a practical matter, energy for societal force must arise in individuals. There is no other place for energy to originate. This does not mean that the *function* of the group is the same as the function of its individual members. Holistic forces of society are more than a compilation of individual contributions. This is an essential feature of the dynamics of law. Ideals that arise from the collective nature of society differ in kind from imperfect, incomplete ideals of individuals, even though energy for enforcement comes from individuals.

To locate energy for law, we need to look more closely at the restlessness which is an inherent part of human nature. Restlessness is the beginning point in understanding human motive force. Many scholars from several different disciplines have noticed the restless human condition, which pushes or pulls people to act.

Restlessness: The Human Condition

St. Augustine said, "My soul was restless until it found rest in Thee," speaking of his relationship to God. Arthur Shopenhauer speculated that all existence is *will*. His use of the word *will* is a bit strange to us. He saw in all of existence, from inanimate objects through the highest forms of life, a *blind striving*. This blind striving, the process of becoming, without awareness of the intended goal, he found to be the total reality of the world of observable happenings. For Shopenhauer, the goal of human existence is to escape from this state of becoming. Nietzsche spoke of the *will to power*. Freud theorized the *id*, which he described as a "cauldron of seething excitement." All of these phrases describe a basic human restlessness. This restlessness, inherent in human nature, energizes the motive force behind most, if not all human activities.

Freud's description of the id captures the basic restlessness I am attempting to portray:

> We can come nearer to the id with images, and call it a chaos, a cauldron of seething excitement. . . . These instincts fill it with energy, but it has no organization and no unified will, only an impulsion to obtain satisfaction for the instinctual needs, in accordance with the pleasure principle. The laws of logic—above all, the law of contradiction—do not hold for processes in the id. Contradictory impulses exist side by side without neutralizing each other or drawing apart; at most they combine in compromise formations under the overpowering economic pressure towards discharging their energy. There is nothing in the id which can be compared to negation, and we are astonished to find in it an exception to the philosophers' assertion that space and time are necessary forms of our mental acts. . . .
>
> . . . Naturally, the id knows no values, no good and evil, no morality. The economic, or, if you prefer, the quantitative factor, which is so closely bound up with the pleasure-principle, dominates all its processes. Instinctual cathexes seeking discharge—that, in our view, is all that the id contains.[31]

Conscience plays no part in this primal restlessness. Freud explains that these activities occur "to obtain satisfaction for the instinctual *needs*." Thus, in addition to the push, there is a goal: satisfaction of needs. Drives push, needs pull, and this distinction is significant.

Freud goes on to show how the ego derives from the id. In a broad sense, the ego arbitrates the needs of the individual in the external world.

---

[31] Sigmund Freud, *New Introductory Lectures on Psychoanalysis*, pp. 103-105.

According to Freud, it channels energy from the id into need satisfying, socially acceptable activity.

One can hardly go wrong in regarding the ego as that part of the id which has been modified by its proximity to the external world and the influence that the latter has had on it, and which serves the purpose of receiving stimuli and protecting the organism from them, like the cortical layer with which a particle of living substance surrounds itself. This relation to the external world is decisive for the ego. The ego has taken over the task of representing the external world for the id and so of saving it; for the id, blindly striving to gratify its instincts in complete disregard of the superior strength of outside forces, could not otherwise escape annihilation. In the fulfillment of this function, the ego has to observe the external world and preserve a true picture of it in the memory traces left by its perceptions, and, by means of the reality-test, it has to eliminate any element in this picture of the external world which is a contribution from internal sources of excitation. On behalf of the id, the ego controls the path of access to motility, but it interpolates between desire and action, the procrastinating factor of thought, during which it makes use of the residues of experience stored up in memory. In this way it dethrones the pleasure-principle, which exerts undisputed sway over the processes in the id, and substitutes for it the reality-principle, which promises greater security and greater success.[32]

Conscience, or super-ego, in turn, is a highly specialized part of ego.

Teleology of Need Satisfaction

Perhaps the destination or ultimate goal exerts a pull, and there is teleological purpose in the happenings of life. Human beings instinctively are active. This enables them to meet basic needs. We are in a continual state of disequilibrium, always seeking stability. Restlessness has its purpose, says psychiatrist C. G. Jung. Usually, the term *causation* means cause and effect. One thing happens that causes another to happen. Jung recognized, in addition to this usual meaning of causation, the validity of teleology, or final causes.

Jung did not reject the idea of causality. Instead he also recognized the validity of another scientific orientation. This orientation is called teleology or finalism. As applied in psychology, it means, in effect, that man's present behavior is determined by the future. Future goals, as well as past events, need to be taken into consideration in understanding a person's behavior. Many of Jung's ideas regarding the development of the psyche are finalistic in the sense that they are goals—individuation, integration, and selfhood,

---

[32] Ibid., p. 106.

for instance—toward which the developing personality is aimed. There is intentionality in behavior, although it is not necessarily always manifested in consciousness.

Jung felt that it was necessary to adopt both attitudes, causality and teleology, in psychology. He wrote, "On the one hand it [the mind] gives a picture of the remnants and traces of all that has been, and on the other, but expressed in the same picture, the outlines of what is to come, in so far as the psyche creates its own future."[33]

The idea of final causes has respectable lineage, since it was included among Aristotle's theories of causation, but it is not a cornerstone of modern theories of causation.

The word *drive* connotes a motive *push* consistent with an endless chain of physical reactions. However, *need* satisfaction implies a *pull*. A need implies the possibility that something will occur in the future that will satisfy it. Stated differently, a need assumes incompleteness that can be remedied. Along with Maslow, I use the term *need* rather than the term *drive*. Need, which connotes a pull or attraction in the future, more accurately captures the restless stirring of motive that moves us toward often ill-defined goals than does the term drive, with its connotative push from the past.

Purpose becomes cause. Examples of the strange call of destiny are all around us. They receive less attention than the more mechanical action and reaction which is the basis of causation in the popular view of physical science. One example of these strange stories is the story of the Capricorn beetle. The larvae lives for three years, burrowing around in a tree trunk. Near the end of its sojourn, it unerringly places itself in the correct position for metamorphosis, just inside the trunk, so the beetle can escape. It even creates a space large enough for the resulting beetle. Robert Ardrey gives the following account:

> The larva of the Capricorn beetle is a tiny wormlike being who starts out life no thicker of body than a straw. He burrows into an oak tree, ingesting wood at the front end and leaving a tunnel behind. You may have seen the same traces in old furniture. For three years he wanders around in the heart of the oak, very much on his own without parental guidance, increasing in size until he is as thick as your finger. About then he is ready to turn into a beetle, and this he will do inside the oak. The problem [is] how the beetle gets out. Only the larva has the capacity to dine off oak. The beetle would be helpless.

---

[33] Hall and Nordby, *A Primer of Jungian Psychology*, pp. 127-128.

Fabre gave long attention to the matter and found that while in the whole three years of wandering the larva would never approach the bark, at the end of his journey he headed directly to it, leaving his tunnel behind him and stopping only when the thinnest film of bark separated the tunnel from the outdoors. Then the larva backs up. Having moved an appropriate distance from the exit, he proceeds to hollow out a chamber not his size but large enough to accommodate the beetle who does not yet exist. The larva's brush with destiny, however, is not yet done. He seals the chamber at either end with a natural cement produced in his stomach. Now, with doors neatly closed, he rasps down the walls of his sealed chamber to cover the floor with a soft down. Using the same wood-wool, he completes the decor by felting all walls a millimeter thick. Now at last his preparations for the accouchement are finished and he lies down and sheds his skin, becoming a pupa which in turn will become a beetle. But the wonders of instinct have not yet been finally recorded. He lies down always with his head toward the exit. Were he to lie down the wrong way, the beetle would be unable to turn around.34

Purpose, unknown to the larva, governed its actions step by step. How could this strange and purposeful chain of events ever have begun?

Can it be that all our restless activities are moving us toward an end? Is this the reason for our restlessness? Are we blindly seeking goals, ignorant of their existence? The possibility that the future pulls us, in addition to the past pushing us, provides a broader explanation for causes of law. Often, we are instinctively and unwittingly drawn to serve purposes of humanity, even when we believe we are serving purely selfish needs.

Every major religion recognizes the basic restlessness of the human spirit. The human being, isolated in individuality, is aware of his finiteness both in time and space. Life is a continuous *process of becoming*. Human consciousness senses its own incompleteness and imperfection, and suggests there must be something more—the perfect, the complete. Locked in individuality, humans cling desperately to existence. An abiding sense of loneliness stirs our restless blind striving, and we seek satisfaction. We do not always, or even usually, know *what* we want.

We seek satisfaction, not knowing what will satisfy. This unshaped restlessness is at the root of all human activity, including activities that embody law. Human development channels these restless energies into patterns that satisfy basic needs. One of those needs is social order. It is possible to identify some of the goals of the blind striving and to place

---

34 Ardrey, *The Territorial Imperative*, pp. 19-20.

them into understandable categories. The categories correspond to the basic human needs. Society captures some of the restless energy to energize principles of law. This satisfies the need for orderliness—a part of the socialization need. We sometimes call the resulting standards *norms*, and forces that shape them *normative forces*. Normative forces arise from interaction among individuals. In the quest to satisfy his own basic needs, an individual must interact with others.

Basic Needs

All human beings share certain basic needs. The human organism has energy to fulfill these needs. There are many ways to classify and describe needs or drives that affect us all. I have chosen five categories. Together, they include almost any imaginable human need.

1) Need to survive. The desire to continue physical existence is innate in human nature. Breathing, eating, and doing everything necessary to survive, comes naturally. The organism has enough naturally given energy to achieve success in these matters.

2) Need for socialization. The human being is a social animal. We fulfill basic needs more easily in cooperation with other human beings. Family is the basic social unit in our society. In ancient times, the family was more extended than now and included common descendants of a patriarch of the clan. The family is paradigmatic of other social structures. We have already discussed conscience formation, which involves the family. Developmental theories show how responsibility to family gradually shifts to the group or society. This is socialization.

3) Need to reproduce. Humankind shares this instinct with everything that lives. For advocates of rationality, we should note that reproduction is not a product of reason. Nature assures the next generation. Natural energy for it is boundless. The desire to reproduce is, in one sense, a continuation of the survival drive. It is *humanity*'s way of surviving. Maturation and hormonal stimuli propel the process of individuation. The reproduction need eventually catapults individuals into new family relationships. The child becomes an adult, finds a partner, and begins a new family. Individuals now play social roles internalized during childhood. The socialization need asserts itself, this time with individuals in new roles. Bambi becomes the Old Stag. Images and ideals are important in socialization processes. By playing roles that society assigns, individuals satisfy socialization needs. These are processes that teach us who we are. From these efforts we gain our identity.

4) Need to achieve maximum potential. A baby does not survive only to be a baby. It is not a matter of what the baby *wants*. Natural activities of the baby just happen to be the activities necessary to cause development and growth. Infants do these things long before they are consciously aware of any desire to grow up. Babies do not reason, "I'm going to exercise so I can grow big like Mom and Dad." They kick and squirm, without knowing the purpose. Nature programs infants to achieve increasing levels of sophistication physically, mentally and socially. Energy to achieve these purposes occurs naturally.

5) Need for meaning. This may be the most controversial need that I include in my classification scheme. The need for meaning is the essence of the religious instinct. Religion is widespread, if not universal in all civilizations. Jungian scholar Robert H. Hopcke reports:

> Jung . . . noted several pertinent facts with regard to religion. First, there is no civilization, present or past, on the planet that has not had a religion, a set of beliefs and sacred rituals. Thus Jung posited that there exists a religious instinct within human beings, an inherent striving toward a relationship with a Something or a Someone that transcends human limitations, a higher power.35

Human beings come equipped with intimations of immortality and infinity. Images and ideals are at the heart of the work of religion. Religion expresses itself in individuals in faith that enables individuals to relate to their ultimate environment. Such faith does not always attach to traditional religious practices. It may take other forms. Nevertheless, there is always faith. Natural energy is available to individuals to *seek* an infinite God in their own way, regardless of prospects for success. The search itself lends meaning to the times, places, and activities of our lives. Since we are discussing motive and human activity, the question is not whether there actually is a God. It is whether or not humankind *seeks* a god.

Needs Confront the World

The Jewish thinker, Martin Buber, wrote an intriguing book, *I and Thou*. In it, he relates modern psychological findings to classical religious principles. The individual—the *I*— is from the moment of birth, mentally involved in differentiation from the rest of the world. The baby notices that he can wiggle toes but not the bed post. As individuals identify

---

35 Hopcke, *A Guided Tour of the Collected Works of C. G. Jung*, p. 65.

themselves, they also identify the "other-than-I": the IT or the THOU. Individuals necessarily encounter this *other-than-I* in five different ways. (1) The individual, consciously or unconsciously, faces the physical world and non-human life. (2) He encounters other people. (3) He meets the other sex. (4) He experiences time, including the future. (5) He encounters the cosmos, including the unknown and the mystery of existence. The five needs that I have described place the individual—the I— into a relationship with these five aspects of the "other-than-I."

Neither the categories of need nor of the other-than-I are clearly defined and differentiated from other categories. They overlap and are intermingled. Categorization is useful to promote understanding of the concept, but both the I and the other-than-I are totally commingled mixtures of the categories that I have identified for analysis. Analysis helps to explain how individuals relate to their environment. Basic restlessness drives or pulls individuals to contend with these five categories. They are the same categories from which individuals must distinguish themselves in the process of individuation. They are the things that can satisfy his needs. From them, he must wrest his continued existence. They are (1) his territory and his food, (2) his group, (3) his sex partner, actual or potential, (4) his future, and (5) his opportunity for vision and meaning. Somehow, individuals must continually reach an accord and balance with each of these five categories.

Here is a paradox. An individual achieves more and more independence through individuation. Nevertheless, he is actually inseparable from these *Other-than-I* categories. As he achieves *individuation*, which differentiates him from these things, he achieves *identity* only in relationship to them. Only as we identify the *other, and make it part of our own mental processes*, do we differentiate ourselves from it.

Maslow's Classification of Basic Needs

Psychologist Abraham Maslow is a leading authority in psychology dealing with motivation based on needs or drives. He described basic needs as follows:

1) Physiological needs;

2) Safety needs;

3) Belongingness and love needs;

4) Esteem needs;

5) Need for self-actualization.36

Along with Jung, Maslow sees the pull of the future as a causal factor. This is his reason for choosing the term *need* instead of *drive* to describe these motive forces. Maslow recognized that basic needs often operate unconsciously.

> These needs are neither necessarily conscious nor unconscious. On the whole, however, in the average person, they are more often unconscious than conscious. It is not necessary at this point to overhaul the tremendous mass of evidence that indicates the crucial importance of unconscious motivation. It would by now be expected, on *a priori* grounds alone, that unconscious motivations would on the whole be rather more important than the conscious motivations. What we have called the basic needs are often largely unconscious although they may, with suitable techniques, and with sophisticated people, become conscious.37

This again shows the importance of unconscious mental operations.

The Continuum of Needs

We obviously cannot separate the socialization need discretely from reproduction or from achieving maximum potential. In fact, Maslow contended that all needs exist in a continuum.

> . . . [A]ll the lists of drives that have ever been published seem to imply mutual exclusiveness among the various drives. But there is not mutual exclusiveness. There is usually such an overlapping that it is almost impossible to separate quite clearly and sharply any one drive from any other.
>
> . . . [T]he only sound and fundamental basis on which any classification of motivational life may be constructed is that of the fundamental goals or needs, rather than on any listing of drives in the ordinary sense of instigation (the "pulls" rather than the "pushes"). It is only the fundamental goals that remain constant through all the flux that a dynamic approach forces upon psychological theorizing.38

These goals or needs are not separate from each other. Moreover, all needs break down into smaller parts. Reproduction divides into sex and child rearing. Survival requires eating, breathing, drinking, etc. In short,

---

36 Maslow, *Motivation and Personality, Second Edition*, pp. 35-46.
37 Ibid., p. 54.
38 Ibid., p. 26.

needs are one continuous whole with many indivisible parts. Each need is not separate from other needs. We describe them in different ways, depending upon what we want to emphasize.

Since needs exist in a continuum, there is obviously more than one way to classify needs. My classification differs from Maslow's. Needs within us correspond to the environment that surrounds us. My classification matches what we call *I* with things that we identify as *other-than-I*. The *Thou* or *it* or *other-than-I* also exists in a continuum. Somehow, the *I* must deal with each of these categories of the *THOU* or the *IT*. This is a useful way to organize the relationship between individuals and the world. Maslow based his classification on his observations of behavior of individuals. He did not try to match needs with total environment. I have dwelt on this point because it is important to see law as a relationship between humans and the total environment. The total environment, of course, includes other people.

Energy for satisfaction of needs is one and undifferentiated. Energy that causes basic human restlessness is interchangeable and can reveal itself in many different ways to satisfy various needs. Energy flows freely from one need satisfaction to another. The energy with which we hunt food can be used to hunt a sex partner. Success in romance can satisfy the need for self-esteem. Separation of needs into different classes takes place at the juncture where the "I" meets the "other-than-I." This makes classification possible. Any classification oversimplifies the complexity of dynamic relationships between individuals, with a continuum of needs, and an environment that presents kaleidoscopic possibilities of need satisfaction.

At different times one need is greater than others. The more urgent need takes priority over others. It appropriates more of the available energy. Maslow described the situation as a *hierarchy of needs*.

> If all the needs are unsatisfied, and the organism is then dominated by the physiological needs, all other needs may become simply nonexistent or be pushed into the background. It is then fair to characterize the whole organism by saying simply that it is hungry, for consciousness is almost completely preempted by hunger. All capacities are put into the service of hunger-satisfaction, and the organization of these capacities is almost entirely determined by the one purpose of satisfying hunger. The receptors and effectors, the intelligence, memory, habits, all may now be defined simply as hunger-gratifying tools. Capacities that are not useful for this purpose lie dormant, or are pushed into the background. The urge to write poetry, the desire to acquire an automobile, the interest in American history,

the desire for a new pair of shoes are, in the extreme case, forgotten or become of secondary importance. For the man who is extremely and dangerously hungry, no other interests exist but food. He dreams food, he remembers food, he thinks about food, he emotes only about food, he perceives only food, and he wants only food.39

The most basic unfulfilled need dominates the personality and appropriates a relatively greater amount of energy available for need satisfaction. A word of caution is necessary in this regard, however. Determinism in behavior does not follow from the hierarchical nature of needs. Only if the differential between needs is great does a single need dominate others. Under normal circumstances, opportunity may play as important a role as need in the unfolding story of behavior. Even if a man is quite hungry, he might forget about hunger if his dinner date invites him in for a drink before dinner, with a romantic twinkle in her eye. Moreover, our perceptions of the cosmos affect actions that we take to satisfy needs. Most Americans would eat rats or dogs only as a last resort, for instance, even though the meat might be quite nourishing. Cattle walk the roads of India among a starving population. Also, a parent anywhere might starve to feed a child. As we will discuss more fully later, there appear to be times when strongly held beliefs seem to prevail over physical needs as a cause of behavior.

Fear, Insecurity, and Social Organization

Any threat to satisfaction of basic needs produces fear and anxiety in individuals. It creates conflicts within groups. The unknown is a source of fear. Security exists when there is no threat to satisfaction of needs. All security is relative and tentative. We consciously know, and unconsciously feel, the lack of permanence in all relationships. The *other-than-I* category is in a constant process of change and becoming. Individuals are constantly on guard against contingencies. Maslow states that we react whenever satisfaction of basic needs is endangered.

There are certain conditions that are immediate prerequisites for the basic need satisfactions. Danger to these is reacted to as if it were direct danger to the basic needs themselves. Such conditions as freedom to speak, freedom to do what one wishes so long as no harm is done to others, freedom to express oneself, freedom to investigate and seek for information, freedom to defend oneself, justice, fairness, honesty, orderliness in the group are examples of such preconditions for basic need satisfactions. Thwarting in these freedoms

---

39 Ibid., p. 37.

will be reacted to with a threat or emergency response. These conditions are not ends in themselves but they are *almost* so since they are so closely related to the basic needs, which are apparently the only ends in themselves. These conditions are defended because without them the basic satisfactions are quite impossible, or at least, severely endangered.[40]

This reaction identifies a source of energy for law. Basic human needs mandate orderliness. Maslow called this underlying need for orderliness a *precondition* to satisfaction of other needs he identified.

In the desire to satisfy needs, we find energized tendencies that bring about law through appropriate social and political structures. Conscience, and fear of consequences, induce individuals to conform to legal norms. But there is also another motivating force that induces conformity. It is part of social interaction and has an emotional base which we cannot describe as fear. Maslow describes this third element.

Let us say that person A has lived for several weeks in a dangerous jungle, in which he has managed to stay alive by finding occasional food and water. Person B not only stays alive but also has a rifle and a hidden cave with a closable entrance. Person C has all of these and has two more men with him as well. Person D has the food, the gun, the allies, the cave, and in addition, has with him his best-loved friend. Finally, person E, in the same jungle, has all of these, and in addition is the well-respected leader of his band. For the sake of brevity we may call these men, respectively, the merely surviving, the safe, the belonging, the loved, and the respected.

But this is not only a series of increasing need gratifications; it is as well a *series of increasing degrees of psychological health*. It is clear that, other things being equal, a man who is safe and belongs and is loved will be healthier (by any reasonable definition) than a man who is safe and belongs, but who is rejected and unloved. And if in addition, he wins respect and admiration, and because of this, develops his self-respect, then he is still *more* healthy.[41]

This factor described by Maslow arises from subtle pressures of the socialization need. Perhaps we can describe it as a reward for good behavior, or respect. Only by following society's requirements can individuals fulfill the need for love and esteem.

Psychological advantages naturally flow from social organization. These advantages include security and overall well-being. They are not merely rational advantages. This point alleviates Freud's concern about

---

[40] Ibid., p. 47.
[41] Ibid., p. 67.

loss of individual happiness to guilt in the advance of civilization. Increased security brought about by social organization offsets the guilt which Freud described as the foundation of civilization. Increased need gratification made possible by an organized, orderly society offsets the individual's loss of coping power to guilt. Freud is right when he says that civilization is dependent on guilt, assuming that the guilt results from a healthy, well-conditioned conscience. Society can gratify needs only when individuals respect the mores necessary to survival and development of society.

Motive force for law derives from security that law provides rather than from fear that it induces. This is inherent in the socialization factor of enforcement. Force is only a temporary partial solution, while security, by its nature, has more sustaining power. The two are inseparable. Energy for force as well as willingness to use force arises from threat to security. Force is more obvious and receives more attention, but it presupposes the existence or possibility of security. Even when law is imposed by conquest, security that motivates conquerors probably has more significance than fear that motivates the conquered, in the panorama of social forces that produce the resulting order. One person does not constitute a conquering army.

Individuals want—indeed need—to control the "other-than-I," from which they distinguish themselves. Control brings about security. This observation is true whether we are talking about raw elements of physical nature or intricacies of life in the society of fellow humans. As used here, *control* includes reaching a dependable accord with the environment, including other people. To control other people does not mean to *master* them. Control as used here simply means to establish a dependable, predictable, and at least somewhat mutually beneficial relationship with others. The Civil Rights Movement was not motivated by a desire on the part of Blacks to master the social environment, but rather to reach a dependable accord with it so that their basic needs could be dependably satisfied.

Individuals control others by the restraint of law. By doing so, it is easier for them to attain their individual needs. They feel threatened if others do not obey law. Therefore, they invest energy into law for the security which their contribution, combined with that of others, can bring. Investment of energy by many individuals produces fear in potential law breakers. Indeed, collective energy is the basis of force itself.

Energy that individuals contribute to society for enforcement of norms does not begin in some *contract* or necessarily even in rational activity. Contribution of energy occurs unconsciously and instinctively. It is the same psychological reaction that causes families or clans to stick together. If there is honor among thieves, as the old saying goes, then this is the reason for it. Contribution of energy to the group is a means of survival—drive number one. It makes possible a means of fulfilling each of the other basic needs. The same psychology contributes to formation of cults and gangs among those individuals who have difficulty fitting into the mainstream of beliefs and values.

Conscience, fear of results, and security for compliance are the motive factors that enforce law. None of them is enough, acting alone. Together, they are a potent arsenal for enforcement of law. They might not enforce the *abbreviation for inch* regulation. However, they work very well for "Thou shalt not kill." We have located in the desire for need fulfillment some more of law's emotional thunder and lightning. These are forces that make law happen. We include these among the answers to the *why* question.

Needs, Economics and Law

Psychological factors lie at the heart of law's motive force. We must grasp them to understand how law works. The matrix of energy producing mechanisms within individuals which we have described energize all societal forces including law, morals, and economics. As individuals accomplish their purposes and desires, the society of which they are units or cells also accomplishes its purposes. Blackstone anticipated this source of energy, but has been thoroughly ignored, probably because his statement is theistic.

> For [God] has so intimately connected, so inseparably interwoven the laws of eternal justice with the happiness of each individual, that the latter cannot be attained but by observing the former; and, if the former be punctually obeyed, it cannot but induce the latter. In consequence of which mutual connection of justice and human felicity, he has not perplexed the law of nature with a multitude of abstracted rules and precepts, referring merely to the fitness or unfitness of things, as some have vainly surmised; but has graciously reduced the rule of obedience to this one paternal precept, "that man should pursue his own true and substantial 'happiness.'" This is the foundation of what we call ethics, or natural law.[42]

---

[42] Blackstone, *Commentaries on the Laws of England*, Vol. I, p. 41.

Sometimes we do not recognize either the immediate or the final purposes of our activities.

A large body of legal writing connects law to economics. Recognition of the role of motive forces provides a psychological explanation for the obsession with economics among legal theorists. Only if we view economics as a social science independent of motive forces can we consider economics the basis of law. All arguments for marginal utility, popular in discussions of distributive justice, simply rationalize "the greatest happiness for the greatest number." Economics necessarily involve the motive to satisfy human needs. Humans exchange goods, including services, to satisfy needs, and exchanges of goods form the basis of economics. When we consider economic theories of law in the light of motive theories of need satisfaction, certain difficulties with purely economic theories immediately appear. Economic theories tend to recognize materialism as the highest human value. If some other need, such as the need for meaning, or the need for order, is the predominant need, then Maslow's hierarchy comes into play. *We can feel threatened and insecure, despite relative security in material things!* It then is the province of law to provide an atmosphere in which these non-materialistic needs can be met. Motive arising from human needs is the direct impetus for law and it is a mistake to skip this human element and connect law directly to economic theory. This observation about the place of economic theory in the motive theory of law does not render economic theories totally invalid or useless. It simply assigns economic theory a proper place. Franklin Roosevelt said, during the Great Economic Depression, "We have nothing to fear but fear itself," thus recognizing the emotional basis of economics. Economics ultimately relate to psychological forces, and to law through those forces. Motive force lies at the heart of economic theory. Economics provide a rational analysis of means of need satisfaction.

Group functions resulting from individual actions differ from individual functions which confer energy. I do my work as a judge in part because the state pays me to do so. However, society pays judges because of benefits to society. Society converts energy of individuals into a new force.

Rationality and Needs

Rationality is a servant of the needs. It is the highest organ of adaptation available in the human repertoire of mental abilities. It has enabled humankind to accomplish unbelievable adaptation in recent history.

Motive springs from needs. Reason mediates between and among alternatives for need satisfaction. Needs and alternative means of satisfaction create an atmosphere in which rationality can operate. The other person, with his needs, is, in a sense, an *object* with which one's rationality works to achieve one's own purposes. The apparent harshness of this observation is tempered by the bonding of love, friendship and numerous other positive affective relations. Basic needs force individuals to relate to each other in ways that produce useful organizations of individuals.

Within individuals, the relationship of rationality to the motive force of law is like the relationship between a rider and a horse. The horse provides strength, and the rider direction. However, there are places horses won't go, and ditches they can't jump. Even worse, by totally excluding any consideration of the necessary motive force for law, modern legal philosophy portrays a jockey without a horse.

No one can deal rationally with every circumstance in life. Habits and customs are important, and essential for satisfying both individual needs and group needs. Habits and customs channel individual energy into corporate purpose. The socialization need is the central need which organizes the others. All needs are easier to fulfill through the advantages of corporateness. However, this is not the point. The advantage of corporateness is an-after-the-fact conclusion. The tendency to operate as a group is natural. The difficult task reserved for rationality is not to create law, but to shape and mold natural impulses that do create law. Rationality must provide balance between the group and individuals and between differing groups in the progressive complexities of evolving society.

The strength of custom comes from the satisfactory way that customs meet basic human needs. To violate custom threatens the security of the group and provokes a reaction which reinforces custom. If the matter is important enough, we articulate it as a principle and authenticate it as law. Some philosophers have even tried to make custom the sole basis of law. Such an approach is an oversimplification, but custom is important. As humans begin to function as groups, it is convenient to repeat the activities that work well. Repetition results in custom. Language reinforces custom by describing a custom in familiar words. Custom thus gives rise to an impulse that can result in law. However, the impulse results from the same psychology that we have been discussing. The group establishes customs, fashions, fads, courtesies and other repetitive forms of behavior which entrench its activities in patterns that satisfy needs. The ultimate weapon in this arsenal is law. Society, through families, schools, churches, and other normative institutions, instills norms that have worked for it into all newcomers.

Rationality is instrumental in directing basic impulses, especially in situations where other means of adaptation prove inadequate. Rationality is not the motive force that makes law happen, but it plays an important part in articulation, authentication, and enforcement of law. Even in those activities, rationality is only one of several factors that bring about results that we know as law.

We should note that the terms *rationality* and *cognition* describe psychological functions. We have concentrated on other *psychological* forces that are usually ignored in discussions of the basis of law. We should not let our fascination with these unconscious forces obscure the *psychological* nature of rationality itself. It has its place, although it is not the motive force of law. Emotional factors are more important in human motive than reasoning capacity, but rationality has its place. The restless human spirit sets the mind itself in motion, as it energizes basic needs. The restless spirit, the mind, and needs meld into a single system.

Needs and Civil Rights

Earlier, I invited the reader to think about the Civil Rights Movement in light of these discussions of conscience and basic human needs. Dr. King was in Birmingham with very specific purposes in mind when he was placed in the city jail and wrote his famous letter appealing to natural law. His appeal to natural law was effective as were his numerous appeals to Scripture, to which I will refer later. But was the appeal to natural law and to religious principle effective because of their rational truth, or were they effective because of their motivational appeal? Dr. King was in Birmingham demonstrating for rights of Blacks to *eat* at public eating facilities, to gain equal *employment* opportunities, and to be treated with *dignity and respect.* In connection with the historic march on Washington in 1963, Dr. King emphasized the need for achievement of "untrammelled opportunity for every person to fulfill his total individual capacity," as well as the need for "housing and employment opportunities."[43] All these fall squarely within the scope of basic human needs we have discussed. Indeed, the reasons for Dr. King's demonstrations embraced matters that Maslow described as a precondition for basic human needs, in the absence of which there is likely to be a strong reaction. Dr. King described the Civil Rights Move-

---

[43] Garrow, *Bearing the Cross*, p. 281.

ment as the *Negro Revolution*. Psychologist Sylvan Tompkins points out that only when conditions begin to improve for a people who have been victims of repression for a long period of time is there likely to be revolution. Only when the possibility of improvement is envisioned and felt will victimized persons give up whatever security and dependability may be included even in a bad situation. In the Civil Rights Movement and its impact on law, we can clearly see forces of human motive discussed in this chapter at work.

In the two preceding chapters, we identified sources of energy for law. Our next task is to describe the labyrinthine courses by which society channels this energy into particular norms. Raw power of motive does not produce orderliness, even though basic human needs demand orderliness. There are other psychological and social mechanisms that channel energies of human motive into norms that produce order. Powerful psychological images lie at the foundation of culture. These images hold social organization and norms themselves in place. They are storehouses and channels for energy allocated to meet human needs. These images are powerful influences in shaping structures of society. In this chapter we show how energies of individual psychology are directed into norms and structure of society. We introduce archetypes and symbols, which are images that attract individual energy into group formation and collective psychology. C. G. Jung is our prime mentor.

Psychologists study basic human needs using objective data. Objects that satisfy needs are external, or outside individuals. Maslow looked at *other people* to see what *they* do. Then he generalized upon his observations about what causes people to behave in certain ways. The matters to which we now turn are more subjective, or introspective. We cannot avoid a certain degree of subjectivity with regard to these highly introspective matters. We cannot literally see the mental structures we are about to discuss. These structures are not observable behavior, and they do not physically exist. Use of words such as *structure* and *mechanism* may erroneously imply something physical. The words are being used metaphorically.

In this chapter, we explore *inward mechanisms* that give additional answers to the *why* question. These inward mechanisms provide the basis for group formation and group dynamics. They show how individuals fit together into groups. We begin to see *how* energy that satisfies individual needs also works to satisfy demands of the group.

As I mentioned earlier, conscience relates closely to the *moral order*, which was the basis of Aquinas' natural law. Basic needs, by contrast, are very *utilitarian,* and Bentham could have used them to talk about "the greatest happiness for the greatest number." Both conscience and basic needs operate largely at an unconscious level. Now we will explore energized forms that shape and organize these unconscious forces. In doing so, we disclose a nexus between natural law and positivism. We begin to move beyond natural law and positivism, by exploring psychological principles whose implications for law have not been explored previously.

Logical Constructs

Psychologists have developed concepts which explain structures of personality that we cannot see directly. Circumstantial evidence leads to the conclusion that these structures exist. We call these concepts *logical constructs.* Logical constructs may or may not have an actual physical situs in the brain or elsewhere. Whether logical constructs have an identifiable physical structure is unimportant. Existence of certain observable facts point to existence of other facts which we cannot see. Certain aspects of behavior consistently evidence the existence of logical constructs. Logical constructs explain certain behavior. Psychology is not the only field that uses logical constructs. They are useful in many fields. The concept of *force,* in physics, for instance, is a logical construct. We can't see force, but we infer its existence because of changes that *we believe* it brings about. Likewise, we cannot see energy. In fact, all abstractions involve logical constructs. Logical constructs of psychology are very important tools for analyzing and understanding our inwardness. They explain what "makes us tick." We can apply them to humankind in general. They explain human behavior. In the chapter on conscience, we met several logical constructs. Sigmund Freud described the *id,* the *ego,* and the *super-ego,* all of which are logical constructs. The *unconscious* itself is a logical construct.

Swiss psychiatrist, C. G. Jung, described individual personality structure using logical constructs that differ from those of Freud. Jung was initially a disciple of Freud, and drew on Freud's concepts. He developed his own psychological theories after a breach between the two of them. Jung's logical constructs for analysis of personality include a fascinating panorama of complexes, archetypes and symbols. Jungian psychology is not simple. There is a vast amount of literature on the subject. I can do little more than introduce concepts essential to my theory. Jungian psychology is pivotal in the theory of jurisprudence that

I am describing. It is here that psychology and mythology meet. The *archetype* and the *symbol* are particularly important concepts.

Archetypes and Collective Unconscious

Jung described archetypes as "typical modes of apprehension." According to Jungian scholar Robert H. Hopcke, they are "patterns of psychic perception and understanding common to all human beings as members of the human race." Hopcke explains:

> The term *archetype* is not coined by Jung, and Jung points out its origin in patristic writings as an "explanatory paraphrase of the Platonic *eidos* " (cw9, I, p.4). Jung's unique contribution was to use the idea of archetype in a psychological sense with reference to contemporary people. Archetypes were for him "typical modes of apprehension" (cw8, p. 137). . . 44

Archetypes operate at an unconscious level in the mind. Jung suggested there are two parts to the unconscious. First, there is the personal part. The personal part of the unconscious reflects personal experience. Hopcke explains:

> Jung thus broadened and deepened Freud's conception of the unconscious. Rather than being simply the repository of repressed personal memories or forgotten experiences, the unconscious, it seemed to Jung, consisted of two parts or layers. The first layer, which he called the personal unconscious, was basically identical to Freud's conception of the unconscious. In this layer of the unconscious lay the memories of everything that an individual had experienced, thought, felt, or known but that was now no longer held in active awareness, whether through defensive repression or because of simple forgetting.45

Secondly, there is a universal part that all humanity shares. The universal part contains the archetypes, or forms. Hopcke explains the collective unconscious:

> However, in using his theory of archetypes to account for similarities in psychic functioning and imagery throughout the ages and across highly diverse cultures, Jung conceived of a second layer of the unconscious, which he called the collective unconscious. This layer of the unconscious was the layer that contained those patterns of psychic perception common to all humanity, the archetypes. Because the collective unconscious was the realm of archetypal experience, Jung considered the collective unconscious layer

---

44 Hopcke, *A Guided Tour of the Collected Works of C. G. Jung*, p. 13.
45 Ibid., p. 14.

deeper and ultimately more significant than the personal unconscious. To become aware of the figures and movements of the collective unconscious brought one into direct contact with essential experiences and perceptions, and the collective unconscious was considered by Jung to be the ultimate psychic source of power, wholeness, and inner transformation.[46]

Archetypes are difficult to explain, without oversimplifying Jung's concept. They are a kind of genetically transmitted predisposition to certain ideas or patterns. Jung himself called them archetypes, apparently because of their similarity to Plato's forms. They are not memory that we inherit. Nevertheless, they make certain images easy to conceive. Hopcke gives the following description of archetypes:

> The archetype itself is neither an inherited idea nor a common image. A better description is that the archetype is like a psychic mold into which individual and collective experiences are poured and where they take shape, yet it is distinct from the symbols and images themselves. In this sense, Jung's concept of the archetype is the psychological counterpart of the Plato's form, or *eidos*.[47]

This connection between Jung's archetypes and Plato's forms underscores the analogy I have drawn between the unconscious and the realm of metaphysics. The conscience is the internalization of the father image, according to Freud. Jung includes the father image among the archetypes. This literally makes the unconscious the situs of the *moral order*. This relationship between Jung's archetypes and Plato's forms allows a modern understanding of important philosophic concepts.

The archetype of the *mother* is a good illustration. While the particular role played by the mother may vary from one culture to another, she has certain basic similarities in all cultures. If the child, because of innate structures, can quickly learn to identify the mother, chances of survival will be greater. Thus the concept of archetypes is consistent with Darwinism. Millennia of survivors have acquired an innate ability to recognize the Mother, as well as other "typical modes of apprehension" conducive to survival.

Archetypes exist within the collective unconscious. They are energy laden. Dr. Jean Shinoda Bolen writes:

> When the archetypal level of the collective unconscious is touched in a situation, there is emotional intensity as well as a tendency for symbolic

---

[46] Ibid., p. 14.
[47] Ibid., p. 15.

expression. Then the usual everyday level of experience becomes altered; there is more "magic" in the air, one can become "inspired," or be "on a crusade." Colloquial expressions acknowledge this change in psychological level: "What the devil got into him anyway?" or "He got caught in the grip of an idea" or "She went out of her mind with fear or rage."[48]

Again the archetype of the Mother is a potent example, with a strong emotional content, but there are many other powerful archetypes as well, with powerful emotional content. While Jung's views of the unconscious are similar to the views of Freud, which we discussed before, Jung's views are quite distinctive. The collective unconscious, which is the storehouse of archetypes, images and symbols, is not a part of Freudian theory.

Jung's concepts of the unconscious and archetypal images play important roles in my motive theory of law. They link individuals to society in a dynamic and formative way. Archetypes are the same for everyone. They are part of the genetic heritage that makes us human. Several archetypes identified by Jung are particularly important to our analysis. They include the *father, mother, self, wise old man, anima/animus, hero, trickster* and *divine child*.[49] Jungian scholars remind us, "There are as many archetypes as there are typical situations in life." Jean Shinoda Bolen's clear description is easy to grasp:

> Jung describes archetypes as "patterns of instinctual behavior," saying that "There are as many archetypes as there are typical situations in life. Endless repetition has engraved these experiences into our psychic constitution." Examples of archetypal situations are those such as birth and death, marriage, mother and child bonds, or heroic struggles. Themes of relationship and conflict raised in Greek tragedies, myths, or modern plays often concern archetypal situations. It is because they touch a common chord in us all that they have universal appeal. The common chord is this archetypal layer.[50]

Jung sometimes called archetypes *primordial images,* and made it clear that personal experience affects them. Dr. Bolen discusses archetypes as primordial images:

---

[48] Bolen, *The Tao of Psychology*, p. 19.

[49] Hopcke's *Guided Tour* provides a short discussion of each of these archetypes, with references to Jung's Collected Works as well as references to helpful secondary sources.

[50] Bolen, *The Tao of Psychology*, pp. 18-19.

Yet another definition of archetypes that Jung uses refers to *"primordial images,"* or archetypal figures that become activated and then clothed with personally derived emotional coloration. This occurs when an emotional situation develops that corresponds to a particular archetype. For example, a person may go to hear a lecture from an elderly man, whose presence and words evoke an emotional response to the archetype of the Wise Old Man. Immediately, that man becomes "numinous" or awesome; he is experienced as being wise and powerful; every word uttered by him seems charged with significance. Accepted as the Wise Old Man, whatever he says is not examined critically. Considered as a source of wisdom, his every word, however mundane, seems a pearl of wisdom. The archetype has become personified—clothed as this particular man, who is given all the attributes of the archetype. Other examples of archetypal figures are the divine child, all-giving mother, patriarchal father, temptress, or trickster—all are symbolic, recurring figures in dreams, literature, and religions.[51]

The "typical situations in life" include situations involving law. Jungian scholars frequently discuss the role of the archetype of the "wise old man." Through millennia of evolution the wisdom of age was important to survival of the group. The shaman or medicine man played an important role. Because of the value of the role, it became archetypal. Now, when we come into contact with an elderly person who strikes us as particularly knowledgeable, the archetype is activated. We cling to his every word, and look to him for guidance. Judges have historically tried to assume this role—even to the extent of white wigs and robes.

The father image is also an archetype, and its importance should be abundantly clear from earlier discussions of conscience formation. The father is an authority figure, and his role is archetypal, which assures great emotional power for the image. In Judeo-Christian writing, God is frequently referred to as *Father*—the ultimate authority figure, and source of law. Clearly, archetypes play a pivotal part in the imagery of law.

Indeed, law itself has all the attributes of an archetype. It is a typical mode of apprehension that has tremendous potential for contributing to survival. We quickly learn that society's methods of problem solving are superior to self-help remedies. However, the matter of social control, involving images of authority, is extremely complex, and we can only allude to them—we cannot completely describe them in a paragraph or two. The entirety of this book can be considered an attempt to describe the archetype of law.

---

[51] Ibid., p. 19.

The logical construct of a singular archetype for law is probably an oversimplification. More likely, there is a group of archetypes and symbols that work together to produce patterns of behavior that we describe as law. Examples of this type of social behavior are plentiful. A rash of neighborhood burglaries prompts a *neighborhood watch*. Suspicion of the existence of a serial killer spawns a strong community-wide defense reaction. Energy that insists upon ordinary law enforcement activity springs from the same motive base.

Individuals, often unconsciously, transfer necessary emotional energy to the group to energize law. The *archetype of law*, located in the *collective unconscious*, is a useful term for describing energized sensitivity of a group of individuals to any action which threatens the group. It receives, stores, releases and acts on mandates, taboos, norms and prohibitions shared by the group to which the individual belongs.

The archetype of the *wise old man* illustrates the importance of appropriate role playing by judges and other law enforcement officials. This imagery suggests the motive underlying law. Officials use symbols and images of authority. By doing so, they evoke a primordial response in individuals in the community. This enables officials to channel collective energy toward achievement of proper ends of law.

The very words *law* and *justice* get their meanings from a rich panoply of archetypal imagery. Archetypal images are not static concepts. All Jungian literature describes them as *energy-laden*. In them, we find the huge storehouse of energy which fuels the machinery of law. They are channels by which individual energy for basic human needs is directed to enforcement of norms of society. The collective unconscious, with its energy laden archetypes is the blue print for society.

It is clear, however, that these energy sources can become unbalanced. They do not merely explain the power of law. These forces also explain mob violence, fanatical religious sects and Nazi Germany. Energy-laden archetypes help to explain the motive force of law. In normal circumstances, they are very useful. Out of control, they are awesome. They can be compared to fire or water. Controlled fire and controlled archetypes are extremely useful; but when either fire or archetypal power rages out of control, as they both did in the David Koresh incident, it is terrible. The same is true of water power—or atomic energy. Power of collective psychological energy, although useful, can rage out of control, as it did in the Los Angeles riots following the Rodney King verdicts.

We will concentrate on archetypes that mold overtly social behavior. Archetypes can apply to other "typical situations" as well. For instance, our experience of space and time is archetypal. Archetypes shape our concepts of roles that are necessary for there to be a society. We will encounter various archetypes as we proceed through the remainder of the book. We cannot discuss each of them here, but can only indicate the nature of archetypes in a general way, and identify some that are important for law. Each culture provides the fund of experience that activates and actualizes archetypes for that culture. There are cultural variations of the mother role, for instance, but they all identify with the same archetype. Archetypes affect how individuals respond to people, images and situations. They are quite important in structuring society. Law is a part of the definition of that structure.

More than any other writer, C. G. Jung provides the bridge of explanations that connect psychology and mythology. In the next section, we deal with mythology in depth. For now, it is enough to say that there is a strong connection between psychology and mythology. Identical archetypes and symbols appear in both. Jung's two layers of unconscious form one basis for Joseph Campbell's contribution to mythology. Campbell quotes Jung's description of the two layers of unconscious at length.

The bridge that connects psychology and mythology operates in both directions. It is the route by which individuals channel their psychological energy to specific social forces. Travelling across the bridge in the opposite direction, social forces arising from mythology of society shape individuals to the mold of their own culture. This shaping or molding includes conscience formation, among other things. Images, archetypes, and symbols freely travel between psychology and mythology. Law uses social force that mythology and psychology combine to create. Archetypes set our expectations of individuals in various roles. They cause needed roles to occur and function in groups. They are sources of energy by which society enforces its norms for individual behavior. Role-playing is normative. The connection between mythology and psychology explains many phenomena in the legal realm which we cannot explain by traditional rational approaches.

Symbols

Symbols are also an important part of Jungian psychology. They are akin to archetypes. Jung found symbols which he believed to appear in dreams of all humans. He noticed that those same symbols also appear in mythology. This is an important connection in the motive theory that I am asserting. Symbols and archetypes that appear in individual mental life connect with symbols and archetypes in mythology. This provides a psychic bond between individuals and culture.

At the risk of illuminating the obvious, let me refer to a few of the many symbols that are of profound importance in law. There are scales of justice, gavels, robes, powdered wigs, red lights, green lights, yellow lights, blue lights, raised benches, formal arrangement of the courtroom, uniforms, badges, ceremonial language, and flags. We could extend the list almost indefinitely. These symbols are significant in Jungian psychology. As mentioned earlier, powdered wigs no doubt seek identification with Jung's archetype called the *wise old man*. Judicial robes are ritualistic, and de-personalize the judge's involvement. The psychological significance of the raised bench symbolizes control. The gavel is probably a direct descendent of Thor's hammer of the mythology of northern Europe.

These outward and visible symbols do not require in-depth discussion. Reflection on personal experience sufficiently exposes the power of symbolism in law. Blue lights on the road behind us cause concern. We feel a tug at the heart strings when *Old Glory* unfurls. The aura of the courtroom instills respect. Fire ravaged the Macon County Courthouse in 1985. Operating from makeshift courtrooms taught me the importance of a formal courtroom setting.

Jung, Kant, Maslow, Piaget and Kohlberg

Jung's archetypes remind us of Immanuel Kant's *a priori* concepts of time, space and duty. Both suggest a *predisposition* to certain types of knowledge. Kant suggests that full blown concepts or categories such as duty, time and space are innate. Jung only suggests innate structures that experience can activate. However, in another sense, Jung goes further than Kant. He suggests that archetypes are *charged with energy*. Energy associated with archetypes is immense, and its release is contagious. Its release activates collective psychology, which causes individuals to support activities of groups of which they are a part. These theories help unravel the mysteries of conscience and other mental functions which partake of the unconscious. They suggest the possibility of genetically precoded mental functions that operate unconsciously. Both Kant and Jung draw on the possibility of a *genetic* basis of certain types of mental functions.

Maslow, who taught us about basic human needs, agrees that certain mental functions are at least partly pre-coded by heredity. Maslow argues:

> Our main hypothesis is that human *urges* or *basic needs* alone may be innately given to at least some appreciable degree. The pertinent behavior or ability, cognition or affection need not also be innate, but may be (by our hypothesis) learned, canalized, or expressive.[52]

Maslow argues that human urges, or basic needs, are *innately given*, rebutting contentions of those who deny such a possibility. Maslow's rebuttal is powerful:

> It was a severe mistake of both the instinctivists and their opponents to think in black and white dichotomous terms instead of in terms of degree. How could it be said that a complex set of reactions was either *all* determined by heredity or *not at all* determined by heredity?

> [I]t is also obvious that nothing is completely free of the influence of heredity, for man is a biological species. This fact, determined by heredity, is a precondition of every human action, ability, cognition, etc., i.e., everything that a human being can do is made possible by the fact that he is a member of the human species. This membership is hereditary.[53]

Archetypes and symbols fit comfortably with Maslow's hierarchy of needs. Archetypes and symbols enable individuals to interpret the social environment. They are parts of the mind that enable individuals to quickly and easily recognize in the external world opportunities to satisfy physiological, safety, belongingness and love, esteem, and self-actualization needs. They also enable individuals to quickly recognize danger or threatening conditions. Although some learning or conditioning may be necessary, archetypes should be understood as a genetic predisposition to this kind of learning or conditioning. Archetypes give structure to the very broad category that Freud called the ego. Freud described the ego as "that part of the id which has been modified by its proximity to the external world. . . . (T)he ego has to observe the external world and preserve a true picture of it. . . ."[54]

Lawrence Kolberg is recognized as one of the leading modern theorists of moral development. He followed the lead of Jean Piaget in

---

[52] Maslow, *Motivation and Personality*, Second Edition, p. 80.
[53] Ibid., p. 81.
[54] Sigmund Freud, *New Introductory Lectures on Psychoanalysis*, p. 106.

formulating definable stages of moral development. In his early writings, Kolberg leaned in the direction of a strong developmental connection between moral development and cognitive development. To grossly oversimplify his thought, we might say that he argued that morals are a product of learning. He called his theory the *Cognitive Developmental Theory*.

Kohlberg later appeared to recognize that moral formation depends upon two types of factors. The first is genetically pre-coded developmental factors. The second is interaction of the developing individual with the social environment. Most of us agree with these basic premises. The problem is that we in western society have little understanding of *what* we get either genetically or from the environment that causes moral behavior. I am now suggesting a broad picture of genetically acquired archetypal structures, and how they affect us. These suggestions are simply extensions of the theory of conscience formation discussed earlier.

Kohlberg's and Piaget's theories are very objective. They are compatible with Jung's theories. Indeed, we could argue that Kohlberg's findings support Jung's subjective theories. Others have noticed this compatibility. James Fowler based his book, *Stages of Faith*, on the Kohlberg paradigm. Fowler suggested that he and other Kohlberg associates had "extended the structural-developmental metaphor in a direction more holistic and inclusive of broader patterns of personality or ego functioning."[55] Fowler argued that Kohlberg's ideas are compatible with those of Erik Erikson. Erikson is a Freudian psychiatrist who advocates a *psychosocial* approach as opposed to a strictly *cognitive* developmental theory.

Fowler felt, as I do, that we cannot separate cognition from affective behavior. Thus, Fowler, and perhaps Kohlberg himself, recognized compatibility between Kohlberg's ideas and those of Erik Erikson. For the same reasons, I contend that the total picture of moral development is not present without including Jung's theories of archetypes, symbols and collective unconscious. It is unlikely that proponents of either group would admit compatibility of the theories. This is not because of *thought content*. It is because of widely divergent research methods used in arriving at the theories, not to mention the common academic predilection to protect one's turf.

---

[55] Fowler, *Stages of Faith*, p. 272.

The Circle of Individuality

Let me suggest a way to visualize some of the things we have been discussing. It has been helpful for me to picture the individual as a circle. The outside world is everything outside the circle. The individual's perceptions of the world is an *internal* picture, constructed by the individual from material drawn from outside the circle. We believe that individuals relate to the outside world through senses—sight, feeling, hearing, taste, and smell. However, individuals do not construct the internal picture in a conscious or intentional manner. The internal world is the one in which the individual really *lives*. We tuck away sensory perceptions, and resulting imagery, in memory somewhere in the circle. We are not conscious of everything stored in the circle. There is a part of our mind that is unconscious. There is mental *equipment*, such as feelings, emotions, and other processes of which we are unconscious. Jung's archetypal images and the two layers of unconscious he describes are within the circle, although all of humanity shares the universal unconscious. Kant's *a priori concepts* are within the circle. All of this is genetic equipment, the *computer hardware*, which shapes an individual's inner picture of *reality*. This is the only reality with which an individual deals directly. Archetypes and symbols interpret, or organize, sensory data. They give it form. Sensory data of a particular culture or subculture funds the actual content and meaning of archetypes and symbols.

These internal structures interact with the outside world. Individuals project the resulting images externally. *Projection* is another well-known psychological principle that we can add to our collection. It explains why we expect others to follow our own standards. Projection is our tendency to interpret actions of others by our own tendencies. We easily understand projection by considering extreme examples. The jealous lover projects unfaithfulness on his partner, when in fact he is the guilty party. The person with a particular moral failing is quick to see the same failing in others.

In normal behavior, the principle of projection causes an individual to expect others to follow his own moral code. Projection, operating in a group of individuals with similar internal standards, produces group standards. The idea of projection is a different way of looking at the same dynamics we have discussed earlier. Projection becomes the individual's external reality. We posit external objects as *things-in-themselves*, meaning things that have actual existence in the external world. We believe that we share this external reality with other beings similar to ourselves. This is why we have an unshakable faith in an external reality.

Although we believe in the world outside the circle, our belief remains inside the circle. Blaise Pascal captured the sobering flimsiness of the ephemeral nature of external *reality* and its social origin.

> And who doubts that, if we dreamt in company and the dreams chanced to agree, . . . and if we were always alone when awake, we should believe that matters were reversed.[56]

Our mental life profoundly affects behavior. Our minds organize data. They bring order out of chaos. They organize the outside world for us so we can live in it—even though the perceptions are really within us. We face that external world with our basic needs. Inward structures aid us in extracting what we need from the external world. The group of which we are part is within us as well as outside us. We assign value, based on archetypal role, to persons involved. In this way we form functioning groups.

We share our perceptions of order, embodied in ideals, with others whom we believe to be similar to our own *self*. Then we project shared ideals of resulting social organization into an external social reality. Most of that social reality consists of shared abstractions that are not at all physical. Individuals change behavior to cope with that shared reality. Shared reality is laden with ideals and archetypes which living mythos perpetuates. This shared reality is the powerful force of culture. It produces social organization, and conditions individuals of each new generation to its norms.

All our meditations about the nature of law must take the dichotomy between internal and external into account. This dichotomy has been well-stated by Fritjof Capra who attributes it to Rene Descartes:

> The philosophy of Descartes was not only important for the development of classical physics, but also had a tremendous influence on the general Western way of thinking up to the present day. Descartes' famous sentence, "Cogito ergo sum"—"I think, therefore I exist"—has led Westerners to equate their identity with their mind, instead of with their whole organism. As a consequence of the Cartesian division, most individuals are aware of themselves as isolated egos existing "inside" their bodies. The mind has been separated from the body and given the futile task of controlling it, thus causing an apparent conflict between the conscious will and the involuntary instincts.[57]

---

[56] Pascal, *Thoughts* from *The European Philosophers from Descartes to Nietzsche*, p. 130.
[57] Capra, *The Tao of Physics*, pp. 22-23.

We call this division the Cartesian system, and it is a major factor in all of western thinking.

The Cartesian division places every individual into one of those circles we described! The rest of us are part of the *outside* for that particular individual. Individuals get feelings of *self-worth* from the reflection of their existence which they see in others. We are images inside their circles, interpreted by their archetypes. Therefore, when we reflect disapproval of conduct because of our own taboos, theoretically the disapproved individuals alter behavior to get our approval, but this does not always happen.

I suspect the existence of a sinister archetype that explains why this does not always work. It is the archetype of the enemy, alien or stranger. This archetype is clearly evidenced in the *gentile*, the *plebeian*, the *barbarian*, the *samaritan*, and others. To deal with the world, we apparently are prepared to ignore or disdain certain classes of people and their opinions. This suggestion is rich in possibilities for explaining a host of strange attitudes and events. At various times and places it has applied to Jews, women, Blacks and others. I have experienced it personally as a southern white male. In any event, we don't particularly care what the *alien* thinks of us.

In addition to specific people whose images are present inside the circle, there is a *generalized Thou*. We worry about what *they* will think, without being specific as to who *they* are. The microcosm includes the individual's parents and significant other people who are close to him emotionally. Later it includes members of the peer group. The generalized Thou usually adds pressure for conformity. However, disapproval by those outside the group can actually be a status symbol within the microcosm. The fact that one does not care what *they* (the generalized Thou) think can actually enhance one's standing in one's own group, especially if *they* have been identified by one's group and internal archetypes as *aliens*.

The process of maturation lessens the impact of feedback in formation of the self-image and conscience. The more completely *individual* a person becomes, the less malleable is his value system. The most formative years are the earliest years, as Freud suggested. After that time, memory and recollection of past feedback plays an ever-increasing role in identity. We construct a personal myth that explains our own origin and identity, and resist identity changes.

Modern thinkers are telling us there is no line around the circle. Observer and observed are one, they say. The part that is mental, and inside, is one with the physical, and outside. Whether the cleavage is real or is part of the anomaly of individual existence is a good question. We must consider the possibility that no such division exists. Jung's collective unconscious is consistent with the idea that there is no line. Observer and observed possibly exist in one continuum. However, the *impression* of division is almost inescapable.

The Archetypal Self

We cannot fully understand the dynamics of the group without understanding how individuals relate to groups. Within the circle which separates us from the outside world, there is something that organizes the perception of *self*. Our senses, in the traditional sense, do not perceive the self. Self is one of Jung's *archetypes*. We cannot even see our own physical image without a *reflection* from a mirror. The perception of self is internal, but it is a product of *reflective existence*—feedback from others. We build it from the reaction of other people to us. It is an *energy laden* image. The self-image is both archetypal and experiential in nature. The task of manipulating *self* in varying social contexts is of utmost importance in understanding motive. Phrases such as *a positive self-image* and *self-esteem* arise from this type of analysis. As we manage the image of *self* in our own groups, the mores, or rules of the group become extremely important. Violation of rules of the group effaces the image of self, simply because *others disapprove* of the violation. This is true, whether the infraction is merely a moral transgression or an actual violation of a law.

Self-image does not actually direct our behavior. It is only one image that affects behavior. Other mechanisms control behavior. Self is merely one of the roles that we manipulate. Understanding the reflective nature of the self-image makes the myth of Narcissus much more meaningful. Narcissus was the lad in Greek mythology who fell in love with his own reflection in a pool. The tragic result was that he could not break away from it for normal, necessary activities. The pool that actually reflects our image is society itself.

We have come full circle. All this information about the self-concept fits in with development of conscience. Freud identified two aspects of the super-ego or conscience: the *ego ideal* and the *taboo*. The ego ideal is a part of the self image. Our discussion of archetypes and symbols underscores the formation of conscience. However, this discussion of *self* and self image involves more than conscience. *Peer pressure*, which is different from conscience, arises in the context of the present discussion.

Peer pressure can act directly on the self-image to affect behavior and induce conformity, without internalization of the values of the group. The need to belong and to be accepted may be sufficient to bring about conformity with wishes of the group, even if conscience opposes the proposed activity. Jung's archetypes greatly expand the role of ideals or images that direct the impulse to law. Ideals are part and parcel of the images that shape our behavior. Unless psychological and social dynamics reinforce a legal rule, it is difficult to enforce. Jung's collective unconscious is richer in images than Freud's concepts. According to Jung, we internalize a whole village, priests, cops, moms and all! He did not talk as much about the father image.

Cultural Relativism

Jung's archetypal images take specific content from the culture in which the individual is reared. This provides a theoretical base for an individual's propensity toward order, in a specific context. Jung's theories provide a plausible explanation for why individuals in a particular cultural group instinctively react similarly to similar stimuli. They all share ideals embodied in the same archetypes. Their latent archetypes have been funded with a common base of experience. This *common* reaction is obviously important as a source of energy that backs legal principles.

Archetypes also leave room for an explanation of evolution of differing legal systems. Different cultures cause the individual's archetypes to be funded with differing contents, although they are energized by the same primordial images. Environmental content furnished by differing cultures varies the specific image of the father, the mother, the self, the wise old man, the trickster and other archetypes. The role of the mother may not be the same in India that it is in Alabama, but they both draw on the same powerful archetype. Personal space and self-esteem, conscience, peer pressure, and other psychological factors may also differ from one culture to another, but they are empowered by the same powerful latent images. However, these images and forces universally underlie motivating forces that result in law and social order.

Archetypes and Civil Rights

In connection with each major addition to the theory that I am developing, I have paused to show how the addition is illustrated in the Civil Rights Movement. Dr. King drew the immense energy of an archetype. He deliberately chose the role of Moses. He saw the "Promised

Land" from the mountaintop, which was a strange prophecy of his own death. He led his people "out of bondage." From a mountain, Moses saw the promised land that he was not allowed to enter. On another mountain, Moses was given the tablets of law. Dr. King drew from the masses the strength of a messiah, in Jungian as well as religious terminology. Dr. King's stated premonitions of his own death heightened the emotional intensity of his image, so that its effectiveness did not end with his death. His prophesies of his own death drew on the image of Christ, who also prophesied his own death. Martyrdom, the death of a beloved leader for the sake of an ideal or a cause, may be one of the most powerful motivating images of all. Dr. King's birthday is now celebrated as a national holiday. Dr. King was a *Hero* in the sense that the word is used in Joseph Campbell's writings on mythology. The power of his speeches illustrates the power of collective representations as described by Emile Durkheim, which we take up in the next chapter. Thus Dr. King himself illustrates the tremendous role of archetypes in lawmaking.

Individual Psychology and Collective Psychology

In this chapter, we continued to develop ideas about how energy and ideals for law come from individuals. Now, we are ready to explore the conversion of individual energy into collective energy. The group uses energy thus generated. However, group function may add entirely new dimensions to the meaning of law. Water power turns a turbine and converts energy into a new form. The group also converts energy supplied by individuals that creates and enforces law, even though it retains some of its original character. The conscience of the group is not precisely that of any one individual, even though it comes from individuals who compose the group. In the next chapter, we will examine group formation and *sui generis* forces that start from the group.

| Chapter 2.4 | Collective Psychology |

In preceding chapters, I discussed how individual conscience develops. I showed that conscience furnishes a part of the force of law. Law finds its roots in individual psychology. Even if psychological functions are responsible for conscience, does this mean that psychological factors are the basis of law? Some will argue that only the strong arm of force is real law. But that causes us to ask about motive for the strong arm of force.

I discussed human needs as the basis for motive. Needs are largely responsible for what we do. Restless energy that pushes us to satisfy needs supplies motive power for all our needs, including law. Basic needs propel us into orderly human relations. Archetypes and symbols shape and direct these motive powers in our lives. They shape us for roles that we play in society as well as roles that we expect of others. Nevertheless, our answer to the *why* question is not yet complete. Why does society force compliance with its mandates?

What are the sources of force and power in a society? The individual's psychological norms translate into a motive force for society through collective psychology. Collective psychology builds upon conscience, archetypes and basic human needs, but adds something new. Collective psychology helps to explain how law gets its motive force. It melds individual energies into a composite force.

Formation of group norms involves far more than a simple conversion of individual norms. It involves more than mathematical concepts of probability. It involves living processes of interaction. Conscience itself results from interaction of individuals with the group. Archetypal roles are the models for structure in society. Archetypes and symbols channel individual energy to enforcement of group norms. Formation and enforcement of norms are dynamic, evolving processes. Collective psychology is an important part of these processes, arising in part from shared archetypes.

Collective psychology is a mysterious force in our lives. Under the influence of a group, we behave differently. Collective psychology is so innate that we are hardly aware of it. We see it in others more easily than in ourselves. Nevertheless, it affects us all.

We shift from psychology to sociology with the discussion of collective psychology. Emile Durkheim argued:

> When we use the word "psychology" by itself we mean individual psychology, and for the sake of clarity in discussion it is convenient to limit the word to this. Collective psychology is sociology, quite simply—why not employ the latter term exclusively?[58]

Development of sociology since the time of Durkheim has not assigned this particular and limited meaning to the word *sociology*. I will use the term *collective psychology*, which is more precise. Durkheim's argument emphasizes the close connection between collective psychology and sociology. Collective psychology is as much sociology as psychology. It forges the link between individual psychology and mythology. Understanding collective psychology is the next step in understanding what makes law work. Emile Durkheim will be our main guide as we explore collective psychology.

Most of us have attended sporting events, such as football games, in which excitement runs high. Caught up in the excitement, we shout and jump up and down. We do everything that avid fans usually do. The response of spectator participants helps create the *home team advantage*. Picture yourself at the same event as the only spectator. Could you become equally excited? This is an example of collective psychology. Collective psychology is contagious. Its contagious nature induces conformity in behavior of individuals.

As television viewers, we are all familiar with scenes of mob rioting and looting. Would any of the participants commit such acts alone? What gives the lynch mob its courage? Most of us have heard a recording of boisterous laughter. We find it difficult not to join in! This is especially true if other people are present and begin to laugh. Anger is contagious. Even yawns are contagious. All of these are examples of the contagious nature of psychology. Collective psychology is discussed in standard texts:

> When people are gathered together under certain rather unusual circumstances, they sometimes indulge in extreme forms of behavior which are not at all characteristic of them under other circumstances. The "lynching mob" . . . offers one illustration of such behavior. Panics, revival meetings, and

---

[58] Durkheim, *Sociology and Philosophy*, p. 54.

"celebrations" provide opportunities to observe other kinds of extreme behavior. Many writers have been so impressed by the intensity of behavior sometimes observed in these kinds of situations that they have concluded that it cannot be accounted for by the established psychological principles. Some writers have therefore tried to formulate specific sets of principles which, they believe, account for "crowd behavior." According to this point of view, there is one set of principles for "normal," individual behavior, and another set for the more extreme forms of "crowd" behavior.

Most of these theories assume, in one way or another, that the individual no longer functions as an individual but is somehow taken possession of by a power that dominates all individuals simultaneously. They seem to act as one person, and even to feel as though they had lost personal self-control. Phrases such as "group mind" have often been used to describe this submergence of the individual into the super-individual power.[59]

A strange aspect of collective psychology is our undeniable tendency to follow a leader. Many people will follow a well-dressed man across the street against the light. They are not as likely to follow the fellow in jeans.[60] Extreme examples illuminate the typical. We have all heard stories about fanatical sects. Often in such sects, collective psychology plays an important part. Jim Jones, leader of a fanatical religious sect, led hundreds of his followers to suicide. The David Koresh incident in Waco and the Los Angeles riots in the aftermath of the acquittals in the Rodney King case have occurred while this book is in progress. Charles Manson, leader of a counter-culture cult of the 1960s, had followers who were willing to obey his every command. Hitler mesmerized the German people. Why do people follow a leader? These examples immediately remind us of the discussion of energy-laden archetypes in the preceding chapter. They are also examples of collective psychology.

A nineteenth-century author, Charles Mackay, wrote a book entitled *Extraordinary Popular Delusions and the Madness of Crowds*. In it he showed how the financial debacles of the *Mississippi Company* and the *South Seas Company* resulted from collective psychology. He also included numerous other stories of the same type. He wrote prior to advent of modern psychology and sociology, which renders his accounts even more persuasive of the existence of collective psychology. His book has been reprinted many times, and is currently in print. Apparently, the

---

59 Newcomb, *Social Psychology*, p. 621.
60 Coon, *Introduction to Psychology*, p. 599

phenomenon that we have described as collective psychology has long been recognized among lay people.

The thrust of my theory is that law thrives on collective psychology. The unusual examples of collective psychology described above merely show its existence. Collective psychology also operates quite subtly in our routine daily activities. It arises from psychological dynamics discussed in preceding chapters. It sets and enforces norms of society. It causes us to confer authority roles on certain individuals to enforce the will of the group. It is part of the motive force of law.

Collective Representations

French sociologist Emile Durkheim described the dynamic force of collective psychology. His book, *The Elementary Forms of the Religious Life*, first published in 1912, is a classic in the field. The book shows the force of mythology in society. It links both sociology and psychology to mythology, and provides an in depth examination of collective psychology.

Durkheim examined the religion of totemism in native tribes in Australia. Totemism involves an identification of a clan with a particular animal or other symbol. For instance, there is a lizard clan, an ostrich clan, and a kangaroo clan, among others. No two clans have the same totem animal or symbol. Each member of the clan personally identifies with the symbolic animal. Clan members believe that they and the totem are the same. Lizard men believe they are one with the lizard.

Each clan celebrates certain rites. There are initiation rites and seasonal rites. Clan members believe that seasonal rites bring rainfall, bountiful harvests, and an abundant supply of the totem animal. Durkheim looked beyond the obvious fact that individuals making up the clan are not lizards, ostriches, or kangaroos. He realized a deeper significance of identification. The identification process enables members to identify with each other. This is neither strange nor difficult. We have sorority and fraternity members who *identify* with each other by Greek letters. We have *Auburn Tigers* and *Michigan Wolverines*. We have Baptists, Catholics, Methodists and Jews. We have Americans, French, Germans, and Poles. The identification process works. We behave in certain ways because of our identity. The concept of duty relates, at least in part, to identity. Identification with the clan animal also enabled differentiation from other clans, which supports exogamous marriage customs, among other things. Identification enabled Durkheim's clan members to form groups and to confirm beliefs held in common. Membership in the group imposed definite social obligations.

Durkheim argues that it is through collective psychology that norms—the moral expectations—of society are energized:

> But it is not only in exceptional circumstances that this stimulating action of society makes itself felt; there is not, so to speak, a moment in our lives when some current of energy does not come to us from without. The man who has done his duty finds, in the manifestations of every sort expressing the sympathy, esteem or affection which his fellows have for him, a feeling of comfort, of which he does not ordinarily take account, but which sustains him, none the less. The sentiments which society has for him raise the sentiments which he has for himself. Because he is in moral harmony with his comrades, he has more confidence, courage and boldness in action, just like the believer who thinks that he feels the regard of his god turned graciously towards him. It thus produces, as it were, a perpetual sustenance of our moral nature. Since this varies with a multitude of external circumstances, as our relations with the groups about us are more or less active and as these groups themselves vary, we cannot fail to feel that this moral support depends upon an external cause; but we do not perceive where this cause is nor what it is. So we ordinarily think of it under the form of a moral power which, though immanent in us, represents within us something not ourselves: this is the moral conscience, of which, by the way, men have never made even a slightly distinct representation except by the aid of religious symbols. (Emphasis added)[61]

Common beliefs form the basis of representations or images. They create the possibility of abstract concepts shared by the group. Clan members base their perception of reality on these representations or images. Durkheim called these images *collective representations*. The word *representation*, as used in the term *collective representation*, may be confusing. In English, the word *representation* has several meanings. As I understand Durkheim's usage of the word, its English synonyms, *picture* and *image* may help to bring his meaning into focus. Thus, a *collective representation* is an image formed and shared by a group. This explanation also shows a similarity between Durkheim's *collective representations* and Jung's *archetypal images*. Collective representations came into being over long periods of time. They result from an immense sharing of ideas and sentiments. Durkheim describes the formation of collective representations:

---

[61] Durkheim, *The Elementary Forms of the Religious Life*, p. 242.

Collective representations are the result of an immense co-operation, which stretches out not only into space but into time as well; to make them, a multitude of minds have associated, united and combined their ideas and sentiments; for them, long generations have accumulated their experience and their knowledge. A special intellectual activity is therefore concentrated in them which is infinitely richer and complexer than that of the individual. From that one can understand how the reason has been able to go beyond the limits of empirical knowledge. It does not owe this to any vague mysterious virtue but simply to the fact that according to the well-known formula, man is double. There are two beings in him: an individual being which has its foundation in the organism and the circle of whose activities is therefore strictly limited, and a social being which represents the highest reality in the intellectual and moral order that we can know by observation—I mean society. This duality of our nature has as its consequence in the practical order, the irreducibility of a moral ideal to a utilitarian motive, and in the order of thought, the irreducibility of reason to individual experience. In so far as he belongs to society, the individual transcends himself, both when he thinks and when he acts.[62]

In this description, we can clearly see a similarity between Durkheim's *collective representations* and Jung's *archetypes* and *collective unconscious* which we encountered earlier. A socially created collective representation can arise much more readily if there is a genetically based archetype to support it. Social existence depends on collective representations. Collective representations reflect the dual nature of humans as individuals and as social creatures. As we pointed out in discussions of archetypes, society exists within the individual. This makes the individual civilized. Humans take on what we describe as human qualities because of these internal images shared by others.

The religious nature of clan activities causes emotional energy to attach to collective beliefs and activities associated with shared images. Durkheim argues that capacity of beliefs to affect behavior depends on belief in their external existence, even though they are obviously contained within the individual minds of group members:

Since it is in spiritual ways that social pressure exercises itself, it could not fail to give men the idea that outside themselves there exist one or several powers, both moral and, at the same time, efficacious, upon which they depend. *They must think of these powers, at least in part, as outside themselves, for these address them in a tone of command and sometimes even order them to do violence to their most natural inclinations.* It is undoubtedly true that *if they*

---

62 Ibid., p. 29.

were able to see that these influences which they feel emanate from society, then the mythological system of interpretations would never be born. But *social action follows ways that are too circuitous and obscure, and employs psychical mechanisms that are too complex to allow the ordinary observer to see when it comes.* As long as scientific analysis does not come to teach it to them, men know well that they are acted upon, but they do not know by whom. So they must invent by themselves the idea of these powers with which they feel themselves in connection, and from that, we are able to catch a glimpse of the way by which they were led to represent them under forms that are really foreign to their nature and to transfigure them by thought.

But a god is not merely an authority upon whom we depend; it is a force upon which our strength relies. The man who has obeyed his god and who for this reason, believes the god is with him, *approaches the world with confidence and with the feeling of an increased energy.* Likewise, social action does not confine itself to demanding sacrifices, privations and efforts from us. For the collective force is not entirely outside of us; it does not act upon us wholly from without; but rather, *since society cannot exist except in and through individual consciousness, this force must also penetrate us and organize itself within us;* it thus becomes an integral part of our being and by that very fact this is elevated and magnified. (Emphasis added)[63]

Beliefs create and reinforce a shared perception of the cosmos. Indeed, according to Durkheim, the very categories of human thinking begin in these shared perceptions of reality.

This same social character leads to an understanding of the origin of the necessity of the categories. It is said that an idea is necessary when it imposes itself upon the mind by some sort of virtue of its own, without being accompanied by any proof. It contains within it something which constrains the intelligence and which leads to its acceptance without preliminary examination. The apriorist postulates this singular quality, but does not account for it; for saying that the categories are necessary because they are indispensable to the functioning of the intellect is simply repeating that they are necessary. But if they really have the origin which we attribute to them, their ascendancy no longer has anything surprising in it. They represent the most general relations which exist between things; surpassing all our other ideas in extension, they dominate all the details of our intellectual life.[64]

If Durkheim is right, then mythology and a shared reality precede conceptual thinking. Durkheim points out that if we did not share

---

[63] Ibid., pp. 237-238.
[64] Ibid., pp. 29-30.

concepts of time, space, cause, number and the like, minds could not communicate. Concepts are at the heart of rationality. But concepts arise from mythological patterns of thought. Since concepts originate in social life, reason itself reflects authority of society and is a moralizing force. In fact, categories of thought, by their very nature, reflect shared beliefs and moral force of the group.

> If men did not agree upon these essential ideas at every moment, if they did not have the same conception of time, space, cause, number, etc., all contact between their minds would be impossible, and with that, all life together. Thus society could not abandon the categories to the free choice of the individual without abandoning itself. If it is to live there is not merely need of a satisfactory moral conformity, but also there is a minimum of logical conformity beyond which it cannot safely go. For this reason it uses all its authority upon its members to forestall such dissidences. Does a mind ostensibly free itself from these forms of thought? It is no longer considered a human mind in the full sense of the word, and is treated accordingly. That is why we feel that we are no longer completely free and that something resists, both within and outside ourselves, when we attempt to rid ourselves of these fundamental notions, even in our own conscience. Outside of us there is public opinion which judges us; but more than that, since society is also represented inside of us, it sets itself against these revolutionary fancies, even inside of ourselves; we have the feeling that we cannot abandon them if our whole thought is not to cease being really human. This seems to be the origin of the exceptional authority which is inherent in the reason and which makes us accept its suggestions with confidence. It is the very authority of society, transferring itself to a certain manner of thought which is the indispensable condition of all common action. The necessity with which the categories are imposed upon us is not the effect of simple habits whose yoke we could easily throw off with a little effort; nor is it a physical or metaphysical necessity, since the categories change in different places and times; it is a special sort of moral necessity which is to the intellectual life what moral obligation is to the will.[65]

Collective representations form the basis of categories of thought. Membership in the group and participation in categories of thinking instill thought processes of the group into individuals. Shared categories are the basis of concepts. A concept is a collective representation. Thus, Durkheim theorized that concepts begin in the social sharing of reality, and carry with them an implicit moral force. Individual observation and thought have no reason to create concepts. Only the prospect of sharing

---

[65] Ibid., p. 30.

information with others gives rise to the need for concepts. The total system of concepts imposes its force on our conduct. We act in accordance with our perception of the world. Our perception of the world is given to us by our social, linguistic, participation in mythos of the group.

In matters touching behavior, collective representations include appropriate emotional tone. The group expects and enforces compliance with its beliefs and requirements. The dynamics described by Durkheim are consistent with psychological dynamics discussed earlier. However, collective representations add a definitely new dimension, which we can call the social dimension.

A definitional approach to collective representations is inadequate. Collective representations are dynamic forces. We must understand their force dynamically, and not just by definition. To understand collective representations, we must understand their effect. They are more than a concept. They explain the origin of concepts. They are more than moral norms. They explain the origin of moral norms. Claude Levi-Strauss, a preeminent French anthropologist argues that *mythological thought builds structure from events, while scientific thought builds events from structure.*[66] His insight, combined with the present discussion, leads to the conclusion that legal thinking has much more in common with mythological thinking than with scientific thinking. Certainly his observation sheds an interesting light on case law, the case method, and *stare decisis*. Cases describe events, and they in turn contribute to the structure of the law. Every case could begin with the classic "Once upon a time there was a..." This narrative approach, from which we glean our metaphors is clearly mythological rather than scientific, if we follow Levi-Strauss' argument.

We will refer to collective representations repeatedly. They are the social counterpart of individual psychology already described. In collective representations we see several themes of psychology that I have developed in earlier chapters, such as the dual nature of humans and the way that dual nature provides the basis for collectivity. Also, there are other themes here that I will concentrate on in later chapters, such as the social nature of concepts and the development of language through mythology. This anticipates a discussion of the role of language in law. In our discussion, *collective representations* join Freud's *super-ego*, Maslow's *basic human needs*, and Jung's *archetypes* and *symbols* and *universal unconscious*. These are all parts of the arsenal of dynamics that

---

[66] Levi-Strauss, *The Savage Mind*.

bring about law. Together they form a complementary system. Each plays a part in structuring society.

Need For Group Formation

As we saw in preceding chapters, each member of a group bestows psychological energy on the group. Archetypes channel this energy into patterns of behavior typical of the particular society. This is the way collective psychology works. The group takes on a life of its own. It sets up its own internal orderliness. It sets norms. By doing so, it alters behavior of individuals composing the group. In addition to pursuing their own happiness, individuals must satisfy the group's needs.

Why do groups organize? Group formation is natural. Social psychologist Argyle discusses formation and organization of small social groups. He shows how group formation occurs in primates other than humans, which suggests natural occurrence of this phenomenon, without involvement of rationality with its *social contracts*.

> A great deal of social interaction takes place in small social groups. Monkeys and apes live in groups, within which children are procreated and reared with various family structures. The work of gathering food and drink and arranging shelter is performed, leisurely social activities occur, and defence against predators is organised (p.27ff). This is presumably an instinctive pattern of behaviour, which has evolved through the survival of those groups and their members that adopted it. Human life is similar: children are reared in families, go out to play with groups of friends, are educated in groups at school; later they work in cooperative groups, and live in families of their own, which form communities, and they pursue common interests in various societies and clubs. . . .(T)he members of small groups work out a pattern of interaction in which all of the members are related as members of the group.
>
> Members of a group will have much in common from the beginning, but it is also found that there is convergence towards shared ways of perceiving and judging, of communication and interaction, shared attitudes and beliefs, and shared ways of doing whatever the group does.[67]

Thus group formation results in a greater ability to satisfy basic human needs. This also explains why groups form norms. Individuals, consciously or unconsciously, *want* and need to organize groups. By organizing, members of the group are better able to satisfy their individ-

---

[67]   Argyle, *Social Interaction*, p. 216.

ual needs. But organization implies—indeed requires—rules. According to Maslow, there is a need to belong. Argyle discusses these concepts:

> Probably the single most important and widely confirmed generalisation about social groups is that they form norms. Our first interest is in why they do this—the functions served by norms and the processes leading to their being formed. * * * [S]hared patterns of behaviour are adopted by group members because this enables them to attain group goals and satisfy interpersonal needs.[68]

Clearly, we need to belong, and by belonging to a group, we are more likely to satisfy our basic needs. However, group participation can be paradoxical. Orderly dissent often supports the needs of groups! Antithetical leaders emerge, offering the group a choice.

The individual lends his skills and services to groups. He also gives more subtle support, by lending the force of his opinions. His opinions, of course, have been structured by the collective representations shared by the group. Opinion coalesces into a powerful force which is the source of authority, according to Durkheim:

> Now the *ways of action to which society is strongly enough attached to impose them upon its members, are, by that very fact, marked with a distinctive sign provocative of respect. Since they are elaborated in common, the vigour with which they have been thought of by each particular mind is retained in all the other minds, and reciprocally. The representations which express them within each of us have an intensity which no purely private states of consciousness could ever attain; for they have the strength of the innumerable individual representations which have served to form each of them. It is society who speaks through the mouths of those who affirm them in our presence; it is society whom we hear in hearing them; and the voice of all has an accent which that of one alone could never have.* The very violence with which society reacts, by way of blame or material suppression, against every attempted dissidence, contributes to strengthening its empire by manifesting the common conviction through this burst of ardour. In a word, when something is the object of such a state of opinion, the representation which each individual has of it gains a power of action from its origins and the conditions in which it was born, which even those feel who do not submit themselves to it. *It tends to repel the representations which contradict it, and it keeps them at a distance;* on the other hand, it commands those acts which will realize it, and it does so, not by a material coercion or by the perspective of something of this sort, *but by the simple radiation of the mental energy which it contains. It has an efficacy coming solely from its psychical properties, and it is by just this sign that moral authority*

---

[68] Ibid., p. 224.

is recognized. So opinion, primarily a social thing, is a source of authority, and it might even be asked whether all authority is not the daughter of opinion. (Emphasis added)[69]

Underlying group formation are psychological forces discussed earlier. They include conscience, basic needs, archetypes and symbols. Archetypes and symbols shape and direct conscience formation and the effort to satisfy basic needs. All these have a part in group formation and operation. Group dynamics are the source of self-esteem and conscience. The group excludes or restricts those who fail or refuse to follow norms of the group. It rewards those who support the group. Members must support aims of the group. All of this is the work of the socialization need.

Group formation also fits with ideas of Freud which we examined earlier. Internalization and parental influence, for instance, which are quite Freudian, are familiar to social psychologists. Each member of the group expects other members to adhere to the same standards that his own conscience dictates, and believes that those standards exist externally and independently of the group. Argyle writes:

> Norms begin as a kind of working agreement among the original members of the group. New members may share the norm behaviour from the outset (and may have joined for this reason); if they do not share it, group processes are set into operation which often result in their conforming. Halla Beloff (1958) distinguished between people simply agreeing and actually moving toward the norm. To the members the norms seem to have some kind of independent existence exterior to the group, and to have a moral quality. Thibaut and Kelley (1959) suggest that the basis of this may be that parents have in the past laid down the rules and arbitrated between siblings. "The newcomer to the group may later move beyond *overt compliance*, in the presence of other members, to *internalisation* of the norms. Whereas previously he would only conform when the group was looking, now he will always do it, will believe it is right, and be prepared to influence or convert deviating members."[70]

Notice the similarity between Argyle's description of the origin of norms and Anna Freud's description of superego formation which we quoted earlier.

The dynamics and psychology of group formation are not merely rational agreements for satisfaction of individual needs. Although group

---

[69] Durkheim, *The Elementary Forms of the Religious Life*, pp. 238-239.
[70] Argyle, *Social Interaction*, pp. 224-226.

functioning is the easiest way to meet individual needs, we must not assume that individuals *choose* to be a part of a group to satisfy needs. Everyone is automatically a part of a number of groups. Group functioning is present at birth and before. By the time an individual starts choosing, he is part of the group and shares its values. Everyone is, by birth, a member of a family, an ethnic group, a language group, a church, a community and any number of other groups. *There is no other option available.* Groups are an integral part of natural human functioning. They are a part of naturally occurring human ecology.

Bonding is natural, and dependency plays a part. Humans may be born one at a time, but they are also born dependent. Thus, even though we are individuals, we are members of a group. Humans remain dependent. Dependency merely shifts from parents to the larger community. Dependency is an externally observable fact. Internal mental structures described in preceding chapters enable us to cope with dependency. Durkheim explains the dynamics of dependency and shows how dependency forces individuals to serve needs of society.

> Now society also gives us the sensation of a *perpetual dependence*. Since it has a *nature which is peculiar to itself* and different from our individual nature, it pursues ends which are likewise special to it; but, as it *cannot attain them except through our intermediacy, it imperiously demands our aid. It requires that, forgetful of our own interest, we make ourselves its servitors,* and it submits us to every sort of inconvenience, privation and sacrifice, without which social life would be impossible. It is because of this that at every instance we are *obliged to submit ourselves to rules of conduct* and of thought which we have neither made nor desired, and which are sometimes even contrary to our most fundamental inclinations and instincts.[71]

Mental structures that enable us to cope with dependency are, at one and the same time, tools and products of evolution. They support survival of the group. Careful examination of moral norms reveals a subtle survival quality. Divine intervention is not a prerequisite to effectiveness. The Biblical command, "Honor thy father and thy mother, that thy days may be long upon the earth" can be understood only in light of this argument. The command does not mean that parents will destroy children who disobey or fail to honor. It simply means that children who follow admonishments of parents are more likely to survive. The argument is both Freudian and Darwinian, and supports my thesis. The

---

71 Durkheim, *The Elementary Forms of the Religious Life,* p. 237.

commandment bristles with archetypes and other principles we have been describing.

Society exacts compliance, one way or another. The *impression* of force asserts force itself. Amassed opinions undergird use of force if force is necessary to exact compliance with rules. But opinion itself asserts moral authority that usually brings about compliance, without need of force. This is because opinions are internal—they are built into individuals as part of the group. As pointed out earlier, individuals must please the group if they are to satisfy their own esteem needs. Durkheim points out that moral authority is more important than actual physical force in exacting conformity.

> Even if society were unable to obtain these concessions and sacrifices from us except by a material constraint, it might awaken in us only the ideal of a physical force to which we must give way of necessity, instead of that of a moral power such as religions adore. But as a matter of fact, the *empire which it holds over consciences is due much less to the physical supremacy of which it has the privilege than to the moral authority with which it is invested.* If we yield to its orders, it is not merely because it is strong enough to triumph over our resistance; it is primarily because *it is the object of a venerable respect.* (Emphasis added)[72]

In group psychology, we see Jung's archetypes in action. The father image, mother image, wise old man, hero, and all the others are on stage. They play their parts. Symbols move the group, and often are deliberately chosen, because of their motive power. Symbols and images permeate our lives, and shape the way we live. But they also embody and enforce group norms.

Durkheim, Jung and Freud

In earlier chapters, we gradually came to focus on the work and theories of C. G. Jung. He showed how energized archetypes are a part of the motive force within individuals. They enable individuals to relate to society. They, in effect, are the *social* part of the double nature of humankind that Durkheim described. There is consistency between Jungian psychology and Durkheimian sociology. The two complement each other. We can find minor inconsistencies if we look hard enough, but the overall consistency more than offsets any possible discrepancies. Any two scholars examining the same data, but theorizing in different

---

[72] Ibid., pp. 237-238.

disciplines, will display some inconsistency. This makes the degree of compatibility between the thinking of these two preeminent social scientists even more remarkable.

Jung and Durkheim have a common denominator in mythology. One can readily visualize the gradual genetic evolution of Jung's archetypes from eons of operation of social life, as described by Durkheim. The evolution always occurs under the influence of prevailing mythology. Jung argues that sociology—social force—derives from psychology. He says mythology is the projection of psychology. Durkheim says just the opposite. He argues that collective representations are introjected into individuals. Some may see this as inconsistency. Which one is right? From our perspective, it is immaterial. Given the nature of biological and social evolution, both are probably right. Evolution occurs slowly, and in small increments. Social progress affects genetic probabilities, and vice versa. The two evolutionary processes, genetic and social, intertwine to such an extent that we cannot separate them. Humans did not come into advanced social systems fully developed. Neither do social, or mythological systems appear overnight. Humans and the systems developed together, symbiotically and slowly. When this does not happen, there can be problems. Modern civilization has encountered less developed societies. Persons from those societies have encountered modern developments. The results can be devastating. Michener's novel, Hawaii dramatizes the dangers of these encounters. This subject requires careful attention. We have learned that the noble savage is not always noble. We have also learned that our so-called advanced civilization gives no license for condescension. Social evolution of collective representations as described by Durkheim is entirely consistent with genetic evolution of archetypes as described by Jung.

Likewise, for our purposes, there is no significant discrepancy between Durkheim's ideas of moral formation and those of Sigmund Freud. Freud's theory of moral formation—formation of the super-ego— is a theory of internalization. Durkheim argues that society is the agent of internalization. Freud emphasized the role of the parents, and his description is quite specific. It includes greater detail that appears to conflict with Durkheim's generalization. Freud described mechanics of internalization that apply to a particular culture. Some scholars believe that his findings were provincial. His patients came from similar cultural settings. Freud certainly did not select his patients randomly, for the sake of scientific research or as representatives of all cultures. Assuredly, there are matriarchal cultures in which the father does not play the exact role in moral formation described by Freud.

Durkheim felt that moral and religious practices are a part of the social internalization that forms conscience. This adds a different dimension which helps to explain the power of conscience. Some may find this to conflict with Freud's theory. However, we must ask ourselves what supports the parent's value system. Without this information, Freud's theory that conscience is the internalized image and commands of parents involves infinite regression. Durkheim fills this gap in Freud's theory. Moreover, neither Freud nor Durkheim professed to be religious. Jung, who did profess religion, attributed deep religious significance to archetypes, which helps to identify archetypes with Durkheim's collective representations. Durkheim was not appealing to religion when he recognized that religion contributes to conscience. He took a dispassionate, sociological view of the matter.

Family, The Basic Group

The basic unit of group formation in society as we know it is the relationship between a man and woman and offspring they produce. The man and woman unite in a strong emotional bond and produce children. It is easier to understand bonding in these relationships than in any other. As Abraham Maslow argues:

> One important aspect of a good love relationship is what may be called need identification, or the pooling of the hierarchies of basic needs in two persons into a single hierarchy. The effect of this is that one person feels another's needs as if they were his own and for that matter also feels his own needs to some extent as if they belonged to the other. An ego now expands to cover two people, and to some extent the two people have become for psychological purposes a single unit, a single person, a single ego. 73

Surely off-spring are included in this bonding. Often parents sacrifice their own desires for needs of their children. Society is a much larger pooling, but pooling starts with family. All bonding processes probably begin with forces and images that start in the family. We cannot overemphasize the central importance of the family. The family is the closed unit that adds new members to the human race; it is the bud on humanity's tree of life.

---

73 Maslow, *Motivation and Personality, Second Edition*, p. 192.

There is "natural selection," to use Darwin's phrase, in the bonding of male and female in the marital union. Maslow affirms that natural impulses combine with rationality to produce a wholesome union.

> Finally, I wish to call attention to the fact that [the principles of bonding which he had been discussing] supply us with another example of resolution or denial of an age-old dichotomy, i.e., between impulse and reason, between head and heart. The people with whom my [self-actualized] subjects fall in love are soundly selected by *either* cognitive or conative criteria. That is, they are *intuitively, sexually, impulsively* attracted to people who are right for them by cold, intellectual, clinical calculation. Their appetites agree with their judgments, and are synergic rather than antagonistic.[74]

The basis of law also lies in the union of natural impulse and rationality. The impulse for law possibly started historically and continues to start socially in family structure.

Civilization began with extension of law and authority beyond the family or clan. This does not erase the crucial importance of organizational forces that arise within the family or clan. Images that arise in the family and clan form the basis for important archetypes. Civilization harnesses energy naturally produced by those structures to accomplish its purposes. Religions have furthered civilization by universalizing principles of family life. Christianity teaches us to love our enemies. It might be rational to kill them. For instance, Hitler died, and everyone was pleased. But we have tried to detach rationality from the underlying dynamics that civilized the world. We have tried to make rationality self-sufficient. This effort is both impossible and foolish. Maslow addresses this question:

> In any case to accept as intrinsic an antagonism between instincts and society, between individual interests and social interests was a terrific begging of the question. . . .Individual and social interests under healthy social conditions are synergic and *not* antagonistic. The false dichotomy persists only because erroneous conceptions of individual and social interests are the natural ones under bad individual and social conditions. [75]

The imagery of orderliness that begins in the family is just as important as rationality in producing an orderly society.

---

74   Ibid., pp. 201-202.
75   Ibid., p. 85.

Collective Psychology and Majority Rule

Collective psychology, of course, is not the same as majority rule. Majority rule assumes the formulation or articulation of a principle, on which each individual forms an opinion, for or against. The very articulation of the issue usually distorts the true impulse. Whoever articulates the issue has already dealt with impulse. The people may have had *no feeling* about the matter before hearing the question. Moreover, group formation, under the direction of collective psychology, has obviously occurred before there can be a vote.

Majority rule, therefore, is quite different from collective psychology. Majority rule is very rationalistic. Collective psychology, on the other hand, is an infectious emotional reaction. It involves unarticulated feelings. Articulation, education and social interaction in general helps to shape those feelings. Collective psychology often involves symbolism and imagery, rather than rational principle. It affects elections governed by majority rule, and vice versa. Nevertheless, the distinction between the two is clear. Majority rule may be a rational attempt to capture the force of collective psychology.

The Social Contract

It is possible, of course, to describe group formation as a social contract in which individuals receive a *quid pro quo* for giving up natural rights. This was the approach of some early philosophers of the Age of Reason. Such an approach is highly legalistic and rationalistic, and helped open the door for legal positivism. The tendency to band together with other people and thereby satisfy basic human needs is natural, however. It is not an artificial result of human intellect as suggested by Hobbes and others. The tendency to band together is not a matter of rationality or logic. Monkeys do it. Ants do it. Cattle do it. Humans do it, also. Many mechanisms involved are completely unconscious, so we cannot possibly describe them as *rational* or *contractual*.

The *social contract* idea is spurious. It is completely circular. The social contract theory defines law in terms of one of its products. Law came a long way before it created the concept of a contract. Contracts are not necessarily law's most important product. Contracts are effects, not causes, of law. They arise from normative force. We *ought* to do what we promise. This moral basis creates dependability and orderliness in society. Why do we honor a contract? That is the question we must ask ourselves. If we know why we honor contracts, then we can probably understand the essence of law. Do we honor contracts because we ought to keep our word, so that there can be dependable social relations? When contracts of adhesion become instruments of oppression, however, the law begins to look for ways to avoid the results of contract. All approaches lead inexorably back to the question of motive. The social contract had less to do with origin of government than the marriage contract had to do with origins of marriage.

If the social contract theory has validity at all, it is at the level of groups rather than at the level of individuals. Individuals form groups naturally. Groups negotiate. It was a *group* of barons who extracted *Magna Carta* from King John. Natural psychological and sociological factors produce original groupings. In a pluralistic society there are many essential groups: families, churches, schools, labor unions, corporations, and local governments. These groups develop naturally as a response to human needs. After development of groups, rationality and agreement at a cognitive level have a place in development of overall governing principles. Negotiations of social order are often conducted by groups, for the benefit of members; but even so, the object remains satisfaction of basic needs. Part of the motive for group formation is to deal more effectively with other groups.

In the sense that I have just described the social contract, the Civil Rights Movement can be described as an effort by Blacks as a group to renegotiate the social contract. However, as we have seen, the Civil Rights Movement found deep motivational support in basic human needs. It called for a renewal of conscience. Thus, the Civil Rights Movement can be more clearly understood as a quest by Blacks for basic human needs than as a renegotiation of some metaphysical social contract. Dr. King took on an archetypal role, clearly identifiable with the role of Moses, who lead his people out of bondage and is identified with origin of law.

In this chapter we have developed the theme of collective psychology. Collective psychology can be seen in mass demonstrations of the Civil Rights Movement. In my immediate area, mass demonstrations occurred in Montgomery and Birmingham, not to mention the historic Selma to Montgomery march. All of these demonstrations helped precipitate major Civil Rights legislation in the mid-sixties. Even more important for our purposes was the mass reaction by non-Black Americans, who became more receptive to the Black People of America, and supported the rightful claims of Blacks. In the next section we will explore the role of mythology in more depth. Even now, if we look closely at changes in law resulting from the Civil Rights Movement, we see the myths that have shaped our culture playing a major role. After all, Dr. King was a man of religion, and he deliberately drew on Biblical imagery.

3 | Mythological Components

The force of law does not arise from rational thought processes, but from deeper aspects of human nature. I have described these forces in the preceding section. However, I have not explained what creates the system and holds it together. There is a naturally occurring higher level of organization for the forces I have been describing than the levels discussed so far. We caught a glimpse of this higher level in the idea of collective representations in the preceding chapter. In the present section, which deals with mythology, we explore the strange ways in which collective psychology perpetuates itself in society and how it enforces the will of the group. Psychology and mythology are the poles of the force field that create law. In this section, I concentrate on mythological systems. We will see how they shape and maintain the psychological components of social control. Discussion of mythology requires additional introduction.

Sacred Stories

I attended Sunday School and church as a child in a small rural church. I became familiar with Bible stories very early. Regular church attendance and involvement in a wide range of church activities along with private study and a couple of courses at Huntingdon College have expanded my knowledge of the Bible. It was not strange that I made a connection between law as described in the Bible and law as we know it today. Biblical law and law as we know it today have much in common.

In the early 1970s, I spoke in several churches as a lay speaker. My topic was the development of law. The law of the Sabbath illustrated my point. The Bible relates in *Genesis* the creation of the world by God in six days. *On the seventh day He rested.*[76] Then, in Exodus, the Sabbath became a part of the law. One of the Ten Commandments which Moses brought down from the mountain is to *Remember the Sabbath Day to keep it holy.*[77]

By the time of Jesus, scribes and elders had interpreted the commandments so that they spelled out many details for daily life. Those in charge of law like to interpret. Jesus found himself in conflict with authorities because of healing a man's withered hand on the Sabbath.[78] In another episode, his disciples were hungry and ate some corn as they passed through a field on the Sabbath. Again Jesus and His group found themselves in trouble with the law.[79] They were not charged with stealing, but with violating the Sabbath.

A theme develops throughout the Bible dealing with the law of the Sabbath. It begins in hazy myth, and as part of a belief system and cosmology. It crystallizes into law and social control. It culminates in a conflict between legalism and the original purpose and intent of law. Jesus' teachings created new collective representations and he knew it. He cautioned his followers that they could not put his *new wine* into their old *wineskins.* His images were more positive than existing restrictive imagery of law. A major part of his teaching was in parables, or simple stories that make a metaphorical point. His parables conveyed vivid new images.

Do laws of the Sabbath have any impact today? Our first inclination is that they do not. One immediately thinks of so-called *Blue Laws,* which prohibit certain activities on Sunday. They are not particularly popular. We seldom enforce them, even if they are still on the books. Certainly, the blue laws are not major influences. However, a part of the wisdom of the law of the Sabbath is that work should alternate with rest. The original narrative gave its main emphasis to work followed by rest. Jewish law required that even *land* lie fallow one year out of seven. We have a widespread custom of labor-free weekends, but there is more. The entire fabric of our wage and hour laws—the 40-hour week—may rest on this early foundation in the Judeo-Christian heritage. Some will argue that wage and hour laws have nothing to do with the Biblical theme, but simply rest on social and moral principles. However, our judgments of

---

[76] Genesis 2:2
[77] Exodus 20:8
[78] St. Luke 6:6-11
[79] St. Luke 6:1-5

right and wrong arise in our mythos, in which the Bible plays a crucial role.

This is precisely the way mythos works. How do members of our society know that certain actions or conditions are *bad*, if not because of the influence of culture? Would such principles have arisen in our culture without the Judeo-Christian heritage? God asked Adam and Eve, "Who told thee thou art naked?" They had eaten the mythical fruit of the tree of knowledge of good and evil. That question is very important.

Where do we get our notions about good and evil? What's wrong with being naked? How do we recognize right and wrong? What we take for *common sense* is much more complicated than we realize. Before Christianity, Romans sometimes left deformed babies in the hills to die. That was probably common sense to them. Does *rationality* tell us it was a bad idea? Apart from our belief systems to the contrary, the practice might still meet all the tests of rationality. Our shared beliefs are important.

Our mythos, or belief system, gives us our basic inclinations about right and wrong. Shared beliefs make "common sense" *common*. The fact that beliefs are present in more than one mind—in a system of shared beliefs—gives them authority. In this section we explore this poorly understood source of values to see how it works. Dr. King drew directly on images and ideals of the Judeo-Christian heritage, both for psychological force and justification for the Civil Rights Movement. He worked primarily through Black Churches. His organization was the Southern *Christian* Leadership Conference, and he rejected suggestions for other names without religious implications.

We will explore the idea that law has some connection with the earliest myths of mankind. I am asserting a connection between mythology and law. Myths are powerful stories that reveal truths. They are not merely fantastic tales portraying events that never happened. I am using the word *mythos* to include more than myths. It includes the Bible, but I certainly am not suggesting that the Bible is a *myth* with negative connotations of untruth, lack of historicity, and the like. The Bible is both directly and indirectly a source of law in our society. It has shaped morality, and morality has shaped law. Thus, the Bible's influence extends beyond its *commandments* as such. But mythos, in the sense that I am using the word, includes not only religious writings and ancient stories; it includes folk stories, fairy tales, legends, nursery rhymes, songs and more.

There are many common themes interwoven in our mythos. In the story of *The Three Little Pigs*, the third little pig built his house with bricks. It withstood the onslaught of the wolf. The story has the same *moral* as the story of the wise man in the Bible. Sunday schoolers know that the wise man built his house upon the rock. Rain and wind could not destroy it. The man who built his house on sand was not so fortunate. Both stories teach us that we should set our lives on a dependable foundation. Such similar themes from widely divergent sources abound in our mythos. They instill in us the values that we hold in common. Those values are the foundation on which our mythos advises us to build our houses!

One explanation for the importance of myths in law is quite simple. Modern laws are usually complex pieces of prose and easily forgotten. Words are easy to forget, unless they rhyme or employ some other literary device. For whatever reason, myths live on in memory. They are rich in imagery. They carry with them many important ideals, including the impulses and themes that we articulate in laws. They are storehouses of value and are therefore durable.

Bettelheim

On one Sunday afternoon in 1977 Bill Russell and Paula Gordon visited in my home. Bill and Paula had started a small TV communications company. I helped them with their legal work, and we had become friends as well as having an attorney-client relation. I mentioned my theory that law arises to some extent from myths and mythology. A few days later, Bill and Paula sent me a copy of Bruno Bettelheim's book, *The Uses of Enchantment*. Myth and psychology are related! Bettelheim vividly described how folk fairy tales affect development of children. Although the idea was not at all new, Bettelheim's book showed me the deep and intense connection between myths and psychology.

I had not yet made the connection between law and individual conscience. Strangely, most of us do not connect *moral formation,* as described by psychologists, and the *moral order* to which Aquinas referred. The larger connection between and among all of these concepts had not occurred to me. If I had written back in the seventies, I would have believed I was writing a book about two unrelated ideas. The first would have been that law arises from mythology, and I would have argued that law always relates in some way to the earliest myths of humankind. The second would have been that law arises from collective psychology. No doubt, I would have mentioned conscience and morals.

However, I would not have connected them with each other or with mythology or collective psychology. Today, I understand that all these matters are closely related. If anything threatens the stability of society, collective psychology releases energy from individuals through conscience, moral sentiment, and collective psychology, for fulfillment of the purposes of law. Law is the mechanism for an orderly release of such energy. Mythos connects and perpetuates these seemingly unrelated ideas. Archetypes, common to mythology and psychology, are mechanisms that store and release energy. This section will explore the role of mythos.

Pirsig

Another fortuitous event added to my understanding of *mythos*. My older son, Philip, attended the University of Alabama, where he participated in the School of Arts and Sciences Honors Program. He read Robert M. Pirsig's book, *Zen and the Art of Motorcycle Maintenance* for a seminar about the concept and role of the university in western society. Philip recognized in Pirsig's book a similarity to ideas that he had heard me talking about and encouraged me to read the book. It was from this book, which I read in early 1988, that I finally began to see the centrality of mythos. Pirsig's book introduced me to the word *mythos*. I will quote material from Pirsig's book which capsulizes the importance of mythos and its relationship to reason. The book centers on de-emphasis of reason in general, which added to my understanding of problems inherent in a strictly rationalistic approach to law. In this section, we take a look at Pirsig's descriptions of mythos. We will see how he relates it to logos.

Joseph Campbell

All of these events together caused me to begin looking for books about mythology, and I discovered Joseph Campbell's works. Friends who knew of my interest began to shower me with copies of Campbell's various publications. It was his work that brought my thoughts on this important subject into focus. In his works, he portrays the vastness of mythos, as well as its dynamic effect in society. Campbell is the most important mentor for this section. He describes the psychological, philosophical, and religious importance of mythos.

As I mentioned in the preface, these ideas did not appear in my own mind in the order that I have presented them here. Why does one remember certain things and forget others? Certain ideas remained active enough in my mind so that I recalled them many years after my initial exposure to them. They all fit into a composite picture. Anyone exposed to all of these ideas at one time would likely associate them. This is not the way the matters came to me. They accidentally dropped into my consciousness, one at a time, over a period of several years. Strange as it seems, these ideas were not part of any literature in law school or in my practice. I probably connected the ideas because they gave meaning to actual events in my life. I doubt that I could have remembered such information as well for any other purpose. I could not intentionally collect the same amount of data in memory unless it were personally meaningful. The existential importance of the ideas to me, in my particular situation, caused me to assimilate them in a quest for personal meaning.

I was slow to grasp the importance of ideas embedded in the word *mythos*. Early on, I realized that our laws often arise from values expressed in the earliest myths of our culture. I was much slower to realize that *all* cultures, *including ours*, has its current mythos. Mythos includes the entire literary and cultural heritage. Mythos is elusive, sprawling, and vague, but it is also dynamic, pervasive and at times, poignant. As Joseph Campbell has written:

> Mythology has been interpreted by the modern intellect as a primitive, fumbling effort to explain the world of nature (Frazer); as a production of poetical fantasy from prehistoric times, misunderstood by succeeding ages (Muller); as a repository of allegorical instruction, to shape the individual to his group (Durkheim); as a group dream, symptomatic of archetypal urges within the depths of the human psyche (Jung); as the traditional vehicle of man's profoundest metaphysical insights (Coomaraswamy); and as God's Revelation to His children (the Church). Mythology is all of these. The various judgments are determined by the viewpoints of the judges. For when scrutinized in terms not of what it is but of how it functions, of how it has served mankind in the past, of how it may serve today, mythology shows itself to be as amenable as life itself to the obsessions and requirements of the individual, the race, the age.[80]

Mythos is closely related to culture. The word is used here to include certain hints not closely associated with the word *culture*. These include history, mystery, religion, romance, and dynamics. While culture includes all these matters, the use of the word *culture* does not bring these things to mind. Likewise, the word *ethos* conveys some, but not all, meanings of *mythos*. Ethos is a static concept, perhaps a cross-section of

---

[80] Campbell, *The Hero With a Thousand Faces*, p. 382.

values of a culture at a particular time. Mythos captures those same values in legends and stories and transmits them in a dynamic fashion. *Mythos* is more amenable than ethos to emotional content that is a very necessary part of our value system.

Mythos is a central, uniting idea in my motive theory of law. Mythos falls generally within the province of anthropology. In formulating my theory, I have drawn on works of pioneer anthropologists. Sir James G. Frazer's *Golden Bough* demonstrates the power of mythos in a unique way. It is a monumental collection of mythological stories and practices. It, in turn has exercised a tremendous influence on literature of the twentieth century. I also found the works of Emile Durkheim and Bronislaw Malinowski while trying to learn as much as I could about mythology.

Mythos unites such widely diverse phenomena as conscience, moral formation, romantic love, archetypal imagery and symbolism, religion, family, relations between the sexes, basic human drives, observations of depth psychology, and collective representations. It pierces deeply into meanings of human nature, but in a non-analytic fashion. I hope that my analytical approach to mythos does no damage to the contribution which mythos has subtly made to institutions of law since the inception of civilization. There may be cause for concern. When I was very small, I pulled up a cutting from a rose bush that my mom and I were trying to root to see if any roots had started to grow. They had, but of course the cutting died as a result of my analysis. All my tears did not change the result. We are quite dependent upon continuance of law's natural dynamics, and I hope that exposure of its roots does not cause its death.

Mythos is the realm in which members of society share knowledge of values and ideals of the culture. It is more than words in books and libraries. Mythos is active knowledge in living minds that impacts on every facet of human activity. Electric utility companies function well, despite the fact that each individual employee does not know every job necessary to their functioning, or even understand electricity. We don't care, as long as the light comes on when we flip the switch. Society operates in an even larger corporate fashion. Mythos painlessly embraces paradoxes and pluralism while undergirding a morality that leads to law and survival of society. Mythos is society's storehouse of knowledge, moral judgment, emotion, language, and many other important aspects of society's existence. None of us have to know it all, so long as the system works; but for the system to work, workable theories and beliefs must be embedded in our system of knowledge, in the grasp of someone in the group.

Mythos and Law

In this section, I expect to cover four aspects of how mythos relates to law. The first chapter pulls together the broad reach of mythos in society. It shows how mythos organizes psychological forces we discussed earlier. I also explore broad philosophical implications of mythos.

The second chapter discusses the connection between mythos and language. This introduces the linguistic aspect of law. The relationship between law and language is deep. The two cannot be separated. Mythos is the bridge between the two. Language allows expression of primordial urges that motivate people to create and enforce law.

The third chapter shows that mythos provides belief patterns that undergird authentication of law. Our belief systems clothe law with appearances of authenticity. Authenticity of law is a product of our shared perception of reality. Survival, and basic needs, underscore the necessity for such beliefs. The fact that our perceptions of law arise from beliefs held in common does not void their reality or importance.

The fourth and final chapter in the section identifies three mythological themes that impact on our modern patterns of belief. They are individuality, rationality, and sexuality.

Mythos

Let's review the discussion thus far and see how mythos fits in. We began our search for law and its motive force by examining conscience. We decided that conscience is very important in securing a central core of compliance with law. We noted the connection between law and morals and suggested that morals relate to conscience. Moral formation is a proper study for psychology, involving unconscious as well as conscious mental processes. Further investigation showed that motive force arises from basic human needs. The need for orderliness is embedded in those needs.

We decided that humans are social animals by nature. Group formation results from natural human inclinations. Findings of modern psychology support this conclusion. This differs radically from the thinking of the early Age of Reason. Hobbes described social life as *artificial*, a creation of the human mind. For him, *rationality* and *agreement* were solely responsible for social life. The life of man in his natural state was "short and brutish," according to Hobbes. This type of thinking infected philosophy of law during the formative period of modern nation states. It was clearly a forerunner of legal positivism.

Norms evolve from group formation to enable orderly functioning of the group. Collective psychology becomes a factor in production of group norms and their enforcement. Motivating force for law and even the content of norms themselves, arise from psychological and social dynamics.

There is a strong and essential relationship between psychology and mythology. Archetypes and symbols of psychology also appear in mythology. Mythos is a dynamic force that causes enculturation. Mythology shapes individual psychology, using archetypes and symbols. Mythology is the culture bearer of values, ideas, mandates, norms, and taboos. It embodies the very language that enables culture to exist as such.

One would clearly expect a strong relationship between mythos and law, based on these connected ideas. Mythos itself proudly proclaims the relation, with pictures of gods handing down laws. Such self-acclamation is not adequate to satisfy the modern externally oriented mind. Such an image is inadequate in the age of rationality. Perhaps the journey we have taken through mountains and clouds of psyche is more convincing. Mythos of each culture contains the culture's value system. It carries values and ideals from person to person and from generation to generation. Mythos relates closely to individual psychological mechanisms we discussed earlier. Mythology and psychology connect through archetypes and symbols that are a part of both.

Bruno Bettelheim captured a perception of the massive concept that I call *mythos* in his book, *The Uses of Enchantment*. He convincingly describes the important role of folk fairy tales in a child's development. Fairy tales provide images which the child uses to resolve difficulties in a creative way. Bettelheim argues:

> For a story truly to hold the child's attention, it must entertain him and arouse his curiosity. But to enrich his life, it must stimulate his imagination; help him to develop his intellect and to clarify his emotions; be attuned to his anxieties and aspirations; give full recognition to his difficulties, while at the same time suggesting solutions to the problems which perturb him. In short, it must at one and the same time relate to all aspects of his personality—and this without ever belittling but, on the contrary, giving full credence to the seriousness of the child's predicaments, while simultaneously promoting confidence in himself and his future.
>
> The child finds this kind of meaning through fairy tales. Like many other modern psychological insights, this was anticipated long ago by poets. The German poet Schiller wrote: "Deeper meaning resides in the fairy tales told to me in my childhood than in the truth that is taught by life."[81]

Fairy tales enable the child to externalize internal conflicts. They enable the child to absorb roles, or ways of dealing with people, that society approves. The meaning of fairy tales is often double. Part of the meaning may be plain, while other parts are not. They address the deepest structures of the child's personality, at the child's level of development and understanding. Bettelheim explains:

> Through the centuries (if not millennia) during which, in their retelling, fairy tales became ever more refined, they came to convey at the same time overt and covert meanings—came to speak simultaneously to all levels of the human personality, communicating in a manner which reaches the

---

[81] Bettelheim, *The Uses of Enchantment*, p. 5.

uneducated mind of the child as well as that of the sophisticated adult. Applying the psychoanalytic model of the human personality, fairy tales carry important messages to the conscious, the preconscious, and the unconscious mind, on whatever level each is functioning at the time. By dealing with universal human problems, particularly those which preoccupy the child's mind, these stories speak to his budding ego and encourage its development, while at the same time relieving preconscious and unconscious pressures. As the stories unfold, they give conscious credence and body to id pressures *and show ways to satisfy these that are in line with ego and super-ego requirements.* (Emphasis added)[82]

Bettelheim's description of the usefulness and effect of folk fairy tales puts them squarely within our concept of mythos. He beautifully describes the meaningful impact of folk fairy tales and their importance. Bettelheim does not claim that fairy tales are the only means by which culture shapes individuals. The word *mythos*, as I use it, includes the total of all cultural forces which shape individuals through written and spoken language, as well as the body language of ritual. Fairy tales are simply one facet of mythos.

We do not have to understand stories for them to work their magic. Stories such as *Cinderella* and *The Ugly Duckling* prepare children for puberty, whether the children know it or not. No doubt, mythos is more effective in shaping values and taboos in children than in adults. Adults do not internalize such matters to the same extent that children do. As a person matures, capacity to reason and choose becomes increasingly important. Individuals still feel pressures and conflicts, but adults have more experience in using rational capacity. They deal with pressures in a different way, but mythos still plays a part. Internalized narratives become the basis of moral judgment. As a judge, I am one of the *king's men*, and I am well-aware of the dilemma of *Humpty-Dumpty* when I try divorce and child custody cases.

The basic orientation which mythos provides children is still present in adults. Adults play out roles acquired during earlier formative years. Myths participate in rational choices of adults. Adults become guardians of mythos. They do not outgrow it, but simply take different roles in it. They use mythos to instill in their children requirements and expectations of society. They may not even be aware that they are doing so. We cannot learn the complex mandates of the moral code by rote memory. Mythos packages values of culture into themes. The themes fund internal

---

[82] Ibid., pp. 5-6.

structures of individuals—archetypes and symbols—with expectations of society. If the internal monitors are insufficient, mythos provides other prompts for the roles. Some prompts are subtle, and some not so subtle.

Origins of Law in Mythology

In the mythologies of all peoples, the earliest references to law always say that gods handed down law. Indeed, rulers claimed their power by divine right. One of the earliest known codes of law is the Code of Hammurabi. A stele discovered in 1901 shows Hammurabi receiving the law from the god Shamash. Shamash is sitting on a mountain. Moses received the Ten Commandments directly from God on Mt. Sinai. These are typical examples.

Ascription of the lawgiving function to gods is important because of the psychological insight that it provides. It confirms the archetypal nature of the source of law. This is an important truth of myths. Assigning authorship of law to deity has the advantage of giving it unquestionable authority. Appearance of externality is important, and association with an energy-laden archetype conveys force to commands of law.

Ascribing law to deity has the disadvantage of making those particular statements of law unchangeable. It is not easy to convince people that gods have changed their minds. Change may require substitution of a new archetype. Perhaps the replacement of the Titan Chronus, of the ancient gods, with scheming Zeus portended the coming of Greek reason.

Thus, we know that in the beginning of history, people attributed law to gods. Yet we fail to see a generalized relationship of law to mythical systems and their psychological counterparts. Since the beginning of the Age of Reason, we have been busy trying to discredit divine origin of law. We fail to realize that we *still have* powerful mythical systems, and they still play a part in the origin and preservation of law.

Our scientific age discredits myths. Our mind-set cannot accept as a fact that law originates in a deity. Such a thought is inconsistent with our belief system. We cannot accept the truth of stories about divine delivery of law. Most people do not believe that God intervenes in human events in that way. Nevertheless, we are overlooking something important. Law begins, in a sense, *in the stories themselves*, and the stories accurately portray our *inward* world. To that extent, they are as true as life itself.

Greeks were among the earliest people to boldly assert the right or power to make law—of governing themselves. This was consistent with the freedom which they had discovered in rationality. In mythos, freedom to choose law created an unrelenting pressure for equality. Freed from the force of divine fiat that establishes *particular* principles, mythos substitutes functional principles associated with justice as its attractive force. Equality, consistency and utility are among those principles. They, too, are created by belief systems. Rationality mediates among principles. Belief systems maintain the principles themselves.

Many modern thinkers deny divine origin of law but then argue that a *higher order*, or *natural law*, or *justice* requires that certain standards exist. What caused *higher order* and *natural law* and *justice* to exist? Where do they come from? Do they come from human beings? If so, what is *higher* about them? Do they come from a majority of human beings? If so, what about rights of minorities? Do they originate in certain elite human beings? If they begin in purely human sources, what makes one idea better than another?

For every priority that we assign, there is an assumption. The assumption of the value of human life is one that we often cite. We assume that preservation of human life is a value. This belief helps us assign priorities. Yet nothing is more certain than physical death. Assumptions arise from mythos. There is no value-free starting point. Most popular assumptions have one principle in common. They support survival of the human race. We want to survive. There is a level of understanding at which survival propensity makes one idea better than another.

Does that mean that human survival is the ultimate purpose of law? Survival for what? Myths take us beyond the short-range goal of survival. They deal with the search for meaning in human existence in the *ultimate environment*, which we can only describe with metaphors. It is a realm of faith. We will discuss these matters in depth in the section on faith.

The Self-Perpetuating System

Mythos shapes individuals, and in turn individuals become units in a system that produces collective psychology. The process is cyclical, or perhaps a spiral may be a more exact analogy, in view of the evolutionary nature of social life. The process involves emotions as well as intellect. An individual's contribution to the will of the whole people is largely unconscious. Culture operates through mythos to shape individuals. Individuals, in turn, collectively energize values, norms, ideals, and taboos of culture. The entirety of the operation is mysterious. Joseph Campbell writes:

In his life-form the individual is necessarily only a fraction and distortion of the total image of man. He is limited either as male or as female; at any given period of his life he is again limited as child, youth, mature adult, or ancient; furthermore, in his life-role he is necessarily specialized as craftsman, tradesman, servant, or thief, priest, leader, wife, nun, or harlot; he cannot be all. Hence, the totality—the fullness of man—is not in the separate member, but in the body of the society as a whole; the individual can be only an organ. From his group he has derived his techniques of life, the language in which he thinks, the ideas on which he thrives; through the past of that society descended the genes that built his body. If he presumes to cut himself off, either in deed or in thought and feeling, he only breaks connection with the sources of his existence.

The tribal ceremonies of birth, initiation, marriage, burial, installation, and so forth, serve to translate the individual's life-crises and life-deeds into classic, impersonal forms. They disclose him to himself, not as this personality or that, but as the warrior, the bride, the widow, the priest, the chieftain; at the same time rehearsing for the rest of the community the old lesson of the archetypal stages. All participate in the ceremonial according to rank and function. The whole society becomes visible to itself as an imperishable living unit. Generations of individuals pass, like anonymous cells from a living body; but the sustaining, timeless form remains. By an enlargement of vision to embrace this super-individual, each discovers himself enhanced, enriched, supported, and magnified. His role, however unimpressive, is seen to be intrinsic to the beautiful festival-image of man—the image, potential yet necessarily inhibited, within himself.[83]

All this underscores the close relationship between mythology and psychology. It is no accident that Freud chose such names as *Oedipus* and *Narcissus* to describe psychological phenomena. The myths from which he borrowed terminology symbolize the psychology he is describing. The myth is not merely an analogy. It is a linguistic *description* of the psychological principle. This point is precisely what is important about mythos. Mythos deals with important, pivotal points of human nature. Symbolic themes of mythology relate directly to archetypes and symbols described by Jung. Mythos activates those psychological archetypes.

Earlier, I described how values of parents become values of children from generation to generation, in a linear fashion. This is part of the dynamics of conscience. Transmission of values and ideals from parent to child, from generation to generation, is lineal. It does not account for

---

[83] Campbell, *The Hero With a Thousand Faces*, pp. 382-383.

the effect of surrounding culture, which obviously affects moral formation *horizontally* as well as lineally.

Mythos supports those same values and ideals, both horizontally and lineally. In a particular culture, one sees, in every direction, archetypes funded with the same values and themes. Culture surrounds individuals with those images. That is not to say, of course, that values and images are without conflict. The cultural system with all its conflicts is workable. Mythos grooms players for each of society's essential roles. We might say it teaches roles, and then pulls the players on stage, and then cues them during the performance. Differing personality types are uniquely fitted to particular roles in society.

C. G. Jung's theories of psychology contained yet another hypothesis that fits into my theory of the holistic, dynamic relationship between individuals and society. He pointed out the existence of psychological types based on mental function. He coined the words *introvert* and *extrovert* which deal with types. Other pairs of opposite types are thinking-feeling, sensing-intuitive and judging-perceiving. These paired types are somewhat mutually exclusive, like being right-handed or left-handed. Psychologists can classify every person as falling within one of the two paired types. Since there are four different pairs, this defines sixteen different personality types. There are additional variations within the sixteen types themselves due to varying strengths of preferences. The analysis helps to determine a person's suitability for certain tasks. Thus, human nature lends itself to the specialized functions of social life. No one is a *complete person*. Completeness arises in the functioning of society. Myths hold the group together and create the characters. Authority figures—judges, legislators, sheriffs, policemen, government officials, soldiers, sailors, administrators and clerks are all there. Exigencies of existence give specific meaning to roles in the context of a particular culture. Typology assigns candidates from membership of the culture to the roles.

Individuals are not born into culture as complete persons. Mythos directs the enculturation process. A child born to English speaking Americans is not likely to begin talking in Japanese. Likewise, our cultures instill more subtle differences in values and ideals. Family and culture instill values of a particular culture into individuals during formative years. In doing so, parents and significant others operate from the mythological systems which nurtured them.

Returning to an analogy we used before, individuals are like computers and mythos like software programs. Significant other persons in an individual's life, such as parents, are *programmers*. Individuals have certain energized capabilities. Society gives those capacities specific content through operation of mythos. These complex, cyclical events are matters we fail to consider when we think about law. We must take mythos into account if we are to understand and improve the design of our legal system.

In a very real sense, mythos is collective intelligence. It is the origin of collective representations that Durkheim described. It is a world spirit or national spirit that incorporates the knowledge and emotions of individuals and molds them into a working whole. Economics and capabilities of large interconnected computers are an almost tangible shadow of this collective intellect or spirit. Corporations intentionally tap into energies and capabilities that mythos provides naturally. Mythos is the spirit and intellect of corporateness that allows individuals to specialize. Mythos is personified by George Orwell's *Big Brother* in his novel, *1984*.

Mythos Unites Motives For Law

The idea of mythos is useful. It captures in one word a matrix of important parts of the motive force of law. It touches and affects formation of conscience, as well as collective psychology, symbolism, and archetypes. It also touches and affects language and other matters which I will discuss later.

Mythos is the substrata of law. Culture stores its values, ideals, norms, taboos, prohibitions and mandates in mythos. No one person controls or even has ability to comprehend all elements involved. Of course, we can develop a general understanding of the parts of mythos that organize the dynamics of law. Mythos is a gigantic function of the entire population. We will never fully comprehend mythos and its operation, as we will never fully comprehend our own unconscious. Yet, like the unconscious of our own minds, to which mythos of society is similar, awareness of its existence can be helpful. In mythos, rather than in some inexplicable metaphysical realm, we find the principles of natural law. Intuitive application of mythos is the growing edge of human understanding.

Survival Selects Principles

It might appear from the preceding discussion that the legislator or judge can just reach into mythos and pull out whatever he or she wants. Earlier discussion of basic human needs, however, shows that this is not true. Society, through its spokespersons, must choose those principles which will satisfy basic human needs, including survival. Only those principles make enforceable law. Lawmakers must consider both utility, which is frequently used to justify positivism, and moral quality, which Aquinas used to justify natural law. Utility and morality are not opposites, nor are they usually inconsistent. Despite the fact that morality is often regarded as *good for good's sake*, there is a haunting quality of survivalism embedded in every system of morals.

There are, of course, overlaps, conflicts, and paradoxes in mythos itself. The role of lawmakers is to tailor the whole fabric to fit needs of a particular culture. Mythos is the whole fabric. Unless they capture the force of beliefs that are firmly woven into the fabric of culture, judicial and legislative pronouncements are mere words. Officials lack the *appearance* of authority. To believers, the shaman or medicine man, judge or legislator appears awesome. To non-believers, he appears foolish.

The idea that law proceeds from mythos may not at first seem important. I may sound like an evolutionist who points to the ocean and says that our ancestors came from it. However, there is more immediate significance to the relationship between mythos and law. *We have our own mythos*. Failure to recognize that mythos and our belief systems are generating and affecting our modern law is a significant oversight. Without that knowledge, we are likely to make laws that won't work— like prohibition. Or we may place burdens on law that it will not carry, such as justice in family law in an adversarial system.

Greeks started the idea that the best government is one that provides the greatest good for the greatest number of people. That principle is still alive and is a major part of legal positivism. A government that doesn't survive is of small benefit to the people. Government can't survive unless citizens—at least some of them—survive. Survival purpose, and satisfaction of basic human needs, are the functional impetus for law and government. They underlie motive. They introduce into law the element of *necessity*. We all agree that law is necessary. Survival purpose, the principle of necessity, limits the choice of the legislator. Survival of the group is the minimum that law can accomplish. We aspire to a system that will do much more. We want a system that will allow and protect maximal satisfaction of human needs. Multiple choices are often presented to lawmakers, and if necessity does not mandate specific principles, it does require a workable group of principles.

In his short book entitled *The Morality of Law*, Lon Fuller made a useful distinction between morality of duty and morality of aspiration. That distinction helps to explain the point that I am making here. Law springs from morality of duty—not from morality of aspiration. There are desirable principles of behavior that do not make good laws. Some enactments are not necessary for survival or for achievement of basic human needs. Others clearly are necessary. Not every idea that legislators happen to *enact into law* is *necessary*. In any event, some form of social control is an absolute prerequisite for civilization, and life itself. This bedrock of *necessity* is a principal factor in enforcing law. We accept principles as law because of their perceived necessity, but perceptions are shaped by mythos.

Ethical choices, choices between good and evil—between just laws and unjust laws—usually operate *within* the limits of the survival principle. If survival is at stake, there is really no choice. We, as a group, will choose to survive. Only the thought that humanity is not worth preserving would promote the idea that justice and survival are inconsistent. This means that legal positivism and natural law are reconcilable. The morals of natural law will always fit into the utilitarian desire to survive, as a matter of necessity. Real morals are seldom inconsistent with survival—either for individual or group.

The survival principle, in the sense that I am using that term, applies to the whole *society* rather than to any particular individual. Many individuals choose not to survive. Some are suicides and others are martyrs. Martyrs die for a group, or for a cause which usually involves a group. Their deaths promote survival of the group. There must be a group for there to be a martyr—without a group to declare martyrdom, the deceased is just dead.

Mythos v. Logos

In Plato's view of reality, logos was the seat of the forms, or ideas or ideals. It is closely associated with, and even symbolizes, rational thinking. The traditional view is that modern Western thought began when Greeks replaced mythology with reason. I am inverting accepted wisdom and asserting the importance of mythos, as a prerequisite to rational thinking. Mythos has not been replaced by rational thinking, but embraces it. In his fascinating book, *Zen and the Art of Motorcycle Maintenance*, Robert M. Pirsig describes the *mythos over logos* argument.

> The term "logos," the root word of "logic," refers to the sum total of our rational understanding of the world. Mythos is the sum total of the early historic and prehistoric myths which preceded the logos. The mythos includes not only the Greek myths but the Old Testament, the Vedic hymns and the early legends of all cultures which have contributed to our present

world understanding. The "mythos over logos" argument states that our rationality is shaped by these legends, that our knowledge today is in relation to these legends as a tree is in relation to the little shrub it once was. One can gain great insights into the complex overall structure of the tree by studying the much simpler shape of the shrub. There's no difference in kind or even difference in identity, only a difference in size.

Thus, in cultures whose ancestry includes ancient Greece, one invariably finds a strong subject-object differentiation because the grammar of the old Greek mythos presumed a sharp natural division of subjects and predicates. In cultures such as Chinese, where subject-predicate relationships are not rigidly defined by grammar, one finds a corresponding absence of rigid subject-object philosophy. One finds that in the Judeo-Christian culture, in which the Old Testament "Word" had an intrinsic sacredness of its own, men are willing to sacrifice and live by and die by words. In this culture, a court of law can ask a witness to tell "the truth, the whole truth and nothing but the truth, so help me God," and expect truth to be told. But one can transport this court to India, as did the British, with no real success on the matter of perjury because the Indian mythos is different and this sacredness of words is not felt in the same way. Similar problems have occurred in this country among minority groups with different cultural backgrounds. There are endless examples of how mythos differences direct behavior differences and they're all fascinating.

The mythos-over-logos argument points to the fact that each child is born as ignorant as any caveman. What keeps the world from reverting to the Neanderthal with each generation is the continuing, ongoing mythos, trans-formed into logos but still mythos, the huge body of common knowledge that unites our minds as cells are united in the body of man. To feel that one is not so united, that one can accept or discard this mythos as one pleases, is not to understand what the mythos is.[84]

Although Pirsig's initial definition of *mythos* is more limited than mine, his application of the term is quite expansive. He uses the word in two senses, both of which are important. First, there is the narrow use. We find our cultural origins in traditional myths of the culture. Second, and more importantly, he makes clear through usage and analogy that *mythos* is a continuing process. It collects and transmits values and taboos which shape culture and individuals who are a part of it. Pirsig also makes note of *cultural differences* among "minority groups with different cultural backgrounds." This is a significant element of our

---

[84] Pirsig, *Zen and the Art of Motorcycle Maintenance*, pp. 315-316.

findings about mythos and its relation to law. We will pursue this matter further in the chapter called *Conflicts in Mythos*.

Mythos collects feelings, passions, truths, biases, taboos, symbols, archetypes, principles of religion, and the very patterns of thought of a people. It imprints all of these on the hearts and souls of individuals who are a part of that culture. It moves through cradle songs, fairy tales, myths, novels, poems, legends, textbooks, short stories, essays, speeches, folk stories, ballads, operas, dramas, comedies, tragedies, plays, histories, sermons, formal education, religious practices, burial customs, ceremonial traditions, orations and in every conceivable (not to mention inconceivable) manner. Mythical messages are spoken, written, chanted, sung, preached, rapped, pantomimed, acted out, and transmitted by body language. Histories collect our myths of origin.

Pronouncements of kings, courts, legislative bodies and bureaucrats and scientists are duly incorporated into mythos. Mythos subjects them to its processes. Mythos sifts its own contents and engages in a collective process of assigning value to those contents. Pronouncements ascribed to gods were particularly significant historically, as are pronouncements of science today. This huge collection of data embodies the value system of culture. It binds culture together in a common mind. It is the projection of C. G. Jung's collective unconscious. It is the source of Emile Durkheim's collective representations and group mind as well as Savigny's volksgeist. It contains the blueprint for every role involved in the entire human saga. It is the basis for Hegel's world spirit and is augmented by mental activities of each succeeding generation.

We transmit mythos through family, Church or other religious organizations, schools, communities, corporations and all groupings that are a part of a culture. Mythos collects in books, libraries, computers, files, and any other places where we store information. Most importantly, it collects in the hearts and minds of people. Through action of mythos, culture instills its values and taboos in individuals.

Mythos v. Reason

Perhaps one reason that our society gives little attention to mythos is that the ancient Greeks displaced the importance of their *mythos* with *reason*. This wholesome accomplishment of the Greeks is an ironic part of our mythos. Our society associates the word *myth* with superstition and lack of truth. Greek philosophers infected our thinking with the bias that *reason* is superior to emotions and passions. Since the time of the Greeks, western civilization has increasingly regarded reason as its most highly valued attribute. We believe that it sets humans apart from the brutes. We regard instincts, emotions, and passions as base. Interestingly, the Christian religion itself sometimes seems to participate in condemning instinctual behavior.

Myths preceded Greek allegiance to reason. They provided a way of explaining and shaping emotional forces. The work of myth, as Bettelheim pointed out, is not at a conscious level. It is not the work of reason. We recoil from the suggestion that instinct, emotion, passion, and myth have any place in the basis of law. The world also recoiled from Freud's theories of infantile sexuality and the unconscious, for similar reasons. We label everything that is not *rational* as *irrational*, with all attendant negative connotations.

Rationality is not virtue, however. I have seen a few intelligent crooks and outlaws who can use rationality very effectively. The smarter they are, the better they are at their evil work. Moreover, we have all known some very fine law-abiding people who were not particularly bright. Some matters very important to our survival are simply *non-rational*. They are neither rational nor irrational. We underestimate the worthwhile work of mythology because it is non-rational. The modern, rational mind discounts the importance of folk tales and myths. This is because of their seeming lack of factual and historical basis, or because of their paganish religious connotations. Whatever the cause, the result is unfortunate.

The cognitive part of our mental processes includes more than rational functions. Mythos provides a fund of knowledge, a data base, from which reason can operate. It provides experience that rationality analyzes. Reason shapes and structures, and works creatively with material provided by mythos. But it ultimately bows to the total organismic response of the individual in which basic human needs play a part. Mythos concerns itself with those seething psychic forces, which we described earlier, as well as with reason. It harnesses those forces to needs of the organismic whole of society. It assures private behavior that preserves society. The function of mythos is of considerable importance to the welfare of humanity.

Mythos embodies the *ethos* or value system of society. Mythos clothes values and ideals in metaphor and analogy. It weaves them into themes. It teaches them in parables. It is not merely a static statement of ethical principle. Mythos shapes and molds the character and personality of individuals. It causes ethical conduct, rather than merely describing it. Mythos often operates through unconscious mental processes, shaping passions and emotions. It uses symbolism and archetypes, the threads that unite mythology and psychology. Heroes of mythology shape and give content to the individual's archetype of the hero. Mythos also gives definition to the roles of father, mother, wise old man, self, trickster, and all other archetypes.

Mythos funds energy-laden archetypes with specific content by indirect, often unconscious processes. The child simply hears and consciously learns the delightful story of Robin Hood. Unconsciously, the archetype of the trickster in the child's mind receives specific content assigned by our culture. Thousands of other narratives contribute to funding of the trickster and all other archetypes. All roles necessary for operation of society receive their meaning in this manner. Then when society needs energy for a particular purpose, it is readily available to enforce the ideals—the needs—of society. Energy is stored in archetypes, and individuals respond archetypically to "typical modes of behavior" with correspondingly typical modes of behavior. When each member of the group responds in this way, tremendous force is created for reinforcement of archetypically expected behavior.

We sometimes describe the rational part of our being as the *light*. This metaphor is universal. It is frequently used in the Bible. Augustine used it. Light stands for reason or understanding. Mythos deals with the dark side of our being as well as the light. Processes of mythos are often unconscious. The dark side of our being can pass through generation after generation of a culture without *coming to light*. We see only one side of the moon, but that doesn't mean that the other side and inside are missing. We may be aware of potent stories involved in a myth. Nevertheless, there are also ideals and symbols that are latent messages. They are hidden behind the luminous surface. They address unconscious, developing mental structures within us. This is the useful function of fairy tales that Bettelheim described. It also applies to other vehicles of mythos. This is how our images of good and bad receive content and meaning. Groups that share a mythos also share perceptions of good and bad.

Even myths that are quite fanciful can carry strong messages. Consider again the story of Robin Hood, for example. The romantic notion of "robbing from the rich and giving to the poor" produces a strong impression. The story instills its values very effectively in a child's mind. The story creates the principle; the principle does not create the story. Robin Hood is *good*, even though he is an outlaw. In mythology, the trickster does not usually carry a bad connotation. The familiar Brer

Rabbit is a trickster. In Native American mythology, coyote often personifies the trickster. In cartoons, the elusive road runner, who constantly outwits Wily Coyote is a trickster. In African mythology, the hare and the spider are tricksters. Often tricksters are heroes of a culture that is not the dominant culture. Within the subgroup, it is alright to trick the dominant culture, and thereby prove actual superiority. Presumed authority that lacks true authenticity is an appropriate target of the wiles of the trickster. Robin Hood was *loyal* to Good King Richard, whose role had been usurped by an imposter. He was the hero of the common person, as King Arthur was hero for aristocracy. Obviously, the role of the trickster is quite important in my theory. The trickster often operates at the interface between conflicting mythological systems. In contrast to Robin Hood, the Sheriff of Nottingham is *bad,* although he represents law. Such images shape our concepts of right and wrong by metaphor and comparison. Metaphor, not logical systems, undergird moral reasoning. Metaphor is the substance of mythology. An *ideal* is as much *image* as *idea*. Mythos does its work at a subliminal level. This is probably why we have underestimated its importance. The Robin Hood story raises interesting questions about authentication of authority. We will return to the matter of authentication by mythos later.

Good and Evil

From mythos we get our notions of good and evil. Mythos provides material with which rationality works. Rationality can impact on the legal system only by feeding sound ideas that promote survival back into the system. In the chapter on conscience I suggested that moral formation comes from introjecting cultural values, primarily from parents into the child. Bruno Bettelheim and Emile Durkheim showed how folk tales and myth fit into this process of moral formation. Nietzsche suggested that *Overman*, the hero of the future, would be *Beyond Good and Evil*.[85] He was dealing with precisely the point that I am now discussing. Nietszche saw that traditional morality derives from mythos, in which he included all religion; and he saw Overman rising above these outmoded limitations. If we, as individuals, actually succeed in casting off myths that shape us, what happens then? New myths must appear if society is to continue. If history is a guide, and it is certainly an important part of our mythology, then new myths are likely to incorporate and expand upon the old.

---

[85] Friedrich Nietzsche, *Beyond Good and Evil*, Translated and Edited by Walter Kaufmann in *Basic Writings of Nietzsche*.

Dr. King was well versed in our mythology, ancient and modern. He drew on the powerful archetype symbolized by Moses the lawgiver. Moses saw the Promised Land—so did Dr. King. Moses brought law down from a mountain amidst thunder and lightening. So did Dr. King in a very real sense. Dr. King's most powerful speeches drew on Biblical themes. To minimize the religious nature of Dr. King's dedication and the role that he played is to accuse him of falsity and fraud in his undertaking. Had he simply said, as President Johnson did, "Come, let us reason together," which, incidentally, is also Biblical, nothing would have happened. More importantly, Dr. King applied Biblical themes in a powerful way to current issues, appealing to basic human needs. The then recent advent of television probably played a major role in his success, and we will explore the role of media in a later chapter.

Words and language obviously are quite significant in law. When we deal with the world of words and language, we are not leaving the strange world of unconscious forces, archetypes, symbols, and collective representations. These logical constructs contain impulses—the forces—that motivate us to law. But without words, we would have no conception of these forces. Words express these forces and guide them into law. For a principle to become law, we must be able to express it in words. The expression in words must capture necessary feelings—motive force—to make law work. How does this happen? Mythos plays a major role in articulating ideals, images, and values that we accept as law. In fact, mythos has played a major role in building language that we use to articulate concepts. Mythos creates words and prepares hearers for the meaning so as to elicit necessary motive force. Study of mythos blends imperceptibly with study of language. The interface between mythos and language is vast and undifferentiated. It would be difficult to discuss either in depth without discussing the other.

Dependency of law on language adds an important new and different dimension to an analysis of law. We will examine some characteristics of words and language which affect their ability to deliver the message of law. Just as language plays a key role in law, it also plays an important part in moral formation. Mythos forms and gives meaning to abstract concepts. We discussed Emile Durkheim's description of this process earlier. Mythos makes language; language is the vehicle of mythos; they are both prime ingredients of law.

Language and Mythos

Mythology and language derive from the same origins. Jakob Grimm, (1785-1863) was one of the German Brothers of *Grimm's Fairy Tales* fame. He was also an early comparative linguist. He showed that German, English and other Germanic languages, as well as Romance languages, Greek and Sanskrit, have a common Indo-European language source. Mythologies of these cultures also have a shared Indo-European source. In Greek mythology, Zeus is the counterpart of Indra in Indian mythology and Thor in the mythology of Northern Europe.

Society stores mythos in words. The Grimms used German language —words—to capture fairy tales which they collected. When one studies a language, one usually studies *literature* of the language. Literature is a part of mythos. Language is the medium for collection, storage, and transmission of mythos. Language of a culture must be co-extensive with the entire communicable experience of the culture. This is a central thought in E. D. Hirsch's *Cultural Literacy*. The people of a society must have a command of the language. Corporate functioning of society depends on it. We must be *culturally literate*. This includes a passing knowledge of literature and history of the culture. Let me express these ideas using terminology we developed earlier. The commonly shared information must include metaphors and themes built on archetypes and symbols of the culture's mythology. Communication based on this shared knowledge is necessary for society to function.

We have analogized mythos to computer software and individuals to computers. We are now introducing an additional element into the analogy: computer language. I realize that I am reversing a metaphor. The expression *computer language* is obviously a comparison to language in the usual sense of the word. There are various computer *languages* with differing capabilities. Likewise, there are various human languages, with differing capabilities. Language of a society must be adequate to express symbolically the collected experience of the society. Differences in language reflect cultural differences.

Language and mythos connect at an even more fundamental level. Mythological systems formed the basis for language itself. Totemic systems formed the basis for classification of the material world. Common belief systems provided a shared picture of reality. Metaphorical application of words in common use to describe everyday events gave rise to abstractions. For instance, the moon was a topic of discussion in all early mythologies. Its phases and periods were observable, and entered into everyday discussions. Its 28-day cycle became the basis for the concept of *month*. We added to the level of abstraction by naming and numbering months. We now use the word *month* as an abstract measurement of time, and seldom think of the moon in doing so. Thus, we abstracted the *month* concept from the movements of the moon, to create an almost independent idea. We seldom think of the moon when someone mentions January! The same applies to concepts of other units of time, numbers, directions and other abstractions that are essential to our way of thinking. Law, justice, morality and related concepts arise from these same sources. We obviously cannot trace language to its origin in the association of vocal sounds with observable phenomena. What we are suggesting is the development of abstract concepts through the metaphorical processes of mythos after language had begun to evolve.

Relationship of Law and Language

Words and language are essential to law as we know it. Mythos is an organizing principle that connects words to underlying psychological forces. A few expressions of law, such as a judge pounding a gavel or a police officer using hand signals to direct traffic, are not linguistic. However, we express the large bulk of law in language. Usually, we express law in writing, despite occasional references to common law as *unwritten* law. In a sense, the socially expected behavior might by described as *unwritten*, and merely evidenced by words, just as Newton's laws of physics exist independently of words that express them. But even such *unwritten* law, when applied, is usually evidenced by written court opinions.

Words are always merely *evidence* of law. Law is not the *words* of a statute or opinion. The words represent an underlying reality that linguists call the semantic reference. Words are merely signs to which we assign symbolic meaning. Words can be well-chosen or poorly chosen to represent the semantic reference, which, for law, is behavior that is either desired or forbidden. Reasons for desiring or forbidding certain behavior relate to our fundamental belief systems, or mythology. We can find roots for our beliefs in early mythology. More importantly, the modern world has belief systems that reflect our perceptions of appropriate social order. Our belief systems are based on and evolved from earlier belief systems, just as language springs from earlier beliefs and associations which were held in common, and shared through intentionally produced sounds.

Can law exist without language? Does orderliness in human relations exist separate and apart from written or oral rules that undertake to govern relationships? Does law exist before air runs over vocal chords and through a mouth and over a tongue to produce certain unique sounds? Does it exist before a listener understands the sound to be a command? Suppose the listener does not know what a *command* is. Does it exist before we print the words? Perhaps these questions sound frivolous, but let's pursue the matter further with examples.

(a) Recall the regulation proclaiming the abbreviation for inch. Was it unlawful to use ditto marks (") on retail package labels rather than *in.* *before* the agency issued the regulation? I suspect you agree with me that it was not. The agency had to issue the words before the regulation assumed any characteristics of law.

(b) Suppose that on the high seas, a sailor is mortally injured, but lingers in agonizing pain. All morphine is gone. There is no ship doctor. There is no hope of reaching help. A long, lingering painful death is certain. The sailor begs his mates to take his life. He is unable to do so himself. The captain gives an order: "No one is to kill that sailor." Nevertheless, the sailor's cabin mate knuckles to the pressure and inflicts painless death with a lethal injection. The ship is not within the jurisdictional boundaries of any country. The captain and crew commandeered the ship to escape a dictatorship that is not a recognized government. Has the cabin mate committed murder? Did the captain's order make a difference? What should be the penalty? Does the need for words here differ in some way from the preceding example?

(c) Suppose an American soldier and a Japanese soldier shipwrecked during World War II. They both wind up on an unclaimed, uninhabited island. The American kills the Japanese. Is he a murderer? Now let me add a fact. They didn't discover each other for 10 years. The war was over and peace treaties signed. Does that make a difference?

(d) A series of cases occurs in State X in which adults with handguns have killed teenagers. Juries freed the adults on pleas of self-defense. A horrified legislature hurriedly passes a law in State X stating that self-defense is no longer a defense. Anyone who kills another human being with a handgun shall be guilty of murder. Such a person shall hang by the neck until dead. Afterwards, a patient known as Ax-Killer escapes an institution for the criminally insane. He heads toward Widow Brown's house. Police issue a statewide alert. Widow Brown hears it on the Christian radio network on her bedside radio. She locks the house and secures the deadbolt on the bedroom door. Ax-Killer chops his way right into the house, using an ax he found in the tool shed. Mrs. Brown's trembling hands clutch the late Mr. Brown's old World War II Army 45. Ax-Killer cuts away the deadbolt. Widow Brown plugs him right between the eyes. What happens at her trial? Does she swing? Did the legislature's words vitiate her *right* to defend herself?

These examples suggest some relationship between words and law. Some of them get into deeper problems of the reality of law, which we will discuss later. For now, just concentrate on the relationship between words and underlying facts in each case. The first one—the abbreviation for inch—is the only simple one. Law did not exist before the words.

Turning to the second example, was the act of the cabin mate murder? Did the captain's order make any difference in the sailor killing case? Suppose the captain had authorized the killing. Could he? How essential is the function of words in the whole process? Do we form our opinions about the case because of the words, or because of some underlying reality?

Did the peace treaties make any difference in the case involving the Japanese soldier and American soldier? Was killing illegal, even though the island was not within the control of any country. Obviously, there were no written laws. Was there any law at all? Can there be law without words?

Can State X outlaw self-defense through legislative enactment? Can a matter as basic as self-defense be outlawed? Are there principles of law that mere words cannot change, even if spoken by the legislature?

Perhaps these deliberately far-fetched examples have increased your awareness that words are mere signs which are used to convey an underlying reality from one mind to another. But are words themselves a *part* of the reality of law? I defer part of the answer to this question to the chapter on authentication, but the question is also pertinent here.

Words and the Reality of Law

The relationship of law to language introduces a new aspect of the reality of law to our discussion. Law, like language, arises out of human relationships. Collective psychology assigns meaning to human relationships. The meanings involve our collective beliefs. Mythos creates and preserves them. Mythos generates and maintains structures of society, drawing on psychological forces described earlier.

Picture an individual like Robinson Crusoe on a deserted island. Is he subject to any law in the sense that we use the term *law*? Until Friday showed up, Crusoe had no one to talk with, and he had no need for social organization or rules. Although motive for law starts in individual conscience and individual needs, law does not exist in one person alone. Law exists in the group. Likewise, language and social norms do not exist in one person alone, but in the group.

As we have seen, abstractions have meaning only in the context of a group that shares them. Building materials for forces that unite groups are in individuals, but the group is more than the collection of individuals. The whole is often more than the sum of its parts. Functions of the entire group differ from functions of individuals comprising the group. This idea is elementary. Nevertheless, it raises some important considerations.

Where do such group functions exist, if not in individuals? Do they exist in collective consciousness or in Jung's collective unconscious? Do they arise from Durkheim's collective representations or group mind? We discussed these ideas earlier. They are a part of collective psychology. They also relate to linguistic aspects of law. Earlier, we examined motive forces themselves. We are now examining the *expression* of forces described by Jung and Durkheim. Words must capture them, if we are to share them.

For example, during the course of a trial (accepted ritual), the judge (archetypal role) must instruct (articulation) the jury (paradigmatic group of twelve, number of months in year, number of hours of day and night, number of tribes of Israel, number of Jesus disciples) on the law (archetype, collective representation). If the offense is murder, words from the judge must usually explain concepts of murder, intent, justification, lesser homicides, self defense, provocation, reasonable doubt, and other related concepts so the jury understands the legal basis for its verdict. All these concepts have a commonly accepted meaning within society. They are powerfully supported by group opinion. In a case with notoriety, the courtroom is often filled with families and friends of the victim and defendant, along with general public. Feeling is intense, but seldom are there unmanageable outbursts. A word from the judge restores order. News media disseminates information about the trial to the waiting public. Words capture feelings, and through a ritualistic process restore an equilibrium and feeling of security in society. Through the whole process, words are bearers of feelings, and operative elements of the group mind.

Language and Concepts

I discussed individual and group thought processes and emotions, conscious and unconscious, in the preceding section. I discussed archetypes, collective representations, and the force of collective psychology. These forces are the motive for law. They are substance that words of law seek to express.

Those same thought processes relate closely to language itself. In individuals, they show the social nature of humanity. They are latent mental structures that support social life. In language, they become clearly societal forces involving more than one person. There is an intimate relationship between law and language. Primordial forces produce the impetus toward law. They precede rationality. We must capture these forces in words for law to have a motive force. Use of language to express desired principles of behavior evidences a new dimension that is clearly social and begins to lay the foundation for rationality itself. This new dimension transcends individual psychology.

The *rational* proceeds on *experience* and enables us to conceptualize. *Writing* and language also proceed on *experience*, providing *symbols* with which individuals can share experience. Rationality and language merge in the *word*— the concept and the sign. Concepts, believed by some to be important in thinking (an individual process) may actually be more important in talking (a *social* process). Words package content of concepts. Consciousness itself may derive from shared experience (concepts) and form the basis of our *reality*. The strongest credibility for our perception of reality is the ability, actual or imagined, to share it with others.

At a deeper, unconscious level, there is a genetic, universal sharing of images, archetypes, or symbols. C. G. Jung taught us this. There is a sharing of archetypes in the universal unconscious. Experience funds latent forms in the shared unconscious. It provides those forms with specific content. These "typical modes of apprehension" become concepts.

Durkheim says that concepts, or categories of our thinking, begin with collective representations. This is reality or experience shared by the group. Words represent Durkheim's collective representations. Words are our means of sharing concepts. Thus, talking, thinking, and indeed knowledge itself arise from a common structure that they all share. Our term *mythos* may be the best word available to represent this common structure. Concepts do not result merely because an individual notices elements that a group of items have in common. More than one person must *share* the impression for it to be a concept. Concepts thus have both an individual cognitive basis and a social, linguistic basis. We use words to represent concepts. Rationality itself is as much social as it is individual.

Concepts are not the deepest mental phenomena. This is an incorrect assumption of Plato, and is still prevalent. Concepts are among the most superficial aspects of our mental life. Logos is the dwelling place of concepts or universals, according to Plato. But concepts actually have to do with how we deal with the outer world. They are tools of the Freudian *ego*, which is the part of the personality that deals with the outer world. They are part of the outermost structure of the personality.

They are the part of the individual that meets the external world and other people.

Thus, logos is not the seat of our deepest reality. It is a facet of our social nature. It does not confirm individuality. On the contrary, it enables us to deal with the external world in a social way. Jung related his archetypes to Plato's *forms* as their psychological aspect. Archetypes are a part of the social side of what Durkheim described as man's dual nature. Logos is not the source and ground of our being. Emotional impulses arise at a deeper level of our individual being than does our rationality. As we move even further inward, the mystery of existence deepens. Taoists describe this deep inwardness as the *inexpressible one*.[86] We cannot express the deepest essence of reality in words. Of course, having said this, I still haven't expressed it!

The cognizable, expressible world which we experience appears to us in paired opposites. We call this division of existence into paired opposites *dualism*. Examples are light/dark, hot/cold, good/bad, and positive/negative. This division enables us to understand by differentiation. It is hard to discern the undifferentiated. If something doesn't move and is not different from anything else, how can we tell it's there? Words can describe both sides of duality. To know good, we must know bad; to know hot we must know cold. The list is endless. Our individual existence simply *is*. Dualism exists at the superficial, conceptual level where words (and concepts) arise. This is the world of words and of social existence. The world of words not only *describes* our social nature, it is a distinct *part of that nature*. Law participates in this duality; its opposite is chaos. This makes law a part of the cosmos in which words are useful. Words reflect a system of order in social life. It is difficult to imagine a non-verbal modern legal system.

Words and concepts are vehicles for sharing experience. They are not intrinsic to the external thing-in-itself. They are essential only to our expression of ideas in *communicable* form. At first, realization that words and concepts are not intrinsic to the external thing-in-itself tempts us to believe that they are totally artificial. However, our mental processes, too, are part of nature. Emile Durkheim points out:

> (W)hen we interpret a sociological theory of knowledge in this way, we forget that even if society is a specific reality it is not an empire within an empire; it is a part of nature, and indeed its highest representation. The

---

[86] *The Wisdom of Laotse*, Lin Yutang, Editor, pp. 41-46.

social realm is a natural realm which differs from others only by a greater complexity.

It is at least true that if these ideas play the role of symbols when they are thus turned aside from their original signification, they are well-founded symbols. If a sort of artificiality enters into them from the mere fact that they are constructed concepts, it is an artificiality which follows nature very closely and which is constantly approaching it still more closely. From the fact that the ideas of time, space, class, cause or personality are constructed out of social elements, it is not necessary to conclude that they are devoid of all objective value. On the contrary, their social origin rather leads to the belief that they are not without foundation in the nature of things.[87]

Words are sounds, but to identify them as *sounds* does not approach their significance, or meaning. As signs or symbols, they add a dimension to reality.

Words are signs. They are means of expressing concepts. They are our chief means of bridging the chasm between our thought world and that of our neighbor. Words generate a mental cosmos that transcends our individual consciousness and is the shadow of external reality that we believe exists. We generate these signs and pass them into a sphere of objectivity that we share with our neighbor, and our neighbor can pull them into his thought world. We say the word; he hears it and knows what we are talking about. Words can carry all sorts of payloads. They convey everything from very simple, tangible concepts, like the idea of *chair*, to very abstract concepts, like the idea of *law*. Words collectively represent the cosmos as shared by humans, but they are also a part of that cosmos. Society uses words to describe behavior that it expects and requires of us.

Emotional Content of Words

Other aspects of language are important to law. Words take on emotive content in their coinage and in their use. Occasionally, we try to change terminology in hopes of escaping the stigma attached to a word. We do not realize that the stigma may arise from the item represented. Alabama changed the name of its "Welfare Department" to "Department of Pensions and Security" to improve its image. When the stigma had attached to the new name, the State changed the name again. This time the name is "Department of Human Resources." I suspect that mere name change is futile. The stigma relates to function, not name. To end

---

[87] Durkheim, *The Elementary Forms of the Religious Life*, pp. 31-32.

the stigma, the attitude of the people of Alabama toward welfare will have to change.

Society expresses collective mandates and taboos as law. The power of words derives from mythos, or belief systems. Society must have an adequate vocabulary to express complex abstract legal relationships. We must experience motive forces and feelings in common. There must be words to describe the common experience or collective representation. Mythos develops and maintains meanings, including motive content. The group weaves words that capture these elusive forces into themes and stories. We have to be able to experience the forces again in words and share the feelings with others. This is what mythos does. From such shared experience, the strength of law finds its way into words.

The concept of law arises from metaphor. Themes and stories draw analogies. Principles such as consistency and equality arise from these repeated themes. The case method itself is a complex series of thematic analogies. We apply one story, or case, to another fact situation believed to be analogous. The word *murder* takes on its powerful meaning from thousands of instances in the annals of human history in which the horror of intentional killing has occurred. Earlier, I argued that law is more a verb than a noun. Now we can see that it is both at the same time. It translates "society requires" or "government forbids." The statement is completed with metaphorical themes.

Words must match the cognitive development of individuals. The population must participate in language, including the emotional content, sufficiently to understand the mandate or prohibition. For full understanding, the people must *feel* the mandate or taboo. Mythos is society's instrument for producing the principle, expressing it in words and conditioning individuals to respect it. Mythos supports and maintains the values, mandates and taboos of society. Mythos connects feelings and forces to words. This makes the words effective.

Non-Verbal Communication

Anyone who has ever been in love knows that not all communication is verbal. We can share love, excitement, fear, and other emotions without words. Non-verbal communication is an important aspect of role playing that is a part of enforcement of law. It has a place in mythos, especially in ceremony, ritual and role playing. Many aspects of law are non-verbal. The ceremonial aspects, raised bench and judicial robe, and all symbols and indicia of authority that we mentioned earlier are non-verbal. Thus, even non-verbal parts of the structure of law relate to mythos, or belief systems. Customs have many non-verbal aspects. Often they are the strata giving rise to impulses to law. Many aspects of behavior, verbal and non-verbal, give rise to impulses that collective psychology transforms into law.

Customs may be considered by some to be non-verbal law, but customs are not cognizable as law until described in words. First, words must describe the custom that we want to be law. Then we must formally authenticate it. Feelings that attach to customs make customs good candidates for law. Identification of a particular practice as *custom* is a start toward putting it in words. *Custom* is a word. When we say that something is a custom, we recognize expectations and feelings that could lead to its adoption as law. Nevertheless, it is *feelings* that count. If something is customary, we *feel* that we *ought not* to do it differently. Custom can be a precursor of law, but as we pointed out earlier, it is not the sole basis of law.

Language and Moral Formation

Language plays an important role in moral formation which we discussed in earlier chapters. Recall the discussion of development of the super-ego. A child begins to develop a conscience during preschool years, before learning to read. Parents instill an important part of the moral code through *oral language*. Written language has little to do with the process. During these early years emotional energy becomes attached to certain basic beliefs in right and wrong. Parents plant seeds for the taboos, mandates and ideals that will govern behavior. Archetypes receive their first contact with experience during these early years. At this young age, children are much more malleable than at a later time. Young children are quite susceptible to values, taboos, and prohibitions of parents. All of this is communicated orally, and by body language; writing plays no part.

Developmental theories describe later stages of moral development. The surrounding culture conditions latent archetypes to its values. A child *speaks with an accent* a language learned after a certain age. Similarly, a moral code learned after a certain age will be more difficult. Stages of moral development succeed each other in a necessary sequence. Perhaps a person who does not get the rudiments of a moral code during these formative years has a *moral accent*.

Similarities between language and moral acquisition may in fact be because they are one phenomenon. The moral code intertwines with the linguistic base. Joseph Campbell noticed the close relationship between language and morals in his work with mythology.

> Sigmund Freud has described as a process of introjection the psychological mechanism by which, in infancy, parental commands are imprinted indelibly on the motivating centers of the will; and the comparative linguist Benjamin Lee Whorf has demonstrated through a number of detailed comparisons to what extent the language learned in infancy determines not only the manner in which one's thoughts and feelings have to be expressed, but also the very patterns of those thoughts and feelings themselves. Hence, even in the solitudes of those remotest fastnesses where the state would seem to have left off, the imprintings of our parish are with us, tattooed on the inside of our skins.[88]

Children get a basic moral disposition during the earlier years, while intellectual development is very incomplete. They can add more complex rules later, similar to the way that they continue to develop linguistic skills. There are several important consequences to these observations. For instance, if parents have poor linguistic abilities, the child may have difficulty in various forms of testing. Also, children with poor linguistic ability may have difficulty acquiring the moral code.[89] If children do not experience and internalize the moral code at appropriate stages of development, they are not likely to abide by it later. Careful articulation of law and moral instructions *in writing* will not replace real moral formation.

The matters we have just mentioned provide a possible explanation for the age-old paradox that to know right is not to do right. Rules learned during later stages of development have little value unless the child gets the foundations of conscience during the earliest years. Rules learned later do not affect behavior the same way unless they attach to an established moral base in individuals. They must identify with motive forces in moral structures gained at appropriate times during development. Individuals must participate in the belief system for it to have its full impact. Mere knowledge is not sufficient.

If parents or parent substitutes know the norms, and are willing to do so, they can instill the norms into the child. However, if parents lack the moral code or the linguistic base necessary for its expression, then it will be very difficult to intercept the problem. The problem will perpetuate itself in the succeeding microcosm of family life. The image of the

---

[88] Campbell, *Creative Mythology*, pp. 88-89.
[89] See "Some Thoughts About the Role of Verbalization in Early Childhood," *The Psychoanalytic Study of the Child*, Vol XVI, pp. 184-188, by Anny Katan, M.D.

parent as an ideal is more significant than actual contents of parental instruction. Therefore, parents must *be* moral and mere knowledge of moral principles is not adequate.

All of these observations about language and the moral code have a definite impact on law. Language is a means of sharing the moral code or values of civilization. Mythos *creates* the meaning of many abstractions included in the value system. Words such as justice, honesty, and truth receive both meaning and value in mythos, or belief systems of culture. Value has to do with emotional importance attached to words reflecting a belief. The emotional element impacts on, and produces, orderly behavior that promotes security and satisfies basic human needs. Moral formation causes individuals to lend the strength of their opinions to group beliefs. It is through language that collective beliefs are shared and passed on.

Once we understand the important role of language in the formation of law, then we can understand some of the functional difficulties of enacted law. Language is not simple. Law as we know it is usually in writing. It becomes accessible to an individual long after the individual develops a moral code. At that time, it may lack emotional force or emotional backing necessary to bring about compliance.

Rules as written may not relate in any way to the moral ideal of a poorly developed individual. This causes difficulty in enforcement. This hypothesis is borne out in experience. The popular belief that criminals are highly intelligent is untrue. Smart crooks are a negligibly small percentage of persons charged with crimes. The criminal justice system packages, bales and warehouses ignorance and illiteracy. The percentage of illiterates in the penal system is far greater than the percentage of illiterates in the general population. These illiterates may have raw mental ability to distinguish right from wrong. Nevertheless, they do not have a linguistic and moral base adequate to cause them to follow requirements of law. They are outcasts in a world that *believes* in rationality and education.

These conclusions are consistent with research. Wilson and Herrnstein, in their book, *Crime and Human Nature*, have reviewed available data very thoroughly. They were searching for character traits that identify prospective criminals. Low intelligence is one important, consistent factor. Wilson and Herrnstein reached a conclusion that is even more important for the theme of this chapter. Criminals register lower *verbal* scores than performance scores in intelligence testing.[90] These findings confirm my subjective impressions of cases with which I deal.

There is no question that requirements of the legal system can extend beyond the preparation or abilities of individuals, both morally and linguistically. In Alabama, the law charges persons accused of "welfare fraud" with *theft of property*. In a typical case, a wage earner moves into the home of the recipient mother after welfare benefits start. The welfare recipient does not tell the agency about the wage earner moving in with her. It is difficult for the recipient to equate that omission with stealing. Nevertheless, the law charges the recipient with "theft of property." The moral and linguistic base for such a law is too sophisticated for the moral and linguistic preparation of the defendant. Defendants don't morally relate the act committed to the crime charged. It doesn't *feel* like stealing. The offense does not relate clearly to the moral ideal involved, so the law does not clearly identify the criminality.

Expressing Principles

What causes us to articulate new legal principles? As new problems threaten the welfare of society, someone in society intuitively recognizes a principle that will solve these problems. He states this *hypothesis* in words and feeds it into mythos by whatever means are available. Poetry, a letter to the editor, a discussion with family or friends, may be the medium. The Civil Rights Movement has provided convenient illustration throughout this work. The speeches and writings of Dr. King are excellent examples of articulation of necessary principles. In our society, lobbying groups formulate their own agendas. Safety standards develop within a particular industry. These proposals find their way into the public eye. Opinion develops. These opinions collect into mythos. Themes and metaphors surround them. Indeed, these opinions, and their supporting themes and metaphors are living mythos. As in Dr. King's case, new arguments usually incorporate and extend existing patterns of belief. They elaborate on existing principles.

A good example of articulation is Rachel Carson's book, *Silent Spring*. She was not a legislator, but her book created an acute awareness of environmental dangers of herbicides and pesticides. Her book, published in the 1960s, caused adoption of new governmental policies and laws almost immediately.

---

[90]　Wilson and Herrnstein, *Crime and Human Nature*, p. 148 et seq.

Feelings arising from experience are difficult to capture in long-term meaningful language. This is especially true if the feeling attaches to an abstraction. Here, emotional content of words comes into play. Importance of thematic preservation of principles also becomes clear in this context. Our stories about events keep principles clear in memory. This is the point of teaching in parables.

Commonly, the harbinger of social change who first suggests a change in law may be a person ahead of his time. Take, for instance, the platforms of William Jennings Bryan, a leader of the populist movement near the beginning of the twentieth century. They included such matters as abandonment of the gold standard and adoption of graduated income tax. They were all later in large part accepted by the major United States political parties and enacted into law. However, William Jennings Bryan never succeeded in his bid for the presidency. Clarence Morris discussed this tendency:

> The public's aspirations do not, of course, spring spontaneously into the minds of the citizenry at the same moment. Men ahead of their times urge law reforms and at first seem to make little headway; later on these proposals catch on and become widely wanted. The first objections to slavery bore no fruit for thousands of years. When John Stuart Mill made common cause with the suffragettes, very few males had shown enthusiasm for woman suffrage. Perhaps, however, Mill was speaking for an inchoate public aspiration to give women full political rights—a subliminal value, already widely shared, though rudimentary. Mill's stand attracted male allies, as humane causes often do. Not many decades later the justice of woman suffrage became the law of much of the Western world.[91]

Similarly, there were numerous precursors of the Civil Rights Movement, such as the events described in *All God's Dangers*, which occurred in my circuit, that failed to attract widespread attention at the time.

A legislator notices the articulated principle, and the motive force supporting it, and causes it to become law. Sometimes a judge recognizes the inherent accuracy and motive force of a principle, and declares it to be law. Of course, it is possible for the legislator or judge to misread the will of the people. They can also misjudge need. They can make a poor choice of alternative principles. In such cases, the enactment or pronouncement will be difficult to enforce as law.

Precise statement of a principle in understandable words is of critical importance in the formulation of law as we know it. Lon Fuller identifies

---

[91] Morris, *The Justification of the Law*, p. 59.

this necessity as part of the internal morality of law. He describes it as one of the principles of legality. I have tried some fairly gory murder cases. In one that I remember, a young lady stabbed a gentleman acquaintance in the heart with a large, ugly, survival knife. Blood squirted into her face from the wound. Merely describing such an incident stirs strong feelings. We express them in a variety of ways. Words such as *yuck* would hardly be adequate terminology for the norm we need to express. Even "Thou shalt not do yucky things" is inadequate. We can imagine angry feelings of the family of the victim. We know how they might express these feelings, but words of vengeance do not work toward orderliness. Against this background, we can hear the thunder and see the lightning that accompany the words, *"Thou shalt not kill."* This principle and belief are fully founded in our mythos and supported by our feelings. I have experienced the eerie quiet in a courtroom filled with people at the beginning of a capital murder trial on several occasions. Feelings are definitely evoked as words that describe the event register in the thought worlds of those involved in the trial.

Law and Development of Language

There are clearly discernible stages in the historical development of law. We can define the stages by the media available for the use of language. These stages parallel development of culture itself. First came the oral stage. The second stage came with the ability to write. Then came paper. Next came the invention of printing. Twentieth century development of electronic media likely foretells the coming of major new developments in law.

Practically all writers agree that law existed before the invention of writing. Indeed, law exists in the twentieth century in oral form in some societies.[92] In the evolution of law, the family unit was the original grouping in which law appeared. Conscience, closely related to parental image, is a basic building block of law. Archetypes of mythology and psychology play out their roles. Thus, development of the modern personality and social structures that support law retraces the historical development of law.

The oral stage apparently evolved from a dimly lit past of totemic or similar modes of arriving at linguistic means of expression. Anthropology documents the religious or mythic background of this development. Members of the tribe or clan expressed and transmitted law by word of

---

[92] See, for instance, Malinowski, *Crime and Custom in Savage Society.*

mouth. Despite obvious disadvantages of such a system, there may have been some advantages. Obviously, an oral tradition required strong mental participation of the society in knowledge of law. In primitive societies, the people couldn't go and "look up" the law. No doubt, they depended on memories of some individuals rather heavily, but there was considerable interest and participation on the part of everyone. Perhaps this is the historical origin of Jung's "wise old man" archetype. Persons with unique memory skills played an important, distinctive role in the group.

Mnemonic devices assisted memory. Groups used verse to bolster memory, as well as proverbs, adages, maxims, aphorisms, and so forth. These are elementary building blocks for mythos. Because of their terseness, alliterative form, symmetry, or other verbal quality they carry authority where a merely logical pronouncement might fail to convince. These devices were as broad as life itself, and addressed practically everything. This type of mental participation in law planted its principles much more firmly in individuals. The Biblical Book of Proverbs provides an example of this literary device. A more modern version is Ben Franklin's aphorisms. "A stitch in times saves nine." "A penny saved is a penny earned." These bits of wisdom are easy to remember. Oral traditions, thus, had a certain stabilizing force that we may have lost in the progress of civilization. Oral law required greater personal involvement than written law. Such memory devices, if comprehensive enough, might be useful today among illiterate prison populations. It would be interesting to use rap to convey moral messages in illiterate prison population. The results might be surprising.

Absence of writing presented several drawbacks. It was difficult for oral law to govern a widespread nation of people. It is also difficult to preserve law from generation to generation. Writing was more dependable and more durable. Writing can be more easily distributed over a broader region, making it easier to govern a large number of people under the same set of laws through broader geographic distribution. Writing also helped transmit law to succeeding generations. Writing made possible the standardization of language itself over a larger area. A more uniform mythos could therefore develop in a much larger area, making possible a more widely shared moral code. Use of writing may have been the beginning of the idea that the sovereign must *obey* law. It provided a more objective standard that existed independently of the person of the king.

Mere writing also had disadvantages, however. Before the printing press, the only way to make copies of laws was by hand. The writer of the Book of Proverbs (if not some disillusioned Medieval monk with a sense of humor) said, "Of making many books there is no end; and much study is the weariness of the flesh."[93] Hand copying was slow and tedious. Multiple copies involved recopying the original. Writing was not available to the masses. The masses still depended on oral means of learning and preserving law.

The next major development came with invention of the printing press. Printing presses made possible mass production of printings. The printing press made possible massive compilation of information, including principles of modern science. Printing presses also allowed widespread sharing of knowledge. This was a major factor making modern nation states possible. Writers have recorded accomplishments of the Age of Reason in words. Ability to store knowledge in printed words is critical to the advancement of civilization. No individual thinker or scientist has been able to accomplish it all alone. Words and various media of communication are essential elements for progress of civilization. Scientists can communicate not only with other living scientists, but also with works of others who have been dead for hundreds of years. Greater and greater specialization has become possible.

Mythos began to progress geometrically with the availability of printing. However, availability of printing further relaxed the degree of actual mental involvement of individuals in the collective knowledge of law. No one had to remember it. Someone could find it in the books. Thus, law became even more externalized. This mental relaxation which began with the invention of *writing* became even more pronounced with the availability of *printing*. Expanding mythos has had its own growing pains. Mythological systems have come more sharply into conflict. Horizons, both literal and physical, which were important limits to ancient mythological systems have fallen in the wake of expanding knowledge. Modern mythological systems are unsure of their limits. Geographic neighbors do not have a common understanding of their mythological limits, although they often subscribe to very different mythological systems.

The twentieth century has brought tremendous advances in technology available for communication. There are exciting possibilities available for articulation and dissemination of law. We probably have not

---

93 Ecclesiastes 12:12.

even begun to use the technology now available. On a more somber note, radio, television, telephone and computers impact on the formative processes of law which we have described. Will we come to a more accurate assessment of the origins of law in human motive? If so, we can intentionally use technology for wholesome development of law. Otherwise, we will rely on a benevolent determinism, and the people who sense the power of modern technology, to evolve the new order of society. Even worse, we may depend on people who control media, but are unaware of its power in the formation of law. A later chapter is devoted to the impact of media.

Language and Nation State

E. Haugen, a modern linguist, suggests that language is a factor in establishing the modern nation state.

> The ancient Greeks and Romans spread their languages as far as their domains extended, and modern imperialists have sought to do the same. But within the modern world, technological and political revolutions have brought every man the opportunity to participate in political decisions to his own advantage. The invention of printing, the rise of industry, and the spread of popular education have brought into being the modern nation state, which extends some of the loyalties of the family and the neighborhood or the clan to the whole state. Nation and language have become inextricably intertwined. Every self-respecting nation has to have a language. Not just a medium of communication, a "vernacular" or a "dialect," but a fully developed language. Anything less marks it as underdeveloped.[94]

Our modern theories of law focus on the nation state. They try to show the relationship between law and the nation state. Basic societal forces I have described bring both law and the nation state into being. If "nation and language have become inextricably intertwined," as Haugen suggests, then so have law and language.

Connections between law, language and government are complex. One point, for instance, that merits attention is what linguists call *linguistic codes*. In linguistics, the word *code* signifies a separate system of speech. In laymen's terms, we might describe this phenomenon in the following manner. In a bilingual society, the more highly developed language—perhaps formally adopted—is the language of law and formal transactions. It is the language that a lawyer uses to talk to clients, or

---

94 E. Haugen, "Dialect, Language, Nation," *American Anthropologist*, Vol. 68, (1966), pp. 922-935.

when litigants talk to a magistrate. At home, the family uses the more familiar local dialect. Psychological principles discussed earlier show the basic moral code to be instilled in the home by parents. Therefore, this linguistic dividing line between law and morals has predictable significance. Of course, if the culture is truly bilingual so that children acquire knowledge and morals of (or should we say *in*) both languages, the effect would be moderated. Even in unilingual societies, different codes exist at different levels of communication. Conversations in open court differ from conversations at home in degree of formality. Indonesia may be an example of results of the dichotomy between familiar and formal language. It is a multilingual nation with a formal language that differs from the language used in most homes. Is this the reason for the significant unrest and lack of orderliness that the nation has experienced in the past?

Freedom of Speech

The discussion in this chapter exposes the need for freedom of speech. Selection of principles to govern a society is not an arbitrary matter. If we articulate and adopt correct principles, the culture will survive and progress. If not, it will likely deteriorate. The level of culture or civilization attained by a people depends on ability to recognize, articulate, and apply correct principles. The penalty is self-operative—no insight, no progress. The Bible declares, "Where there is no vision, the people perish."[95]

There must be a free exchange of information and expression of ideas. This is the only way we can be sure that someone will suggest principles needed for survival and solution of the next problem. This is the powerful message delivered by John Stuart Mill in his small book *On Liberty*. "[T]he peculiar evil," Mill wrote, "of silencing the expression of an opinion is, that it is robbing the human race; posterity as well as the existing generation; those who dissent from the opinion still more than those who hold it."[96] New answers come from unexpected sources. Few would have picked Abe Lincoln, Dr. M. L. King, Jr., Dr. George Washington Carver, Rachel Carson or others like them to carry the banner for civilization. Nevertheless, they picked up the banner and advanced it.

---

[95] Proverbs 29:18.
[96] Mill, J. S., *On Liberty*, p. 33.

At last, we have reached the point where many discussions of legal philosophy begin. We are ready to consider *formal authentication*. We are ready to consider how groups of words, such as "Thou shalt not kill," or, "Thou shalt not steal," or, "the abbreviation for inch shall be 'in.'" become law. Is it the words themselves, because of their dignity or their emotional content, that cause legal recognition? Although some words lend themselves to such a purpose better than others, words cannot be the source of their own authenticity as law. Is it a matter of who says the words? That is certainly a consideration, but not a completely satisfactory answer to the question. Other questions bear on the issue also. Is it a matter of precisely *what* the words express? Is it the nature of underlying reality symbolized by the words?

Let's think again about the examples given in the preceding chapter. Are some acts, such as intentionally killing a human being, so obviously asocial that prior words are not necessary to make such activity *illegal*? First year law students will immediately think of the *principle of legality*. Society should not punish anyone for an act not declared illegal before its commission. This necessity of prior declaration of the principle sought to be enforced is a generalization of the *ex post facto* principle. Reference to the principle is good legal reasoning. In connection with our examples, many non-lawyers would also think of the principle of legality. However, the principle of legality cannot solve the problem of authentication. After all, the common law crimes of murder, theft, burglary and others, originated without legislative enactment. We are exploring authentication of law itself, and the principle of legality is a *legal* principle. Where did *it* come from? If we knew that, we would have our answer. Are there *rules* by which we can authenticate other rules? If so, where do they come from?

These general questions indicate the nature of our quest for authentication. If we try to use a legal principle to authenticate other legal principles, we become involved in an infinite regression. The principle of legality is not simply logical, or the product of pure reason. Philosophers might say that the requirement that laws be published before being enforced is a necessary but not sufficient reason for law. In some instances, such as the atrocities of Nazi Germany, prior pronouncement may not even be necessary.

Did the captain's order not to kill the sailor in the example of the mortally wounded sailor discussed in the preceding chapter make any difference? Was it law? If so, what principle of nature, or of law, authorized the captain to make such rules? Was it because he was captain? What made him captain?

Are some acts, such as murder, burglary, and theft, so obviously bad as to need no prior condemnation? We raised this question earlier. A closely related question is equally important. Are certain activities so inherently lawful that no one can declare them illegal? We refer to such matters as *rights*. Most of us believe that self-defense is an absolute right. Remember Widow Brown from the preceding chapter, who was barely able to get a shot off to avoid the ax. Other rights are far more controversial, and often not so clearly visible in human nature.

We need to make one more point to introduce authentication. The American and the Japanese soldiers were just two people on an *ungoverned* island. Earlier we meditated about war, the end of hostilities, peace treaties, and their effect. Now we approach a deeper question. Must there be a *society* for there to be law? Must there be a government? Suppose the two soldiers meet, and realize they have no rules. They adopt rules, including a rule against killing each other. One of them kills the other anyway. What happens then? Must there be an organized society, including people other than those actually involved in the dispute, who enforce the will of a group, for there to be law? It presents an interesting question doesn't it? Is the origin of law purely social, or is law of metaphysical origin? Are laws part of an external reality, or simply products of the collective mind of the group? What does formal enactment add? Are laws there because we make them, or are they built into nature itself?

The Problem of Authentication

These examples and questions help us to visualize the problems of both articulation and authentication. The questions posed by these examples have no simple solutions, and they go to the essence of the nature of law. We need to be very specific about the nature of *authentication* itself. The examples we discussed in the preceding chapter enable us to reach general conclusions about authentication. These general conclusions are points of departure for various contentions in existing legal philosophy. All existing legal philosophy tries to show what causes a particular principle to have the character of law. In short, what makes law authentic?

One can look to the nature of a reality underlying the words. This, of course, is the natural law position that we discussed earlier, which approach holds that only certain naturally occurring realities or concepts partake of the nature of law. In short, we can *look to content*. For instance, almost everyone condemns unprovoked killing, stealing, and other such offenses.

A corollary is that when one looks to the nature of the underlying reality, or content, certain propositions *cannot* be law. It would be difficult, for instance, to outlaw self-defense. We call self-defense a *natural right*. There are other natural rights also, but the right of self-defense probably best illustrates the kind of right that legislation can never eliminate. I am using self-defense to represent the entire group of natural rights, simply because it seems so "self-evident." Other rights include, for instance, freedom of speech, religious freedom, freedom from unwarranted governmental intrusion in private matters, and others. Some asserted rights are not nearly so clear as self-defense.

These two arguments concentrate on *what the principle states* or the nature of the *underlying* reality. The problem with such an approach is *who decides?* Who has authority to "look to the principle?" Who decides whether a particular proposition is law? Authenticating the authenticator is as difficult as authenticating the principle itself.

Another approach is to look at the *source* of the principle. This is the argument of legal positivism. Advocates of this approach argue that if a principle emanates from a source that has authority to make law, then the principle is authentic. Law is simply what a court or legislature decides it is, if the court or legislature has authority to decide. Such an approach immediately involves law in a relationship with the nation state, which really begs the question. What authenticates nation states? Ironically, despite phrases such as "deriving their just powers from the consent of the governed," recognition by other nation states seems to be the most important criterion for a regime's claim to legitimacy. Perhaps this is additional evidence of the inadequacy of an individual nation as the source of law. Nazi Germany was an independent nation with apparent power to make law without interference from other nations.

Proponents of the *source* argument, of course, have not overcome a problem of circular reasoning and infinite regress. Who authenticates the authenticators? One argument is that authenticity of government comes from consent of the people. Surely the people themselves can establish vehicles for making authentic law. But what part does *custom* and *conquest* play, if lawmaking authority is purely a matter of agreement or consent? Further, what are the rights of minority groups who do not agree that the vehicle is authentic? Is the putative consent absolute or is it conditional? If conditional, who decides when the condition has been violated?

Proponents of the *source* argument also meet another difficulty. Does the nature of the underlying reality matter at all? What if the *authentic* source enacts something really stupid? If the legislature outlaws self-defense, what happens then? If we look to content, we are back to the argument that underlying reality is the source of law's authenticity.

Assume that we have an appropriate vehicle for enacting law. The people agree upon a constitution that provides for a representative lawmaking body. Also assume that the legislative body exercises sound judgment in making laws. Are there naturally occurring rules that regulate the lawmaking process? If so, this would simplify the problem of authentication. Then the lawmakers would only have to identify the *authenticating* rules. The problem is how to recognize authenticating rules. Who identifies them? What authenticates *them*? H. L. A. Hart, for the legal positivists, and Lon Fuller, for the advocates of natural law both seem to argue for certain principles that authenticate other principles. Hart describes a sort of hierarchy in which secondary rules establish rule making power, and set limits on governmental power. Fuller describes an internal morality of law that includes principles which must be met for law to exist. Both analyses are highly useful and instructive. No doubt, within the belief systems that undergird authenticating processes, there are logical or hierarchical structures pursuant to which certain principles authenticate other principles. The fact remains, however, that mythos—our belief systems—provide the processes for authentication.

Let's state the problem a different way. Does the legislator *discover* law, or does he *make* law? Lon Fuller discusses *made vs. implicit* law in his short but informative *The Anatomy of Law*. If the legislator or judge makes law, what does he make it from? If he is to discover it, where does he look? Are laws found in nature? Does he look to the Bible or Koran? Does he look to Aquinas' moral order? Do we find law in custom? Is law purely a matter of utility? How do we recognize law when we see it? We could go on and on with possible sources, but that is not necessary. No doubt you now understand what I mean by *authentication*. No explanation of authentication proposed so far provides a satisfactory explanation for law. These are simply restatements of existing arguments concerning the nature of law. The discussion of authentication has carried us back to natural law and legal positivism, which we summarized earlier. We are ready now to move forward and show the authenticating role of mythos, or belief systems.

Mythos, Belief Systems, and Authentication

The method of authentication in antiquity was to place the origin of law with the gods. Mythological accounts of receipt of law from gods are many. We cited two examples earlier. Most of us are familiar with the Biblical account of Moses receiving the Ten Commandments from God on Mt. Sinai. A stele discovered early this century shows the Sun God handing a code of law to Hammurabi. Author W. A. Robson lists numerous such accounts.[97] It may be impossible to say that such a belief was universal, but it was clearly widespread in early societies. We could describe this method of authenticating law as based on mythos. However, such a conception differs considerably from the theory I am advancing. To say that law derives from mythos in the ways that I have described is not to attribute law directly to a god.

Ascribing law to the gods was consistent with the world-view of early people. They believed unquestioningly in their gods. So, authentication of law actually resulted from their *belief systems*. Assignment of the origin of law to the gods gave it unassailable authenticity. Changes in law were more difficult. The gods don't change their minds that easily. Nevertheless, the benefits of unassailable validity are significant.

We do not have to accept the factual basis of a myth that gives a particular account of the origin of law. The way that law arises from mythos does not depend on accuracy of the account. It depends on the sharing of beliefs. We have our own mythos and shared beliefs. We authenticate law the same way the ancients did: through our belief systems. Faith is as important to us as it was to them. Governments derive their just powers from the beliefs, not the consent, of the governed. As we will see in a later chapter, faith is unavoidable. The question is not whether we will have faith, but rather what we will believe.

No doubt, ascription of law to the gods occurred a few generations after the alleged event. Perhaps *fathers* and *mothers* passed the informa-

---

97 Robson, *Civilisation and the Growth of Law.*

tion along to the children. This helped to identify the origin of law with those archetypes of Jungian psychology. Probably, the leader of the clan, or medicine man, or some other *wise old man* reinforced the image of law and authority. Let me make it clear. *They* believed that their gods gave law to them. *I* believe that their mythos—their conception of the cosmos and nature—gave law to them. Their beliefs included a particular belief in a deity. The connection to divinity gave motive force as well as authenticity to law.

Formality, rituals, and ceremonial aspects of their religion were not only important in making law, but in preserving law. I am suggesting that this mystique is characteristic of how the group—society—interacts with individuals to produce law. There is always some rite, some ceremony, some ritual involved in authentication and preservation of law. Law arises from human nature, as described by Jungian psychology and Durkheimian sociology.

Thus, both the position of the natural law advocate and that of the legal positivist are products of operative mythos. They are both aspects of a larger social reality of the type described by Durkheim. Durkheim captured the essence of the authenticating power of mythos in the following passage:

> We say that an object, whether individual or collective, inspires respect when the representation expresing (sic) it in the mind is gifted with such a force that it automatically causes or inhibits actions, *without regard for any consideration relative to their useful or injurious effects.* When we obey somebody because of the moral authority which we recognize in him, we follow out his opinions, not because they seem wise, but because a certain sort of physical energy is imminent in the idea that we form of this person, which conquers our will and inclines it in the indicated direction. Respect is the emotion which we experience when we feel this interior and wholly spiritual pressure operating upon us. Then we are not determined by the advantages or inconveniences of the attitude which is prescribed or recommended to us; it is by the way in which we represent to ourselves the person recommending or prescribing it. This is why commands generally take a short, peremptory form leaving no place for hesitation; it is because, in so far as it is a command and goes by its own force, it excludes all idea of deliberation or calculation; it gets its efficacy from the intensity of the mental state in which it is placed. It is this intensity which creates what is called moral ascendancy.

> Now the ways of action to which society is strongly enough attached to impose them upon its members, are, by that very fact, marked with a distinctive sign provocative of respect. Since they are elaborated in common,

the vigour with which they have been thought of by each particular mind is retained in all the other minds, and reciprocally. The representations which express them within each of us have an intensity which no purely private states of consciousness could ever attain; for they have the strength of the innumerable individual representations which have served to form each of them. It is society who speaks through the mouths of those who affirm them in our presence; it is society whom we hear in hearing them; and the voice of all has an accent which that of one alone could never have.[98]

Authentication involves both what is said and who says it. Both source and underlying reality are important. Authenticity arises from mythos of culture. For a principle to become law, these two aspects of authenticity must coalesce. The *person or body that speaks* must be authentic. The *principle spoken* must also be authentic. Authenticity for both comes from shared beliefs of the population. Both must meet requirements of mythos of the culture before the culture will accept the principle as law.

The speaker must occupy a properly authenticated role, which mythos accepts. In our society we authenticate the role by election or appointment. An outsider examining these processes might describe them as ceremonial. Typically, a legislative proposal requires three ritualistic readings. Formality is observed. A required percentage of legislators ceremonially cast their votes, and then the measure is believed to be law. Departure from the prescribed ritual casts questions on the results.

In primitive cultures ceremonies were different. Our ways would appear as strange to primitive societies as theirs do to us. If Moses had descended from the mountain, called the people to order, and asked for a roll call vote, the golden calf might have won. Likewise, if a bearded guy with stone tablets came down from a mountain and said he had the law, and started breaking up our golden calves, we would likely lock him up. Both the asserted proposition and the person(s) doing the talking must activate our archetypes—or collective representations, as Durkheim calls them. Failing in this, the principle itself will fail as law. It will lack emotional backing which is essential to its effectiveness. There is no question that we believe in law, but why do we believe in it? Law identifies in some way with our deepest representations of social reality. This makes it authentic. Law is a *collective representation* in Durkheimian terminology. The function of ritual is to identify the principle with the current system of belief.

---

[98] Durkheim, *The Elementary Forms of the Religious Life*, pp. 237-238.

I need to underscore the non-reductionist nature of my position. I am not saying "law is nothing more than a product of collective psychology," or "law is purely a human social function." To capture in a few words psychological dynamics of the immediate causes of law does not dissipate the mystery of its ultimate sources. Ultimate sources demand all of the awe of life itself. Law arises from our mythos, as the laws of the ancients arose from theirs. However, there has been improvement. Obviously, laws of modern civilization are in many ways superior to those of primitive, superstitious tribes. Modern law provides a framework for meeting basic human needs of millions of people. If it fails to meet those needs, then law and government itself are subject to challenge on those very grounds. I suggest that this explains failure of the central government in the Soviet Union. Our perception of reality is in some way superior to that of our predecessors, but this is because we have built our system on theirs. This is not a contention that all social order evolves along the same lines. It merely acknowledges that our early mythos is part of our present mythos. We have built on the foundation of our own literal and cultural ancestors. We are further along the journey of a progressively deepening understanding of ourselves and our environment. Unfortunately, we may have less understanding of our connection with nature, and we may have to rediscover it. Nevertheless, the ultimate mystery of it all is unavoidable. What is the source of this brighter perception of reality that we have achieved? What is the nature of that reality itself? These mysteries we can't reduce.

To summarize, ancients believed that God was the source of law. Thus, they looked to the source of the words of law for authenticity. It was important for there to be an external source of law. They may have assigned the words to the source long after the alleged delivery of the words took place. There is often a delay between dictation and transcription. Regardless of the so-called *facts*, the belief system supported the law. Whether delivery of the law by a god occurred in the precise manner described in the myth is not terribly important. Assignment to the deity solved the problem of authentication, and the existence and usefulness of the rule is no less a mystery than any other part of creation. Nevertheless, there obviously were human sources who, because of their position or images, occupied a special role in the intuitive receipt and delivery and protection of law.

Were these ancient lawmakers who ascribed law to the gods fakes or deceivers who deliberately misled their followers, as Frazer seemed to assert in *The Golden Bough*? We reach such conclusions only by assigning to those ancient leaders a mental capability far more advanced than that of their followers. Only by making them Connecticut Yankees in King Arthur's Court can we be so unkind to them. They were adjusting to their environment, including the social environment. That environment produced the very representations with which they dealt. They, like our judges and lawmakers, usually acted in the most sincere manner that they could muster. We engage in our own pretensions. Legal fictions are abhorred only after wearing out their usefulness. A hundred years from now, legal history will probably look upon our civil justice system, with its contingent fees, and lawyers financing lawsuits, with the same disdain that we look on bounty hunters of the last century. Right now, we seem to have no better alternative for remedying corporate immorality, however. And plaintiffs lawyers are *bringin' 'em in, dead or alive!* To understand that the ancients acted in sincerity, we must appreciate the evolutionary nature of mythos. We must understand its dependency on custom and tradition. We must empathize with their respect for wisdom of the elders who had given them these customs and traditions. Survival over eons of time involved keeping to set ways.

When cultures commingle, with a gradient between their comprehensions of reality, manipulation of mythos for individual or group advantage becomes possible. Cicero, the great Roman Jurist, thought that it was necessary to cause the masses to believe that the gods were responsible for law.

> So in the very beginning we must persuade our citizens that the gods are the lords and rulers of all things, and that what is done is done by their will and authority. 99

"The powers that be are ordained of God," and "Render to Caesar the things that are Caesar's," were probably Constantine's favorite Bible verses.

Since ascription of law to the gods gives law authenticity, there comes a time when a degree of manipulation becomes possible. Manipulation is clearly possible in our times. Against the background we have described, this possibility only adds a new level of complexity to the process of authentication. Even if masses of people submit to tyranny at the edge of the sword, because they *believe* they will be put to death for

---

99 Cicero, *Laws Book II, The Great Legal Philosophers*, Edited by Clarence Morris, p. 52.

insubordination, law is built on a system of belief. It is not those who are killed, but those who survive that are governed.

Obviously, Cicero knew that the gods were not the direct authors of the laws for which he sought authenticity. Equally obvious, he believed that those principles really were laws. What was *his* authenticating principle? Earlier we quoted Cicero's eloquent description of the role of conscience in the enforcement of law. Suffice it to say that Cicero looked to the enlarged mythos of his own day for the authenticating principle.[100]

Common Law and Civil Law

Modes of authentication vary from nation to nation, although there is some commonality in groups of countries. Roughly speaking, English speaking countries follow the common law system. Continental Europe follows the civil law system, which descended from Roman law. In the common law system, courts play a prominent role in law*making*. Civil law countries often try to use comprehensive codes, so that, at least theoretically, the legislative body is more important than courts in lawmaking. Civil law gives more deference to the *code* and the scheme of law which it reflects than do the common law courts. Common law courts rely more heavily on case precedents. You will recall the earlier discussion of the case method used in our law schools.

In a sense, the case method is a highly specialized system of mythology. We use the stories of events of former times to resolve present controversies. The case method builds structures from events, which Claude Levi-Strauss describes as characteristic of mythological thinking. The very essence of law is to provide structure, and it builds that structure from events described in cases.

Differences between common law and civil law are somewhat superficial concerning the problem of authentication. The difference between the two raises a question as to which governmental agency should be responsible for making law. However, the distinction between the two does not show the deeper psychological and sociological factors of authentication that are at the heart of the problem. Both are dependent upon belief systems of the people for their acceptance and authenticity. Mythos may very well have something to say in choosing the governmental agency authorized to make law, however.

---

[100] Cicero, *The Nature of the Gods*, translated by Horace C. P. Mcgregor, pp. 147 et. Seq.

At this institutional level, where we discuss whether courts should make law, or whether the lawmaking function is reserved to the legislature, the conflict between natural law and legal positivism often finds expression. Natural law advocates, you will recall, contend that law arises beyond the pale of government—either in the moral order or in the scheme of nature. Legal positivists argue that law is the product of properly constituted government. We have shown that the real process of authentication subsumes both of these positions. However, at the institutional level, where the arguments about which *agency* or branch of government has lawmaking power, we can actually debate the rhetorical question of whether we will have a government of laws or a government of men. The result of this exercise in mental gymnastics is a matter of concern. It disguises the real dynamics of authentication in the American legal system.

The common law tradition very clearly grew out of a natural law background. John Austin described legal positivism in *The Province of Jurisprudence Determined* in 1832. *Blackstone's Commentaries*, which arrived in America in the 1770s, stated the natural law basis of the common law. According to Blackstone, courts do not make law, they find it. If the court could not find law in precedent or statute, then the judges looked to natural principles. The greatest reliance was on precedent.

In the rare instances in which courts did not follow precedent, it was because the earlier case was a *mistaken* view of the law. In this way, you will notice, common law judges were careful to respect *collective representation* (to follow Durkheim's terminology) of law. Common law judges drew on mythos in their selection of principles that would resonate with collective representations, or archetypes, of law. They protected the appearance of their archetypal role by a conservative stance. Conservatism, as expressed in the doctrine of *stare decisis*, was the hallmark of authentication of traditional common law.

Even so, it was clear that, from time to time, courts changed law. New law came into being as a result of court decisions. How were John Austin and legal positivists to get around this problem? After all, the legislative branch makes law, and courts simply apply them, according to the then accepted theory of government. To ignore the obvious reality of court-made law would have labelled the legal positivist school as rather naive. Austin met the problem head on. He frankly admitted that courts make law. Courts are authentic officers of the sovereign, entrusted with the function of deciding cases. It lies within the province of courts to make law. When judges make law, they are duly commissioned agents of the sovereign. Of course, this same argument extends in our times to regulations made by administrative agencies. The only question for the positivist is whether the judge or regulator has authority from the sovereign. So the legal positivists declared it openly: *courts make law*. Humans make law. Governments are made up of humans.

This development now seems little more than recognition of an obvious reality. Courts *do* make law. Nevertheless, against the background of the actual dynamics involved in authentication, there is a problem with this approach. It has to do with how the court's appearance relates to collective representations and archetypes. The legal community accepted the empirical conclusion of positivists. The courts began, perhaps a bit timidly at first, but with ever-increasing temerity, to admit that they made law. They began to assert that they were very proper agents to do so. Once positivists brought the Trojan horse of the judiciary inside the citadel of the legislature, the siege was over. The foundation of the American dream of *separation of powers* and a *representative democracy* shattered, although it remains a part of our mythos. The problem is with authentication of the spokesperson. It made sense to hold that courts had the final say in interpreting the Constitution. *Marbury v. Madison* established this point. Ironically, the case also clothed the court with a certain authenticity in its lawmaking role, so long as the Constitution is used as the authority for the principle sought to be established. We believe in the constitution; we believe it is the prerogative of the courts to interpret the constitution, and this belief blends imperceptibly with the positivist belief that courts make law. The courts abandoned the conservative approach of traditional common law. The conservative stance had protected the role of judges in their lawmaking functions. Leaving that conservative position assured an ideological struggle for the ultimate power to make law.

The problem is not at all a simplistic one. The lawmaking role of judges violated some images of our mythos in certain particulars. After all, we believe in a representative democracy, where duly elected representatives of the people make the law. In other ways, however, courts identified with the lawmaking images of our mythos. The courts, more often than not, spoke the will of the people. They correctly identified collective representations. They were in fact the "voice of society" while artifices of legislative experimentation broke down. Judges assumed the priestly role, dealing directly with mythos, and extracting its wisdom, without the intervention of the legislature and its representation of democracy. Samuel Enoch Stumpf describes the dilemma well:

There are times when a moral right has not yet been legislated but becomes relevant for the first time in the course of a controversy in the judicial process. The judicial process involves both finding and making, for where there is no specific statute or precedent governing a controversy, a moral norm is sought, and when it is discovered, or when the process of judgment has matured under the influence of a moral norm, this moral norm is transformed into a legal norm by judicial recognition, interpretation, and application.[101]

So what is the problem? The problem is in the institutional structure. In the United States, where we appoint federal judges for life, there are no guarantees of restraint. Power originally assumed in strict compliance with mythos will not necessarily remain in check. It will not necessarily remain responsive to the people. By short-circuiting the deliberative processes of legislative action in a democratic republic, we risk non-responsive law, beyond control of the people. Confirmation proceedings in the U. S. Senate in recent years, including the debacle involving the confirmation of Supreme Court Justice Clarence Thomas, does little to assure responsiveness. The processes of confirmation and impeachment are far too cumbersome to assure real responsiveness, once it is admitted that federal courts make an immense amount of law. The dreams of advocates of autonomous law originating in courts are dangerous. To say the least, it appears to be an elitist position. Courts, by making law, can be unresponsive to needs of the people as easily as they can serve as an arbiter between government and individuals. Fortunately, we have been blessed throughout most of the history of the United States to have conscientious judges who have tried to be responsive to the needs of the people.

Over the last two centuries, however, the position of natural law advocates has reversed itself. Natural law is no longer the fortress of conservatism in law. It has become the basis for advocacy of individual rights. This is a natural response to the threat to individual liberty posed by positivism. However, this shift removes advocates of natural law from the ranks of conservatives who guarded against encroachment of court-made law. The change has been a very gradual one, occurring over a period of two hundred years, which happens to coincide with the history of the United States as a government organized under a constitution. The Constitution itself has achieved mythical significance as the oracular authority for judge-made law. This result is deeply ironic for a

---

[101] Stumpf, *Morality and the Law*, p. 238.

document that was intended to establish separation of power and to limit federal lawmaking! The distinction between the actions of the court in invalidating Congressional law and in declaring positive law should be carefully noted.

Creation of Law and Separation of Powers

Roscoe Pound discussed creation of law and the doctrine of separation of powers.

> In the eighteenth century, it [the theory that only the legislature can make law] was given scientific form in the theory of separation of powers. The legislative organ made the laws. The executive administered them. The judiciary applied them to the decision of controversies. It was admitted in Anglo-American legal thinking that courts must interpret in order to apply. But the interpretation was taken not to be in any wise a law making and the application was taken not to involve any administrative element and to be wholly mechanical. On the continent, interpretation so as to make a binding rule for future cases was deemed to belong only to the legislator. The maturity of law was not willing to admit the judge or jurist could make anything. It was not the least service of the analytical jurisprudence of the last century to show that the greater part of what goes by the name of interpretation in this way of thinking is really a law making process of supplying a new law where no rule or no sufficient rule is at hand. "The fact is," says Gray most truly, "that the difficulties of so-called interpretation arise when the legislation has no meaning at all; when the question which is raised on the statute never occurred to it; when what the judges have to do is, not to determine what the legislature did mean on a point which was present to its mind, but to guess what it would have intended on a point not present to its mind had the point been present." The attempt to maintain the separation of powers by constitutional prohibitions has pointed to the same lesson from another side. Law making, administration and adjudication cannot be rigidly fenced off one from the other and turned over to a separate agency as its exclusive field. There is rather a division of labor as to typical cases and a practical or historical apportionment of the rest.[102]

Pound's comments are typical of American jurists and legal theorists earlier this century. They not only admit that courts make law but justify it on a principle of necessity. Sometimes statutes *are* unclear, and need interpretation. I cannot eagerly adopt the guessing game for courts when legislative meaning is unclear. Lack of clarity is sometimes real. At other

---

[102]   Pound, *An Introduction to the Philosophy of Law*, pp. 102-104.)

times "lack of clarity" enables the court to substitute its judgment for that of the legislature. It does so because it *disagrees* with the principle.

The culmination of all of this came in the Warren Court years. Page after page of pure positive law rolled off the Court's printing presses. The *Miranda* opinion, almost a hundred pages long, gave detailed positive instructions as to what a village police officer must say before questioning a suspect in a criminal case.

Legal Realism

In all that has just been described, there is a threat to the authenticity of law and the legal system itself. A primary concern must be preservation of the institutional framework of law. We can accomplish that goal only by recognizing the dynamics necessarily involved in law's authentication. These dynamics are not law but the substrata from which law arises. We must recognize the power of a people to speak through its mythos, and arrange institutions that are faithful bearers of that voice. *Courts are not necessarily that voice.*

We can understand legal realism best as the very skepticism about courts which we are describing. First the realists buy the positivist position that courts make law; then they have apoplexy when they realize that judges are human and base their decisions on their particular perceptions. Jerome Frank and others believed that opinions of courts rationalized the judges' conclusions, without giving the real reasons for results. Thus, the realists reasoned, the pronounced principle had little to do with the actual outcome in the case. It would be better, they further contended, for the courts to forego pretenses and deal rationally with the underlying problem—*the reality*. My contentions admit much of the realists' argument. However, hardened belief systems that motivate decisions are not as malleable as realists believed. The greatest difficulty with the realist position is that it simplistically assumes a reality shared by all, and fails to come to grips with the problem of the fragmentation of reality itself with which we are grappling in this volume. Each subgroup has its own perceptions, which, for that subgroup, is *reality*.

The legal realist approach, taken to its limits, will destroy the very essence of law as we know it. It will convert courts into mere problem-solving agencies, responding to each problem on a case-by-case basis. Such an approach brings on the unmanageable burden of litigation under which we are now sinking. Legal realism, then, is no more than a manifestation of the problem of authentication. For anyone who believes there is continuing validity to *law*, legal realism and its progeny are causes for concern. Current emphasis on "alternative dispute resolution" must be carefully examined in this light. If alternative dispute resolution places the solution of each problem on a case-by-case, problem-solving basis, and fails to acknowledge underlying principles, it is likely to fail. If the legal system is not solving problems adequately, we must make it do so, using and recognizing legal principles.

Autonomous Law

Legal realism has had a considerable impact on legal thinking in this century, with one offshoot being the idea of *autonomous* law. Some recent writers find the source of authentication of judge-made law in the mirage of *autonomous* law. This theory holds that "separation of law and politics" provides a role for an independent judiciary as a check on the power of government. The theory is an interesting one:

> The separation of law and politics is the master strategy of legitimation. It is the way autonomous law brings legitimacy both to itself and to the political order. The strategy has two aspects. First, a foundation is laid for subordinating politics to law. In the regime of autonomous law the actions of the organized political community are not self-legitimating. The political elite may make decisions and deploy resources, but the question of whether those acts are lawful requires a separate assessment. The work of government and of political leadership has to do with solving problems, mobilizing resources, and winning consent. There is always a potential strain between action and legality. Autonomous law provides a forum for scrutinizing that strain and rendering a judgment on it. To that extent, law institutionalizes a principle of restraint in the exercise of power.[103]

Clearly, such writers are referring to *court-made* law. Ultimately, of course, courts are not *autonomous*, nor is law autonomous. In fact, any effort by a court to act in such a capacity politicizes the court, and undermines the court's authority. Courts are a function of government, with salaries paid by taxpayers. Courts can become the *politically elite*, from whom the people need the protection contemplated by the constitutional plan of checks and balances.

The law*making* process *is* politics. Making law involves courts in politics, with all of its ramifications. Law, if it is to be authentic, must have the motive support of psychological and sociological forces within society. Only democratic structures can assure continuing responsiveness of law to aspirations of the people. The idea of autonomous law lacks

---

[103]   Nonet and Selznick, *Law and Society in Transition: Toward Responsive Law*, p. 59.

both the checks of political accountability and the conservatism of traditional common law as safeguards against oppression.

Nevertheless, the imagery of autonomous law is interesting and helpful in understanding how law becomes *authenticated*. As long as the people accept the idea of autonomous law, everything will be fine. As long as courts *truly* draw on the moral base, and on our collective representations, the people will accept pronouncements of courts as law. The idea of *law*, which clothes those pronouncements with authority, is a collective representation, with much power of persuasion.

Any change in law is a threat to acceptance of the law as amended or changed. A certain amount of conservation or hesitancy to change law is natural and desirable. Thomas Aquinas made a shrewd observation:

> Human law is rightly changed, insofar as such change is conducive to the common will. But, to a certain extent, the mere change of law is of itself prejudicial to the common good: because custom avails much for the observance of laws seeing that what is done contrary to general custom, even in slight matters, is looked upon as grave. Consequently, when a law is changed, the binding power of law is diminished, insofar as custom is abolished.[104]

Wisdom literature from the Bible proclaims, "Whoso breaketh an hedge, a serpent shall bite." We cannot foretell the consequences of changing the law. Changing the law is, metaphorically, an invitation to the snakes. If adverse results from changes in law are difficult to anticipate, they are even more difficult to correct.

Moral Order and Moral Formation

Aquinas argued that law arises from the moral order. Many legal writers recognize the relationship between law and morality,[105] or law and public opinion or law and public aspiration.[106] They recognize that there is a connection between such factors and the authenticity of law. Dr. King correctly tied law to morals. However, legal writers do not usually admit or suggest a connection between law and *individual conscience, basic human needs*, the *unconscious, archetypes*, and *collective representations*. The connection with mythos goes undetected. This oversight is beyond explanation. Anthropology made the connection long ago. Perhaps anthropologists have been hesitant to apply their

---

[104] *The Great Legal Philosophers*, p. 77.
[105] See, for instance, Stumpf, *Morality and the Law*.
[106] See Morris, *The Justification of the Law*.

findings to the so-called modern civilized world. Their studies often relate to "savage" societies, such as South Pacific Islanders, American Indians, and Africans. In addition to the work of Durkheim, on whom we have drawn heavily, there is important work by Malinowski, Levi-Strauss, and others. Their work points to the conclusions I am drawing. For English speaking people, the oversight is even stranger. *The Golden Bough*, by Sir James G. Frazer, is the starting point for examination of mythology in anthropology. It has also been influential in literature of the twentieth century. It clearly influenced Campbell, but it also impacted on many other twentieth century authors.[107] An important thrust of *The Golden Bough* was to show the relationship between mythical rites and authority figures. Somehow, public opinion or morality referred to by legal writers appears as if by magic, without origin. P. S. Atiyah, in *Law and Modern Society*, argues that law must *persuade* if it is to be effective. He recognizes the futility of physical force in long range enforcement. This is a good point, but does not go far enough. We must understand *how* law persuades and *why* it persuades. We must understand motive force. The writers give little attention to factors underlying development of morals in individuals and the projection of individual morals into collective psychology. Legal philosophers ignore the development and collection of values in mythos and propagation of values through mythos.

For Aquinas, the moral order was directly of metaphysical origin. He had no knowledge of moral formation in the modern sense of the word. Thus, Aquinas could not include the *functional* basis of the motive force of law in his natural law theory. Today, we try to find the basis of moral values and law in rationality. Rationality is amoral—morally neutral. Rationality builds sand castles, but the sandy beach was already there. There must be a *substance* for rationality to deal with, and mythos—shared beliefs woven into a thousand narratives—provides that substance. Ronald Dworkin strikes a glancing blow at this problem in *Law's Empire*. He creates an imaginary community, whose members follow "rules of courtesy." Rules of courtesy deal with such matters as when it is necessary for peasants to take off their hats. Then he develops an "interpretive attitude" with regard to the rules. The difficulty with such an approach is its totally artificial nature. There are *actual* customs, *actual* myths, *actual* forms of behavior, *actual* motive forces; and it is from these that actual law arises. People *actually believe* certain things. Law is not

---

[107] See Vickery, *The Literary Impact of The Golden Bough.*

merely the procedural things that courts do to aspirations of society. Law incorporates and includes those aspirations as its substance.

There is unending debate about the relation between morality and law. Stumpf discusses the relation of law and morals:

> There may be serious questions over whether anything can be gained by demonstrating that there is such an intimate connection between law and morals. Bentham wondered just what Blackstone had achieved by arguing that the natural law places limits upon what the positive law can control. Bentham's objection was that if it is held that there is a close connection between law and morals, the effect will be for people to identify their moral obligation with their legal duties. And to say that the law already contains its moral justification is to stifle any serious criticism of the law.[108]

Actually, both morality and law spring from the same fountainhead: individual conscience and basic human needs. This is true, even though group formation adds new dimensions. Both law and morality are pronounced and preserved in mythos and belief systems of society. One difference between law and morality is that in questions that are purely moral, individuals may have a choice. Some propositions are necessary for survival of society or more adequately meet basic human needs. In these instances, society itself makes the choice, and these propositions become law. In other matters, society may have a preference, but not insist upon it in all instances. These are morals. Unfortunately, legislators and courts do not always understand this distinction. It is not correct to say that law is a societal matter, while morals are individual. Both are very social in nature. Perhaps the difference lies in the structures of society to which they relate. Law in modern society relates mainly to the nation state as its institutional repository. Structural repositories of morals are fragmented: families, churches, occupational groups, and others. It is interesting to wonder if our distinction between law and morals would be as pronounced if a dichotomy between Church and State had not occurred historically.

Collective psychology is the fountainhead of both morals and law. Through collective psychology, both law and morals gain ascendancy in society. There can be good laws and there can be bad laws. Legislators and courts can make mistakes. Moral judgment is still there to take issue. Laws can contribute to morality, but more often morality is the basis of law. So even though there is a considerable overlap, both law and morals

---

[108] Stumpf, *Morality and the Law*, p. 111.

have their scope of operation. Too often, however, we see morals purely as a means of criticizing bad law. We do not recognize that morality is also part of the motive force of good law. The force of moral persuasion plays a significant role in authentication of law, just as Aquinas urged; but moral persuasion arises through moral formation as described by modern psychology. It does not arise purely from a God created moral order, to be interpreted only through authority of the Church.

The Goal of Authentication: Acceptance

The goal of the rituals of authentication is to achieve acceptance of law in human motive. Mere intellectual assent is not enough. To achieve acceptance, law must initially arise from primal urgings of individual conscience and basic needs. Otherwise, law must identify with that position through processes of persuasion. Mere rational understanding of legal principles may be some small beginning toward acceptance of law. The ultimate test is whether the principle relates to aspects of human nature consistent with the culture in which it exists or which enacted it. As Clarence Morris states:

> The character or tone of a society affects its values. The ethos in which men live plays a part in determining their aspirations. Law making is a response to felt needs, and legislators and judges are tenants-in-common, along with the rest of their society, in the culture of their time and place. Though logic and the principles of sound legal reasoning are norms applicable to all societies, each local public's aspirations inevitably differ in some details, and therefore justice will also differ somewhat from place to place.[109]

Inadequately accepted laws lack power of enforcement. The power for enforcement arises from broad scale acceptance. Enforcement of unaccepted law is erratic and inconsistent. As Morris points out:

> Even apart from the intrinsic desirability of lawmaking that seeks to implement public aspirations, there are two forces that tend to direct lawmaking into this channel. (1) Laws that run counter to public aspirations, and therefore do not seem just to the public, are often enacted in vain. Laws purporting to advance pruderies widely rejected are likely to be widely disregarded; breaches of such laws are only sporadically prosecuted. Speed traps are for tourists who are caught but once; home folks usually ignore them with impunity. This point, of course, can be over stressed. Unjust licensing laws may effectively exclude deserving and qualified men from trades and professions. Unjust taxes may be collected from people unready

---

[109] Morris, *The Justification of the Law*, p. 14.

to rebel. (2) Legislators acting singly are helpless. Those who want to espouse legislation of extremely wide and complicated import usually attract few allies.[110]

Law must have a basis in mythos and be within the linguistic base of society. Collective representations are its foundations. Law must find a basis in human motive. If law does not meet these requirements, it cannot find wide acceptance among the people and will be difficult to enforce. Cicero argued:

> What of the many deadly, the many pestilential statutes which nations put in force? These no more deserve to be called laws than the rules a band of robbers might pass. . . [111]

Formally authenticated lawmakers can overlook a necessary principle. Organized government may fail to perceive a needed principle, or may fail to enforce it, even though the people recognize the need. In that event, unused power of mythos is an open invitation to vigilantes, protests, and other *unofficial* group efforts. Traditional theory among white southerners attributes such a cause to the rise of the infamous Ku Klux Klan. Unused power of mythos may be partly responsible for cult and gang formation, which is becoming an increasing cause of concern.

---

[110] Ibid., p. 44.
[111] *The Great Legal Philosophers*, p. 51.

Even in modern society, mythos has a continuing relationship to law. Like other cultures, we are not fully aware of our operative myths. Exposure of the meaning of myths softens their effect, and prepares the way for the next evolutionary stage in mythology. Mythology is a product of our faith systems. Every culture has its operative myths, and each has its faith systems. In this chapter, I will identify mythological themes that deeply affect modern American society.

If we recognize that certain themes and popular beliefs are mythical, we may also recognize the importance of other myths that have sustained our culture. Many individuals disapprove certain aspects of our mythological heritage that are important for our welfare. They write off important aspects of our belief systems as unimportant myth. Often the persons who write off the importance of myth are the very ones whose beliefs are so deeply embedded in economics, science, or some other modern theme that they do not even realize that they are acting out a faith. If we can reintroduce the importance of the mythos that constitutes the core of our culture, wiser judgment may result. Recognition of the importance of mythos as the basis of belief systems will give human reason material with which it can work. One way to reintroduce the importance of mythos is to show that modern beliefs are based on mythological themes. In highlighting certain mythological themes that are now popular, I am not claiming that they are exclusive. There are other mythological themes with varying degrees of importance.

Myths of Individuality

The leading modern expert on mythology is the late Joseph Campbell. Campbell identified a central theme of modern myths as *individualism*. I could not agree more. Nothing has more impact on modern western civilization than myths of individualism. Durkheim referred to the *cult of individuality* in a non-critical manner. Individualism is a mythical theme that expresses itself in hundreds of different ways. It is the central theme in almost every modern story.

Campbell sees individualism emerging from stories that originated during the Middle Ages, particularly the Arthurian legends and the quest for the Holy Grail. Parcival is the most frequently cited account. Campbell draws on many other sources as well. A review of all the data on which he bases his findings is well beyond the scope of this work. Campbell has done a masterful job, and I simply refer the reader to his works for a discussion of the roots of the myth of the individual. Many other thinkers and writers share Campbell's findings and conclusions. Perhaps Nietzsche developed the theme of individualism to the extreme, in *Thus Spoke Zarathustra*. Nietzsche's theme of the *Overman* is almost a caricature of individualism.

We need not look to erudite philosophical and legendary sources for myths of individualism, however. Superman and Wonderwoman in Saturday morning T.V. programs are great examples. So are the white hat heroes of a thousand western movies, Zane Gray Heroes, Abraham Lincoln, and hundreds of rags-to-riches stories. In the South, there is Robert E. Lee and Stonewall Jackson. We can also add Leonardo Da Vinci, Martin Luther King, Jr., Rosa Parks, Jack Kennedy, Mickey Mantle, and Paul "Bear" Bryant. The list is endless. We tell their stories. We make up songs like *Casey Jones* and *John Henry* about heroes. A frequent theme is the individual competing with a machine. John Henry, the hero in a ballad, was a railroad worker who drove spikes in competition with a "steam hammer." Heroes like Casey Jones *use* machines, if only to be killed by them to become martyrs. We embed these stories in our mythos. They are our mythos. They are our heroes. In all these stories, the hero archetype is at work.

At their best, myths of individualism place before us examples for emulation that pull us onward toward our own fulfillment. One basic need is to achieve maximum potential. Myths of individualism, told a thousand different ways, are undoubtedly one of the strongest shaping motifs in our society. They draw on the need to achieve maximum potential, if not the quest for meaning itself, for its energy source. The archetype or image of the hero and of the self get specific content from culture. They are powerful images that shape much of the behavior of individuals in our culture. Recall that a part of the power of myth lies in imagery—in symbolism. Jung identified the *hero* as one of the archetypes. The hero is the archetype of individualism. The archetype of the hero is in evidence in all literature. Campbell entitled his best seller *The Hero With a Thousand Faces*.

Dangerous Propensities of Individuality

Myths, while very useful in preserving values of culture, can have dangerous tendencies. In Alabama and around the country there are lots of *rugged individualists*. Often, they own powerful pickup trucks, with a rifle across the rear window. They arise at 3:00 a.m. in suburbia to catch a country boy's breakfast of bacon, eggs and grits at a local all-night place. Then they drive 40 miles out an interstate highway to the woods before daybreak and shoot a deer. There's absolutely nothing wrong with any of this so far. I hunted deer with a club for many years, so I am describing friends for whom I have the highest regard.

The point that I am making is the paradox of self-esteem that this activity involves. This person feels very *individual* as he engages in these activities. He confirms his individuality by listening to country music on the radio. If he is lucky, he may hear Hank Williams, Jr., sing *A Country Boy Can Survive*. However, he doesn't know where material came from that built his suburban house. He doesn't know where the pig and chickens were that furnished breakfast. He hasn't the slightest notion where gasoline for his truck came from. He cannot make a truck or rifle. He doesn't know how the radio works. A real individual would need none of these instruments of society. Why does an individual need a radio, for instance? In short, corporate fabric surrounds and enmeshes our hero, even as he feels most individualistic. I have deliberately chosen an example from my own surroundings. I could have chosen the black-jacketed motorcyclist seeking escape, the bearded protester seeking justice, the jogger seeking the elixir of youth, or a thousand other examples from our society. The mythological character of the "individual" becomes very apparent as we see specific individuals totally immersed in society.

There is a problem in this obsession with individualism. Joseph Campbell describes it as follows:

> The problem of mankind today, therefore, is precisely the opposite to that of men in the comparatively stable periods of those great co-ordinating mythologies which now are known as lies. Then all meaning was in the group, in the great anonymous forms, none in the self-expressive individual; today no meaning is in the group—none in the world: all is in the individual. But there the meaning is absolutely unconscious. One does not know toward what one moves. One does not know by what one is propelled. The lines of communication between the conscious and the unconscious zones of the human psyche have all been cut, and we have been split in two.

The hero-deed to be wrought is not today what it was in the century of Galileo. Where then there was darkness, now there is light; but also, where light was, there now is darkness. The modern hero-deed must be that of questing to bring to light again the lost Atlantis of the co-ordinated soul.[112]

The dangerous tendency of individualism arises from the effort to advance individuals at the expense of society. Considering the problem from a holistic view of society, we simply cannot do it. Advancement of individuals goes hand in hand with advancement of society. Had Einstein been born a thousand years earlier, he may have passed for an idiot. Whatever he might have been, he would not have been a nuclear scientist. Thus, even the most productive individuals are dependent on their own culture.

The role of complete individuality is untenable. It overextends the archetype of self. We are not independent. We are social animals. We are part of a population. Our extreme pressure for individual meaning, separate from the group, can have serious side effects. Pursuit of the image of individuality results in an ever-increasing feeling of loneliness and separation. *Self-actualization*, so highly touted by Maslow, only works *if* the individual establishes satisfactory relations with other people. Individualism can splinter the social fabric.

The quest for individuality is, at best, cyclical. Joseph Campbell writes:

But there is another way—in diametric opposition to that of social duty and the popular cult. From the standpoint of the way of duty, anyone in exile from the community is a nothing. From the other point of view, however, this exile is the first step of the quest. Each carries within himself the all; therefore it may be sought and discovered within.[113]

Thus, individualism, seen in its most favorable light, is the beginning point of the next higher round of socialization:

This is the stage of Narcissus looking into the pool, of the Buddha sitting contemplative under the tree, but it is not the ultimate goal; it is a requisite step, but not the end. The aim is not to see, but to realize that one is, that essence; then one is free to wander as that essence in the world. Furthermore: the world too is of that essence. The essence of oneself and the essence of the world: these two are one. Hence separateness, withdrawal, is no longer necessary. Wherever the hero may wander, whatever he may do, he

---

[112] Campbell, *The Hero With a Thousand Faces*, p. 388.
[113] Ibid., p. 385.

is ever in the presence of his own essence—for he has the perfected eye to see. There is no separateness. Thus, just as the way of social participation may lead in the end to a realization of the All in the individual, so that of exile brings the hero to the Self in all.[114]

The individual is inseparable from his social context.

Sexual Myths

A second mythical theme deeply embedded in modern society is sexuality. Perhaps we can view sexuality as a corollary of individualism. It certainly relates to individualism, but has a different focus. The hero always has his heroine and vice-versa. This is also an idealized theme which has roots in the Middle Ages. Both Joseph Campbell and Robert A. Johnson, a Jungian psychologist, use the medieval story of *Tristan and Isuelt* as a point of departure to introduce the myths of sex roles.

Robert A. Johnson presents an interesting Jungian analysis of the romantic love theme in his short book entitled *We*. According to Johnson (and Jung), both male and female are born with a full set of emotions and traits. We associate some emotions and traits with the masculine image, and some with the feminine image. The masculine role stresses analytic skills, aggressiveness and the like. The female image involves nurturing, feeling and a more submissive role. To achieve the male *role* type, the male represses the feminine characteristics. Repressed characteristics do not disappear but become a part of the man's unconscious. Repressed feminine characteristics unite in the man's unconscious to form an idealized image of *woman*. Likewise, repressed male characteristics become the *ideal* male within the unconscious of the female. Jung calls the *ideal* female repressed within the male the *anima*, and the *ideal* male repressed within the female the *animus*. These images are archetypes with immense energy.

When a man falls in love, he projects the repressed, idealized image of woman onto the actual, flesh and blood object of affection. The situation is just the opposite when a woman falls in love. She projects the ideal male onto the object of her affections. An energized bonding results. The results can be disastrous, since the *actual* love object may not measure up to the idealization. The idealization is an archetype. When the princess kisses the frog, he may still look green, slimy and warty to the rest of the world. In the princess' wonderful world of projection, he becomes a prince. I see these results repeatedly in domestic relations

---

[114]   Ibid., p. 386.

cases. Actually, the attachment to the image can become *worship*. It is not the workable sexual attraction between male and female. The archetype is more like a god than a human. The power of these images is strong and very evident in American society. When experience overcomes the projection, as sometimes happens, unhappiness results. Flesh and blood cannot measure up to the ideal.

Our society reflects the mythological theme of romantic love and the anima/animus archetype in thousands of ways. Dime store novels, country and western music, advertisements, movie stars, the Virgin Mary, Miss America, Cinderella, Snow White, Superman and Lois Lane, and football heroes and majorettes, are a few examples. The list is endless. The stories of heroes usually involve the romantic love scene. The archetypes *animus* and *anima* are alive and well in the world today, supporting a huge mythology.

Sexuality Robs Religion

In our society, overemphasis of individualism brings a burden of loneliness and separation. The individual seeks to discharge this burden in the warmth and comfort of romantic love. The problem is that the romantic love object cannot measure up. He or she is not a god or goddess. At the same time, we deny true religious impulse. Denial of religion directs all energy of the religious drive; i. e., the need for meaning, toward the romantic love object. A diversion of an important flow of energy occurs. It won't work. It is idolatry. It deprives life of meaning. Robert Johnson suggests that we should treat members of the opposite sex as such, and should put religion back in Church, or other appropriate religious practice.[115]

This whole theory helps explain why we do not understand religious symbolism very well. Religious symbolism was once very powerful, but today it often evokes little or no response. Our modern myths rob religious symbolism of its energy, and the displaced energy overflows into *romantic love*. Romantic love has its own set of symbols, mythical forms, and images.

To say that the theme of sexuality has a large amount of motive capability is probably the understatement of this century. The imagery of romantic love melds into mythology of individualism. This image, described in a thousand mythological themes, provides the warmth, the

---

[115] Johnson, *We*, pp. 165-166.

mystery, the impetus toward *belonging*. These comforting forces are missing in the icon of the individual.

Any fan of country and western music should be able to identify at least a hundred songs that vividly portray *worship* of the opposite sex. Interestingly, this theme has dominated country and western music since World War II. It was at about this time that large numbers of women joined the work force, first to aid the war effort, and later, to provide additional income. The divorce rate has gone up. Our mournful country music is telling us something. The theme is not subtle or hidden. One recently popular song says, "Come on Baby; don't say maybe; I've got to know if your sweet love is going to *save me*." Then there was, "You are my *special angel*, sent from up above," and, "There goes my only possession; there goes my *everything*." Not to mention, "When a man loves a woman, *she can do no wrong*. . . ." The songs even express the pervasive loneliness of individualism which was mentioned earlier. "I am, I said, to no one there; And no one heard at all, not even the chair; *Leaving me lonely still*. . . ."

Listen to any radio station with these thoughts in mind. Mythos is there, active and powerful. It teaches themes of individualism and sexuality. It teaches roles we are to play, and we play them according to the script. Not far beneath the surface of many country and western songs is the mournful grief of broken families, which is an unerringly accurate portrayal of society. These comments are not intended to criticize, but to recognize this useful art form. We can learn much from it.

Rationality

Individualism and sexuality express themselves religiously as humanism. Secular humanism as a value system established itself by using the powerful image of the individual. It idealizes (and possibly idolizes) the worth, potential, rational capacity, etc., etc., of the individual human being. Please do not think that this is a hasty conclusion without foundation in fact. Auguste Comte is one of the founders of sociology. He has had considerable influence in the social sciences. In an introductory note, Monroe Beardsley writes the following of Comte and his ideas:

> Probably no previous philosopher realized so fully the capacity of the concept of humanity as a whole to serve as a basic ethical concern for each person, and as a religious object. * * * And for all the fantastic and idiosyncratic elements that he came to attach to his original idea of a "religion of humanity" (his Catholic training led him to think that his humanistic

religion must be furnished with a priesthood, a "positivist calendar" of secular saints' days, a catechism, devotional gestures, and prayers), his essential idea of man's obligation to all his fellow men, and each man's oneness of destiny with the whole of the human race, past and future, has, in considerable part by the efforts of Comte himself, become a vital and effective religious ideal in many parts of the world.[116]

The principal archetype of this humanist religion is the hero. The self-image also contributes. Animus and anima are in the cast. Father, mother and child archetypes are not nearly as strong in the shaping mythology.

Rationality is the ultimate extension of this idealization of the individual. I suggest rationality as a third theme of modern myths. Reason is the most powerful weapon in the arsenal of the hero. Despite our obviously finite capacities, it is in rationality that we try in modern society to break through to the infinite. We see no limit for human rationality. Faith in Reason is the religion of modern science. Ultimately, it is no more than faith in our own finite selves. The rationality theme finds its expression in many forms in our mythos. Science fiction, space adventure, and most of the adventures of heroes are examples. Of course, the rationality theme is not missing in adventure stories for children. Lassie's great appeal lies more in her keen wit than in her loving disposition, so we project rationality onto the animal world. To sum up, the hero always wins because he is smarter, and he always gets the girl, although often for a one night stand rather than happily ever after.

Perhaps the cause for dislocation of religious energy into sexual romantic love relates to our faith in reason. Reason, like all gods, is a jealous god, and insists that we condemn traditional faith. Nevertheless, rationality is cold, crystalline, and uncaring. Rationality has the sympathy of a lawn mower. It says, "I will let you believe in me infinitely, but fate sets the plan of your life. Your thoughts are meaningless chemical and physical graffiti. I do not and will not love you." A member of the opposite sex does and will. For the lonely individual, questing for independent, rational existence, but finding only loneliness, the allurement is irresistible. Thus, the predominant mythological themes of our times produce an explosive combination.

---

[116] Beardsley, *The European Philosophers from Descartes to Nietzsche*, p. 731.

Other Products of Loneliness and Emptiness

C. G. Jung described emptiness as the crisis of the modern world. Victor Frankl emphasizes the importance of man's search for meaning.[117] Emptiness arises from inability to achieve the godlike state of individuality. Our quest for individuality isolates us from humanity. So we become prisoners within the walls of our individuality. We often try to escape from this miserable plight through sex, as was suggested above. Drugs and alcohol also temporarily break down these walls of the prison of individuality. They ease the pain of our separation. They soften the intensity of our loneliness and calm the frantic id pressures that are seeking release from this solitary confinement. The solution to such problems lies in reestablishing our bonds with humanity and with God. The bond with humanity has always been a part of the Christian faith. Christians are to love the Lord with heart, soul, mind and strength, and neighbor as self. They pray for God to forgive trespasses, "as we forgive those who trespass against us." If we can't love the neighbor whom we have seen, how can we love God whom we have not seen? All of this is New Testament mainline teaching.

We experience comfort in the warm touch of a friend, with no sexual overtones, but given to express concern. There are times when only the touch communicates. Comfort of religious experience and faith gives meaning to the otherwise endless, meaningless chain of cause and effect that is objective human experience. The quarrel of the Church is not with humanism. The Church invented humanism. The quarrel is with *secular humanism* that idolizes humanity and human rationality.

Humanist Values Based on Tradition

Modern mythological themes of individuality, rationality, and sexuality form the basis of what we sometimes call secular humanist values. The term *secular humanism* has taken on an emotional content that labels its users as narrow or perhaps fanatically religious persons. However, the literal meaning of the term is valuable in distinguishing non-theistic humanism from the humanism expressed in religion. The Christian religion has many *humanistic* values. Those values are persuasive in our society, and non-believers subscribe to many of them. There is an extensive group of people, many of them highly intelligent, who profess no religious faith but who obviously believe in the *human* values that

---

[117] Frankl, *Man's Search for Meaning.*

arose from religious tradition. Therefore the term *secular humanism* is a meaningful descriptive term.

Many values of secular humanism are the direct outgrowth of the Judeo-Christian heritage. This demonstrates the evolutionary nature of mythos, and culture itself. Tolerance, equality, intrinsic worth of every individual, a non-judgmental attitude and probably most values of humanism have their origin in Judeo-Christian values. Nevertheless, there are differences between religious values and their secular offspring. The basic difference lies in the ultimate view of reality. Each system hooks onto the infinite or the ultimate environment. The non-religious humanist hooks onto crystalline, ice-cold infinity of rational principle. It is a mere product or extrapolation of our own intellect. He connects to an amorphous, changing society with no purpose but its own continual existence. The more traditional religious person hooks onto a warm, living principle, a God who created all and takes a continuing personal interest in human affairs. The difference in perspective is real, and has significant impact on moral formation.

Impact on Law

Do the powerful mythological images and forces of individuality, sexuality and rationality play a part in the formation of our law? Of course, they do. The value system of culture comes from mythos. Mythos places its imprimatur on members of society. We described how this takes place in earlier chapters. Based on those mechanics, we can expect our mythos to have significant impact on specific contents of law, and the force of law.

I have shown the role of rationalism in law throughout the text. Rationality is the principal mythological basis of the legal system itself. We describe law as the *rule of reason;* the standard for conduct is the *reason*able person; proof beyond a *reason*able doubt is required for criminal convictions, and the list could go on and on. Individuality appears in law in endless contentions about *individual rights.* This is the source of ideas expressed in court opinions that cause many members of the public to think that the legal system protects criminals rather than victims of crime. The sexuality theme is abundantly clear in the plethora of divorces and child custody disputes, as well as many other issues.

Other Mythological Themes

At the outset of this chapter, I was careful to state that choosing these three dominating themes does not exclude others, and there are many others. For instance, materialism, and beliefs about economics, are fertile fields of inquiry. I have not attempted to systematically discuss these topics, since I believe that they are not central, but derivative issues. I believe that they are reflections of our values and belief systems. As we discussed the themes of individualism, sexuality, and rationality, you may have noticed that each of these mythological themes has roots in the Middle Ages. In a similar manner, there are mythological themes that have been undercurrents during the modern era. Some of them will be dominant themes in the future. It is hazardous to guess which ones will gain ascendancy. I believe, however, that some themes of the future are beginning to emerge.

One of these ideas is a revamping of our thoughts about our relationship to nature. Rationality has sought to control nature. Instead of the destiny of *control*, in the future we will become more concerned with finding our place in nature and respecting its life-giving forces. This theme has, in fact, been an undercurrent throughout the modern era, giving rise to some of the thoughts of Pascal, Rousseau, and Montesquieu. It has shown itself in romanticism, the theory of evolution, transcendentalism, and various forms of existentialism.

The trend of this theme is that we humans are a part of nature and that we must find our place in it. We must respect nature, and try not to let our rationality destroy it and us. The idea that humans are a part of nature, rather than something above nature, has likely come of age, and its mythology is beginning to spawn from our perceptions of this necessary relationship in the ultimate environment. This, of course, is one of the major themes of the present volume. The idea of natural ecology in which humans are merely a part of nature, stands in stark contrast to themes of individualism and rationality that have dominated the Western world for five centuries.

4 | Territoriality: A Case Study

E arlier, I argued that we find the basis for law in human motive. Norms themselves derive largely from collective psychology. Basic human needs give impetus for development of norms, and supply law's motive force. Jung's archetypes help to shape and direct motive forces of human nature toward specific social images which are ingrained in our psychic makeup. I also endorsed Emile Durkheim's idea of *collective representations*. The term describes shared social images that result in law. Jung's archetypes and Durkheim's collective representations may be one and the same phenomena described from differing vantage points. Together, they form a powerful psychosocial explanation for the force of law. Basic human needs act through those images to induce corporateness which is the essence of social life, and *ergo*, law.

Recognition of basic human needs as part of the motive force of law has two important effects. First, it clarifies a part of the motive basis for law. Natural law advocates argue that law that is not moral is just not law. I contend that, in a practical sense, law that does not include motive power for enforcement is not law. I am speaking of law as a force; not as a formality. I am not inviting courts, for instance, to invalidate principles enacted by the legislature because the court finds the principle lacks motive force. Secondly, recognition of basic human needs as a part of law's motive force introduces the element of survival into law. Survival, in turn, introduces *necessity* as one attribute that defines law. Social order is necessary for society's survival. Survival propensity of law makes the theory that I am describing quite consistent with Darwinism.

I have painted a big picture of the dynamic processes of law. Now it's time to put that picture into a frame—a big frame. The frame into which these processes fit is *territoriality*. It is a frame as big as the populated earth itself. Study of territoriality is a specific application of motives of psychology and sociology that I have already introduced. There is an ongoing debate about whether humans have a territorial instinct. The college textbook that I used as a student in 1963 did not even mention territoriality. The concept has found its way, grudgingly, into more recent texts, including later editions of the same text that I used. Similarly, collective psychology was not well understood and accepted at that time, but is better understood now. C. G. Jung received no mention in my college text, either, but is included in later texts. The importance of mythology is also better understood now than it was a few years ago. This strange combination of developments may explain why the theories described in this volume have not appeared earlier. For some strange reason, ideas that are pivotal in motive theory of law have only recently received broad acceptance. Territoriality fits in well with the system of motives, archetypes and collective representations that we have been describing. We will explore these relationships in this section.

Some results of territoriality are rather obvious.

(1) Territory defines *populations.*

(2) Populations create *mythos.*

(3) Mythos creates and reinforces *conscience* through family, as well as *collective psychology* through larger groups.

(4) Conscience establishes the *moral base* of the population through group dynamics and collective psychology.

(5) The moral base and collective psychology that supports it are foundations for the legal system.

(6) This entire holistic system promotes survival of the population.

What do we mean when we say that territory defines populations? Territoriality largely determines whether a particular man will meet a particular woman and whether they will have children. This, in turn, determines the speed with which desirable genetic characteristics become incorporated into a population. In short, territoriality determines genetics of populations based on sheer mathematical probabilities. Evolution proceeds through breeding populations, rather than individuals. Robert Ardrey, author of *The Territorial Imperative*, concluded that what he called *biological morality* exists for survival of the population of a particular species. He argued that territoriality produces biological morality.

The analysis outlined above is a very mathematical approach, based on genetics. Even in that very terse outline, we can see important relationships between territory and motive forces that result in law. But there is a deeper significance to territory. Territory is not merely physical location. Territoriality is an unconscious motivating factor of inestimable importance in formation of morals and law. Territoriality describes the relationship between the maturing, individuating person and the environment itself. Environment specifically includes the territorial area of the person's group. Moral formation happens at a particular place. *Home* is important, as family is important, and home is a place. We will explore this *psychological* aspect of territoriality in Chapter 4.1. Robert Ardrey is the prime mentor for this discussion.

As in most deep-seated psychological factors, psychological territoriality has its counterpart in mythology. Many mythological themes surround and underscore the importance of home and homeland. The heroine of *The Wizard of Oz* says over and over "There's no place like home." A well-known song has those same words as its title. Even the extraterrestrial *E. T.* talks about home. *Home* clearly has archetypal importance, expressed both in psychology and mythology.

Territoriality expresses itself in mythology in more subtle ways, dealing with organization of space. Myths organize the cosmos. We assign special value to certain space. Myths reflect this special value. Our beliefs organize the cosmos for us. Mircea Eliade, and his book *The Sacred and The Profane*, is the prime source of ideas for Chapter 4.2, which deals with *mythological territoriality*.

Eliade's approach is totally different from that of Ardrey. I believe that interaction of the two viewpoints is complementary. Neither Ardrey nor Eliade appeared to relate his ideas to those of the other. Against the background of psychology and mythology that we have already discussed, however, the ideas of Ardrey and Eliade fit together well.

Territoriality is a psychological principle, reflected also in mythology, that gives rise to specific legal principles. In the final chapter of this section, I show that territoriality is a paradigm for the theory that I am presenting. Psychological principles other than territoriality also give rise to legal principles.

Many animals in the wild stake off their territory in various ways. They repel intruders with force. Polar bears in captivity reportedly cannot live long without the moat that separates them from the visiting public. Too close exposure to the public causes nervous disorders for the bears. They must have a certain amount of privacy—a certain amount of space or territory. Examples of territorial behavior in the animal kingdom are plentiful, and there is ongoing debate as to whether humans are territorial.

Robert Ardrey described the *territorial imperative* in his popular book with that title, published in the 1960s. In it, he surveys the world of nature to expose the dynamic concept of territoriality. The book is fascinating. Ardrey argues passionately that the human species is territorial.

> Man, I shall attempt to demonstrate in this inquiry, is as much a territorial animal as is a mockingbird singing in the clear California night. We act as we do for reasons of our evolutionary past, not our cultural present, and our behavior is as much a mark of our species as is the shape of a human thigh bone or the configuration of nerves in a corner of the human brain. If we defend the title to our land or the sovereignty of our country, we do it for reasons no different, no less innate, no less ineradicable, than do lower animals. The dog barking at you from behind his master's fence acts for a motive indistinguishable from that of his master when the fence was built.[118]

Ardrey describes territoriality in species ranging from exotic birds to salmon, giving scores of interesting examples of territoriality. He makes a forceful argument for existence of an "open territorial instinct" in mankind. His contention for existence of an *open territorial instinct* is reminiscent of the Jungian argument for archetypes, and the Durkheimian argument for collective representations, and is quite similar to those two concepts. It also resembles Kant's *a priori* ideas. Ardrey distinguished *open instincts* from *closed instincts*. A closed instinct mandates

---

[118] Ardrey, *The Territorial Imperative*, p. 5.

certain deterministic, rigid behavior. Open instincts, on the contrary, are open to conditioning from environment. An open instinct is similar to what we described earlier as a genetic predisposition to duty. The effect of territoriality is strong attachment to a defined geographic, area or place.

Unexplained motive patterns which Ardrey describes, such as the homing instinct in certain species, afford ample evidence of the mystery of final causes. Many aspects of behavior are quite difficult to explain using traditional "cause produces effect" type logic. Territoriality certainly does not explain all human behavior, as Ardrey himself admitted.

> In a way it is a pity that we must isolate from all that rich carpet of human impulse a single pattern for contemplation. No man or other animal lives as other than a whole being. If I am a dominant male lion with a vast impressive mane, then at once I am a predator seeking candidates for my next meal, or I shall grow unbearably hungry; I am also prey, and I must keep a wary nostril for men carrying guns, or I shall end up decorating somebody's wall; I am a proprietor, and I must keep rival lions out of my hunting territory, or game will grow scarce; I am a husband, and when one of my wives comes into heat then I must entertain her; I am a father, and with due regard to future lion generations I must brook no nonsense from my cubs while teaching them all I can; and I am also a social being for, sad to confess, I am deathly slow on my feet and an appallingly bad hunter except at close quarters, so I am dependent on the assistance of my wives and my friends, and whether I like them or not I must somehow get along with them.

> If I am a lion I am many things at once, and if I am a man I am even more. And so it may seem a temptation toward unreal simplification to select a single aspect of the human condition with which to absorb ourselves. And indeed it is most surely a temptation and an almighty hazard. In precisely such fashion some have reduced men to a sexual symbol, and others have excavated him like a kitchen midden, as if he were nothing but a cultural accumulation, and still others have embalmed him in economic determinism, like many of our friends on both sides of the iron curtain. Shall we not when we are done have reduced him to a walking territorial principle? Well, I can only say that I find myself dedicated to man's elevation, not his reduction; to his desimplification and not his distillation to a pale white definitive liquid. I shall do what I can.[119]

Ardrey was wise to limit the all-encompassing effect of territoriality. We have already shown that many other psychological factors bear on human conduct, and I use territoriality as one example. Territoriality is a

---

[119] Ibid., pp. ix and x.

good subject to isolate for more detailed consideration. It is an excellent example for exposing relationships among psychology, mythology, and law.

Personal Space

Closely associated with psychology of territoriality is the psychology of personal space. Humans require a certain amount of space for survival. Space for the body itself is obvious, but additional space is necessary. We could not live long in a plaster of Paris cast. Cliches in the vernacular such as "breathing room" and "elbow room" recognize the need for living space. Space is necessary for survival.

We recognize personal space in subtle ways. Everyone in a group in an elevator faces the door. To do otherwise has definite psychological implications.[120] We make certain signs of apology if, because of crowding, we cannot turn around and face the door. The problem is invasion of personal space. Standing face to face in close quarters produces discomfort for people who are not intimate.

Jurors tend to return to the same seat in the jury box. Usually, this happens naturally, without prompting. When a non-conformist juror changes seats after a recess, it causes mild upset to other jurors. He or she has invaded their territory. Church pews are often the subject of territoriality. Church members lay claim to a particular pew. I have heard stories of the usual occupants of a particular pew asking an unsuspecting visitor to move from their pew! In our homes, most of us occupy the same seats at the table at all family meals. In the den, daddy has his chair. All these are examples of territoriality. We could possibly describe these events some other way. Orderliness, self-esteem, and the like could explain them. Despite other possible explanations, however, there seems to be a central characteristic of territoriality in the human species. Space does not allow a lengthy argument about the existence of territoriality in humans, and I am simply agreeing with those who contend that humans are territorial.

Home and the Homing Instinct

Central to the idea of territoriality is the concept of home. Ardrey gave many illustrations of the homing instinct, involving many varieties and species of animals. All of us have known examples of dogs and cats that have returned home despite overwhelming odds. A catchy tune

---

[120]   See Fast, *Body Language*, p. 22.

years ago called *The Cat Came Back* captured this proclivity of felines. Perhaps because humans think and are reflective, we believe that we do not share territorial instinct of lower animals. Consciousness obviously thinks it is responsible for most behavior. We are not fully conscious of our attachment to territory.

However, *home* is one of the brightest in our repertoire of images. If the father image helps us form our image of God, home is certainly the analog of heaven. In popular gospel music, such terms are often interchanged. Home is not just people whom we associate with our place of residence or place of origin. It is the place itself. True, we become melancholy when we miss people from the old house and old community. However, the call of territory itself is also real. I was eight years old when we moved away from the two room house in which I was born to a larger, more comfortable house. The family was the same, and everyone was there. Nevertheless, I experienced homesickness for the old place for a while after the move.

Sentiments of attachment expand to include a larger geographical area as we mature. School, churches, restaurants, stores and mills take their places in sentiment. As we grow older we often return to scenes of childhood. Is it mere idle curiosity that brings us to engage in such activities? No, we relate to our territory as we do to our group. Eventually, our nation, our *homeland*, seizes the power of territoriality. Territoriality becomes patriotism, and the nation state is the beneficiary. All of this is a part of and arises from our cognitive and emotional organization of the cosmos.

Legal Implications of Territoriality

What could territoriality possibly have to do with law? First, let's consider property law. What is the elaborate system of Anglo-American law of real property other than an effort to *stake off territories*? Did God lay the world off in one-mile squares? Were those squares merely discovered by surveyors in early days of this country? This question provides an interesting analogy for proponents of legal positivism, who would say that neither a given set of land lines nor a given set of rules is a product of nature. However, this argument underestimates the importance of psychological tendencies that require both land lines and rules, and produce them in our belief systems. Obviously, God did not physically lay out land in the pattern of modern surveys. We have imposed on geography a rational, mathematical, geometrical system of descriptions. Motive to do so is innate, however. This is paradigmatic of the entire legal system, which is composed of rationality superimposed on innate motive factors. To show that a pattern of dealing with the world is human in origin does not eliminate mystery and necessity for faith until we solve the enigma of human existence.

It is difficult to offer any explanation of real estate law that does not resolve itself to some aspect of territoriality. We combine modern geometrical designs, carefully surveyed angles, lines and curves, with primordial urgings of territoriality. In this combination of emotion and reason, we see an example of the essence of law. Once a land line is laid out, and we come to believe in it, we are ready to fight for it. Territoriality and real estate law illustrate the principle for which I am contending. Motive forces of psychology, shaped by socializing tendencies, are foundations of legal principle.

Understanding this relationship of psychological principle to law is important. In my rural circuit, land values are now somewhat greater than they were a few years ago, and this gives rise to disputes about land lines. New owners frequently assert claims to property where previous owners had allowed problematical lines to go unchallenged because of ties of friendship and neighborliness. I have tried many cases involving land line disputes. Frequently, the quantity of land actually in dispute is worth no more than a small fraction of the cost of litigation. There is no way to view the litigation as *rational* from an economic viewpoint. Parties spend thousands of dollars disputing an area that may not be worth $500. When pressed on this point, the stock response from litigants is "It's a matter of principle." Lawyers say, "The parties couldn't reach an agreement. There is no way to resolve the matter but to go to court." Feelings of parties in such cases are very intense—far beyond what any *reasonable* assessment of the problem justifies.

Understanding psychology of territory helps to resolve legal disputes about land lines. Psychoanalysts hold that transferring unconscious matters to consciousness allows patients to deal more effectively with their problem. If the patient becomes conscious of repressed matters that are manifesting themselves in mental disturbances, he can accommodate to the problem. This helps resolve the disturbance. It works. It also works in land line disputes! I have found in many cases that a mere discussion of rational, economic implications, such as splitting the difference between two claimed lines, has little impact. Proposed economic solutions seldom work in land line cases. However, a discussion of such factors *combined with* discussion of the psychology involved often brings about a settlement. I don't really know whether wild dogs urinate on bushes to stake their territory or not. I've read that they do. When land line litigants begin to see themselves in this light, however, they often reevaluate their differences!

Recruits to Israeli Armed Forces take their oath of office atop the rock of Masada. There Jewish zealots made a last heroic stand against Hadrian's Roman legions and fought to the death. Symbolically, recruits are pledging to do the same to defend their territory. There can be little doubt that psychological territoriality is a major organizing social force with significant impact on dynamics of law.

Territoriality affects many areas of law other than real estate law. It becomes patriotism for nation states, and positivists believe nation states to be the source of law. However, before we develop further the connection between psychology of territoriality and law, we need to follow up another point. Throughout earlier chapters, we have insisted on a strong connection between mythology and psychology. We have suggested that mythology shapes psychological formation of individuals born into a particular society, so that group norms can be effective. If our hypothesis is correct, then we should be able to find territoriality reflected in mythology.

When we talk about territoriality, we are not dealing with simple geometric space with fungible economic value nor with the homogenous space of physics. Mircea Eliade has shown that for certain purposes, space is not homogeneous and interchangeable. Certain space has more *value* than other space. He referred to such space as sacred space. Eliade argues:

> For religious man, space is not homogeneous; he experiences interruptions, breaks in it; some parts of space are qualitatively different from others. "Draw not nigh hither," says the Lord to Moses; "put off thy shoes from off thy feet, for the place whereon thou standest is holy ground" (Exodus, 3, 5). There is, then, a sacred space, and hence a strong, significant space; there are other spaces that are not sacred and so are without structure or consistency, amorphous. Nor is this all. For religious man, this spatial nonhomogeneity finds expression in the experience of an opposition between space that is sacred—the only *real* and *real-ly* existing space—and all other space, the formless expanse surrounding it.[121]

Personal space in our mythology also has psychological energy. The foray of a pulpwood cutter across the property owner's perception of "the line," is not merely an economic problem. It is a violation of personal space. It is an assault or invasion. It is personal. It violates the territorial imperative.

An old country doctor delivered me into this world at home. My parents gave his name, Philip, to me. The doctor lived several miles away and maintained an office a few steps from his home in a plain, frame structure. For the folks in that community and time, that office was the destination in time of illness. If one could only make it to Dr. Lightfoot's office, there was hope. There was confidence that his medicine would help. The office was a mysterious place to us. It was special. There were medicinal odors, and an awesome aura enveloped the place.

---

[121] Eliade, *The Sacred and the Profane*, p. 20.

In time, the doctor died. My older brother married his granddaughter and they live in the doctor's old home. The old office still stands. It is a collecting place for unused furniture and other *garage* or *attic* items that one never uses but can't bear to discard. I have often pondered the disappearance of the power of the place. I still feel a tinge of awe when I visit the old place, even amid collecting dust and disabled furniture. I had similar feelings visiting an old church that had been deconsecrated. The psychological non-homogeneity of space is all around us, if we are but sensitive to the matter. The emotional pull is there, of course, whether we are conscience of it or not; but it is not unusual for us to be unconscious of important psychological forces.

Why are Gettysburg and Arlington important to us? Is it purely because of historical interest that we visit historical battlefields and tombs of our fallen leaders? I think not. I believe there is a mystery that attracts us, built into the human psyche. It is a part of what Eliade described. Religious pilgrimages to Holy Lands are clear examples of the attractive power and value of mythical space.

Christians bury their dead with the head to west, facing east. This custom is widespread, if not universal. A Black man who had retired in Detroit moved to Macon County into the community in which I lived. He was murdered in what reports described as a "gangland style" killing. His family buried him on land that he owned, intending to begin a family burial plot. They aligned the grave north/south, rather than in the customary east/west fashion. One of our Black friends expressed deep concern that they buried him "cross-wise to the world."

Mythology Organizes the Cosmos

It is interesting to speculate how humans first got a conscious sense of spatial organization. How did they learn to communicate directions such as north, south, east, and west, using those abstract terms? The burial ritual, head to west, facing the rising sun, with its attendant emotion, may have preceded the abstract concept of *east*. This speculation reminds us of Durkheim's theory of collective representations and the origin of categories. It also is a good example of how *mental* phenomena impress themselves on physical data. After all, besides our need to interpret and explain, where does north exist physically? Where is west? These are not terms that relate to a physical reality. They are terms that enable more than one person to share in an orientation. They are pure abstractions, and exist only in our minds, and are useful only because *we all* share them.

Mythology provides a beginning point in the process of orientation. An individual might know how far and what direction to travel to get from a village to a particular lake or grove. He would have to be personally familiar with the points. The individual might even have a *sense of direction*. However, without mutual orientation, abstracted to words, one person would have difficulty describing a route to someone else. Actually, many animals have a sense of direction. However, there is no evidence that they communicate directions to others in abstract terms. So far as we are aware, they know nothing about *north, south, east and west* as such.

This system of orientation or organization, along with others, including law itself, begins in mythology. Belief systems of early people establish (1) a center of the world, (2) the four directions, and (3) horizons, beyond which there are great dangers. All of these are important aspects of territoriality. Myths of origin also connect groups of people with a particular territory. Even though our perception of the cosmos is much more complex than these simple components, our thought processes have not discarded these components. They remain a part of our orientation. First we will explore the idea of the *center of the world*.

Establishment of the Center of the World

Human perception or experience of space, or territory, is an organizing principle. Mythology reflects the primordial psychology of space, as well as of time. Eliade shows how mythology is an organizing principle, spreading from a mythologically established center of the world. Eliade summarizes some of these matters:

> [T]he religious experience of the nonhomogeneity of space is a primordial experience, homologizable to a founding of the world. It is not a matter of theoretical speculation, but of a primary religious experience that precedes all reflection on the world. For it is the break effected in space that allows the world to be constituted, because it reveals the fixed point, the central axis for all future orientation. When the sacred manifests itself in any hierophany, there is not only a break in the homogeneity of space; there is also revelation of an absolute reality, opposed to the nonreality of the vast surrounding expanse. The manifestation of the sacred ontologically founds the world. In the homogeneous and infinite expanse, in which no point of reference is possible and hence no *orientation* can be established, the hierophany reveals an absolute fixed point, a center.[122]

---

[122] Ibid., pp. 20-21.

A legend of how Alabama got its name illustrates the *center of the world* principle. I take it verbatim from my seventh-grade Alabama history book. This legend is entirely innocent of mythological interpretation by the authors. However, its mythological meaning and quality are perfectly clear.

> Many years ago, before any people lived in what is today the State of Alabama, an Indian tribe was said to have wandered over the continent of North America seeking the most desirable location for a permanent home. At the close of each day a camp site was selected. Here the chief thrust his staff into the soil. The following morning, the band moved in the direction in which the staff was leaning; that is, if the staff leaned toward the north, the band moved in this direction; if it leaned west, the group travelled that day in a westerly direction. But, one morning the staff was standing straight; during the night, it had not moved in any direction. So, seeing it, the chief said, "Alabama! We will go no farther. This is a good land. Here we rest."
>
> Alabama is an Indian word. It is said to mean "clear the thicket," which suggests making a permanent home, in terms of one task that confronted many of the first settlers.
>
> Years later, the words, *Here We Rest*, were made part of the Great Seal of the State.[123]

The fact that I remember this story forty years after I first heard it speaks to the unusual power of the mythological theme. Precisely the same theme is reflected in the story of the Israelites following pillars of fire and cloud.

Eliade describes how several different religions organize the cosmos, emphasizing the importance of the center of the world, or *axis mundi*. Eliade contended:

> To us, it seems an inescapable conclusion that *the religious man sought to live as near as possible to the Center of the World*. He knew that his country lay at the midpoint of the earth; he knew too that his city constituted the navel of the universe, and, above all, that the temple or the palace were veritably Centers of the World. But he also wanted his own house to be at the Center and to be an *imago mundi*. And, in fact, as we shall see, houses are held to be at the Center of the World and, on the microcosmic scale, to reproduce the universe. In other words, the man of traditional societies could only live in a space opening upward, where the break in plane was symbolically assured and hence communication with the *other world*, the transcendental world,

---

[123] Parks and Moore, *The Story of Alabama, A State History*, pp. 3-4.

was ritually possible. Of course the sanctuary—the Center par excellence—was there, close to him, in the city, and he could be sure of communicating with the world of the gods simply by entering the temple. But he felt the need to live at the Center *always*— like the Achilpa, who, as we saw, always carried the sacred pole, the *axis mundi*, with them, so that they should never be far from the Center and should remain in communication with the supraterrestrial world. In short, whatever the dimensions of the space with which he is familiar and in which he regards himself as situated—his country, his city, his village, his house—religious man feels the need always to exist in a total and organized world, in a cosmos.[124]

The center of the world is a place where there is a break in the plane of the three tiered world. Apparently, the perception of a three tiered world is widespread in mythology. It consists of the upper world (heaven), the middle world (the earth's surface), and the underworld. The underworld is not always associated with hell or evil forces. The ordinary world opens to the sacred. Earth communicates with heaven. This gives the world authenticity. Eliade went on:

> [W]e could say that the experience of sacred space makes possible the "founding of the world": where the sacred manifests itself in space, *the real unveils itself*, the world comes into existence. But the irruption of the sacred does not only project a fixed point into the formless fluidity of profane space, a center into chaos; it also effects a break in a plane, that is, it opens communication between the cosmic planes (between earth and heaven) and makes possible ontological passage from one mode of being to another. It is such a break in the heterogeneity of profane space that creates the center through which communication with the transmundane is established, that, consequently, founds the world, for the center renders *orientation* possible. Hence the manifestation of the sacred in space has a cosmological valence; every spatial hierophany or consecration of a space is equivalent to a cosmogony. The first conclusion we might draw would be: *the world becomes apprehensible as world, as cosmos, in the measure in which it reveals itself as a sacred world.*[125]

Eliade's excellent work conveys the strong psychological/mythological nature of our attachment to territory. Eliade continued:

> But since to settle somewhere, to inhabit a space, is equivalent to repeating the cosmogony and hence to imitating the work of the gods, it follows that, for religious man, every existential decision to situate himself in space in

---

[124] Eliade, *The Sacred and the Profane*, pp. 43-44.
[125] Ibid., pp. 63-64.

fact constitutes a religious decision. By assuming the responsibility of creating the world that he has chosen to inhabit, he not only cosmicizes chaos but also sanctifies his little cosmos by making it like the world of the gods. Religious man's profound nostalgia is to inhabit a "divine world," is his desire that his house shall be like the house of the gods, as it was later represented in temples and sanctuaries. In short, this religious nostalgia expresses *the desire to live in a pure and holy cosmos, as it was in the beginning, when it came fresh from the Creator's hands.*[126]

Joseph Campbell echoes his findings. It is a pattern consistently found in mythology. Campbell tied territoriality specifically to mythology.

> For a culture still nurtured in mythology the landscape, as well as every phase of human existence, is made alive with symbolical suggestion. The hills and groves have their supernatural protectors and are associated with popularly known episodes in the local history of the creation of the world. Here and there, furthermore, are special shrines. Wherever a hero has been born, has wrought, or has passed back into the void, the place is marked and sanctified. A temple is erected there to signify and inspire the miracle of perfect centeredness; for this is the place of the breakthrough into abundance. Someone at this point discovered eternity. The site can serve, therefore, as a support for fruitful meditation. Such temples are designed, as a rule, to simulate the four directions of the world horizon, the shrine or altar at the center being symbolical of the Inexhaustible Point. The one who enters the temple compound and proceeds to the sanctuary is imitating the deed of the original hero. His aim is to rehearse the universal pattern as a means of evoking within himself the recollection of the life-centering, life-renewing form.[127]

Campbell also describes the mythology of directions and horizons, both of which are important for our purposes. Campbell continued:

> Ancient cities are built like temples, having their portals to the four directions, while in the center place stands the major shrine of the divine city founder. The citizens live and work within the confines of this symbol. And in the same spirit, the domains of the national and world religions are centered around the hub of some mother city: Western Christendom around Rome, Islam around Mecca. The concerted bowing, three times a day, of the Mohammedan community throughout the world, all pointing like the spokes of a world-extensive wheel to the centering Kaaba, constructs a vast, living symbol of the "submission" (*islam*) of each and all to Allah's will.

---

[126] Ibid., p. 65.
[127] Campbell, *The Hero With a Thousand Faces*, p. 43.

"For it is He," we read in the Koran, "that will show you the truth of all that ye do." Or again: a great temple can be established anywhere. Because, finally, the All is everywhere, and anywhere may become the seat of power. Any blade of grass may assume, in myth, the figure of the savior and conduct the questing wanderer into the sanctum sanctorum of his own heart.[128]

Thus we see that mythology organizes territory of a particular group by providing a center, directions, and horizons or boundaries.

Directions

Emile Durkheim explains the origin of directions, fitting them into his sociological origins of categories as collective representations.

(S)pace is not the vague and indetermined medium which Kant imagined; if purely and absolutely homogeneous, it would be of no use, and could not be grasped by the mind. Spatial representation consists essentially in a primary co-ordination of the data of sensuous experience. But this co-ordination would be impossible if the parts of space were qualitatively equivalent and if they were really interchangeable. To dispose things spatially there must be a possibility of placing them differently, of putting some at the right, others at the left, these above, those below, at the north of or at the south of, east or west of, etc., etc., just as to dispose states of consciousness temporally there must be a possibility of localizing them at determined dates. That is to say that space could not be what it is if it were not, like time, divided and differentiated. But whence come these divisions which are so essential? By themselves, there are neither right nor left, up nor down, north nor south, etc. All these distinctions evidently come from the fact that different sympathetic values have been attributed to various regions. Since all the men of a single civilization represent space in the same way, it is clearly necessary that these sympathetic values, and the distinctions which depend upon them, should be equally universal, and that almost necessarily implies that they be of social origin.[129]

It is easy to understand how the concept of *direction* originates in myths. American Indians of the southeastern United States were sun worshipers. There were many legends about the sun. These legends brought into focus the *direction* from which the sun always appeared, and the direction in which it disappeared. These directions were noticeable, consistent, and communicable. Mythical stories did not explain so much as make these directions communicable.

---

[128] Ibid., pp. 43-44.
[129] Durkheim, *The Elementary Forms of the Religious Life*, pp. 23-24.

Orientation to the right arm and left arm, while facing in the direction of the rising sun, rounded out the four directions. In Indian mythology, colors sometimes represented directions. This is a method of abstraction.[130] We frequently use color codes to create filing systems. With these abstractions came a sense of direction that members of the tribe could share in words.

Horizons

Establishing horizons was of considerable importance in the organization of the world. Mythology dealt with this important matter. For instance, Romans recognized a god of boundaries, *Terminus*. The point is not that *nothing* exists beyond the horizons, but that *danger* exists beyond horizons. Beyond horizons lie unknown and fearful beings. Beyond horizons lies the *wasteland*. The wasteland theme recurs in mythology and literature. Campbell, in his *Creative Mythology*, presents interesting modern applications of the theme. T. S. Elliot's famous poem bears that name. The modern world has lost some of the geographic significance of the wasteland theme, but the theme's psychological force now evidences itself in other ways. For a person not included in the culture, or not accepted in mythos of the culture, the very country of residence may be a wasteland.

Horizons served the very useful function of keeping the tribe or clan together. Campbell describes the matter well.

> With the personifications of his destiny to guide and aid him, the hero goes forward in his adventure until he comes to the "threshold guardian" at the entrance to the zone of magnified power. Such custodians bound the world in the four directions—also up and down—standing for the limits of the hero's present sphere, or life horizon. Beyond them is darkness, the unknown, and danger; just as beyond the parental watch is danger to the infant and beyond the protection of his society danger to the member of the tribe. The usual person is more than content, he is even proud, to remain within the indicated bounds, and popular belief gives him every reason to fear so much as the first step into the unexplored. Thus the sailors of the bold vessels of Columbus, breaking the horizon of the medieval mind—sailing, as they thought, into the boundless ocean of immortal being that surrounds the cosmos, like an endless mythological serpent biting its tail—had to be cozened and urged on like children, because of their fear of the fabled leviathans, mermaids, dragon kings, and other monsters of the deep.

---

[130] Lankford, *Native American Legends.* This book contains an excellent collection of American Indian legends originating in the Southeast.

The folk mythologies populate with deceitful and dangerous presences every desert place outside the normal traffic of the village.[131]

Implications of horizons are many. People beyond the horizon may not be due the same respect, for instance, as people within the perimeters. Claude Levi-Strauss writes:

Primitive societies have, and not without justification, been said to treat the limits of their tribal group as the frontiers of humanity and to regard everyone outside them as foreigners, that is, as dirty, coarse sub-men or even non-men: dangerous beasts or ghosts.[132]

He goes on to show that totemic classifications may tend to break down these frontiers and "promote an idea something like that of a humanity without frontiers." These ideas expressed by Levi-Strauss and Campbell also support the idea of an archetype that I suggested earlier of the *enemy*, or *stranger*. The archetype has lots of names, such as *gentile*, *barbarian* and even our gentle word *foreigner*. The word *foreigner* often takes on unfavorable emotional coloration. For purposes of the present discussion, this is significant because of the obvious territorial association. There is a certain element of truth, and definite propensity for survival in these orientations. The modern mind has not escaped this primitive orientation. We are often fearful of neighborhoods beyond our own.

Metaphorical *horizons* can be a limiting factor in today's world for many people. This is a commonly used figure of speech. For instance, we say that education expands a person's horizons. However, the modern absence of actual physical horizons or boundaries poses its own set of problems, including possible loss of identity. Massive consolidation of community based schools may have a negative impact on identity and moral formation. Thus, territoriality is a matter that deserves careful attention. Mythology and psychology of territory are important parts of our way of thinking. They organize the world in which we live.

Myths of Origin

Myths of origin add an interesting insight into the mythology of territory. Myths of origin operate at several different levels. For instance, there are myths that deal with the origin of earth and skies, or the cosmos. All great religions have their holy places and they are quite rele-

---

[131] Campbell, *The Hero With a Thousand Faces*, pp. 77-78.
[132] Levi-Strauss, *The Savage Mind*, p. 166.

vant to this discussion of territoriality. Conflicts in today's world certainly evidence this point. Although these myths are quite important, they are not our immediate concern. Local, perhaps more primitive, myths of origins of groups demonstrate more clearly the connection between psychology and mythology of territory. Once the point is made, it is easy to understand how the great religions have an even more far-reaching impact. They are more abstract and mystical.

Myths of origin are widespread. Often myths from widely separated locations take an identical form or theme, even in very diverse cultural settings. One such widespread myth of origin has the ancestor of the clan emerging from the earth. Malinowski reports such myths of origin among the Trobriand Islanders.[133] Lankford provides the following legend from the Creek Indians who occupied the area in which I now live.

> Of their Origin or coming into the Country, some old Mingoes [chiefs] relate, that they lived under the Earth in great Darkness and saw no Sun; they hunted, but got nothing, they lived upon Linowa (Mice) which they killed with their Hands; the Ground Hog had worked a Hole through the Ground, through which some of them crept out, ran about upon the Earth, and finding a dead Deer, they brought the Meat into the Earth: the good Taste of it, and the Account of how light and fine it was upon the Earth, brought them to the Resolution, to go out of their dark Place; some stayed behind, those coming forth, began to plant Corn etc. etc.[134]

The close semi-historic attachment to the soil helps to explain their "passionate love of the soil."[135] Malinowski sums up this attachment to the soil and puts it into perspective. He shows how all of this ties into social order, including the legal system.

> The traditional feeling of a real and intimate connection with the land; the concrete reality of seeing the actual spot of emergence in the middle of the scenes of daily life; the historical continuity of privileges, occupations, and distinctive characters running back into the mythological first beginnings— all this obviously makes for cohesion, for local patriotism, for a feeling of union and kinship in the community. But although the narrative of original emergence integrates and welds together the historical tradition, the legal principles, and the various customs, it must also be clearly kept in mind that

---

133 Malinowski, *Primitive Psychology*.
134 Lankford, *Native American Legends*, p. 111.
135 Levi-Strauss, *The Savage Mind*, p. 243.

the original myth is but a small part of the whole complex of traditional ideas.[136]

Myths of origin integrate with myths of the center of the world, the horizons, the wasteland, the four directions and others. Together, they produce a socially useful web of belief that serves the social order of the clan or tribe. They provide a common orientation, which, through more complex myths and beliefs, establishes a basis for communication. Thus, shared beliefs direct emotional energy into useful social channels. It is not my purpose to present this configuration as a universal schema of belief. There are other myths of origin. Myths vary in content and in the way they fit together. The important point is the social significance of the myths as the source of organizing principles. Configuration of the cosmos, and the place of humanity in it, is an important function of mythology. It would be possible to show, in a similar fashion, that our orientation in time originates in mythos.

Territoriality and Identity

Eliade, Campbell, Durkheim, Malinowski, Levi-Strauss and others plumb the depths of psychology and mythology of territory. As their analyses unfold, it becomes clear that *psychology* of territory relates closely to mythological themes of humankind. The present discussion confirms earlier discussions of psychology and mythology. The moral base includes territoriality as a part of its foundation. Territoriality and the population concepts which it affects, involve the perception of the self—of identity. Territoriality tells us who we are and helps to define our relationships to other people. I am an American from Tallassee, Alabama, for instance. More importantly for the purpose of my identity as author of this book, I was born in Macon County, Alabama. Place of origin is frequently the historical source of proper names. Thomas Aquinas' name identifies the Italian village which was the home of his family.

The importance of this point is easy to overlook or underestimate in our highly mobile society. I have known several seemingly detached people, for whom the desire to own a small piece of land assumed a dimension far beyond reason. Their number includes members of the military and Methodist preachers. All of us need a place where we belong. One problem of mobility and seeming detachment is the loss of

---

[136] Malinowski, *Primitive Psychology*, p. 44.

connection to territory. Territorial attachment fits with Maslow's *belongingness* need.

The importance of territory is clear in the living mythology of the modern world. Popular songs lift the appeal of *home*. Songs glorify states, rural life, small towns, and dozens of other territorial designations. Nationalism appeals to the *homeland*. Regional identification, such as the *South* or the *North* demand identification and allegiance in folklore. Countries such as Ireland, Scotland, Italy, China and Greece and the continent of Africa have a strong call on their nationals and descendants of nationals living in the United States. Establishment of the nation of Israel, and immigration there by Jewish people from all over the world, is a poignant example of territoriality. Its continuing impact on the surrounding area after more than forty years of existence evidences strength of territoriality. The involvement of mythos is obvious. Without an Old Testament, there probably would be no modern Israel.

Territory makes a moral demand that we protect our own. We are urged to buy American products. Even as the cold war with communism subsides, American economic competition with Japan and Europe heats. We are concerned when *Americans* are detained or mistreated by other governments. We look to our government to protect *American* interests. All of this harks back to territoriality. Through territory, we relate to each other.

Interaction of the psychology and mythology of territory organizes space for us and allows us to orient ourselves. Territorial orientation produced by interaction of psychology and mythology of territory is a beginning point in defining our relationship to other people. We traditionally relate more favorably to those close to us than we do to those far away. Mobility of the modern world has blurred this distinction and the morality of solidarity that it engendered. Nevertheless, archetypes and collective representations of the old mythology and psychology linger, and exert profound influence on behavior. These remnants of mythology, deeply embedded in psychology help to form the basis of our social order. As we will see in the next chapter, territoriality lends its motive force far beyond the realm of real estate laws.

<table>
<tr><td>Chapter 4.3</td><td>Territoriality, Psychology and Law</td></tr>
</table>

Chapter 4.3	Territoriality, Psychology and Law

In this section, I am demonstrating how a particular psychological trait—territoriality—can result in specific law. I am using this specific trait to illustrate the motive theory of law that I described in preceding sections. In this chapter, I will show that territoriality is a psychological force that undergirds several areas of law. Territoriality is a good example of the relationship between psychology and law, since the relationship between territoriality and legal principles it supports is relatively easy to grasp. I discussed its rather obvious tie to real estate law earlier. However, territoriality supplies motive force to areas of law other than real estate law. Specific legal principles may draw motive force from more than one psychological trait. Likewise, one trait can support more than one legal principle. Therefore, it is not always easy to isolate a legal principle and show that it is supported by a particular psychological trait. Territoriality demonstrates just such a connection between law and psychology.

Territoriality appears in criminal law. A plea of self-defense is not available if the defendant has a safe route of escape. The defendant has a duty to retreat, if he can do so safely. However, the duty to retreat before using force to repel force ends at the defendant's *home*. When the defendant gets to his own *territory*, (in this instance, the home) the duty to retreat ends. Burglary and trespass also arise from territorial considerations. Both are offenses against territory. Again, in criminal law, we deal with *illegal searches and seizures*. Which warrantless searches are illegal? Searches of areas in which the defendant has a *right to expect privacy*. Does that sound familiar? It is pure territoriality secured by law. It is a guarantee of space for individuals, into which society may not intrude. This territorial security reminds us of the preconditions to need satisfaction suggested by Maslow.

Likewise, the tort of *invasion of privacy* may have a territorial foundation. The territorial paradigm has clear implications in this relatively new cause of action. Courts base this tort on an inherent right of privacy, in part. Privacy is a facet or analogy of *personal space,* or territorial allocation. Concepts of venue and jurisdiction are centered in territoriality.

In mobile modern society, a driver takes his personal space with him. There are interesting theoretical implications to this insight. We have a *side of the road.* The vehicle to the right has the *right of way.* One can *follow too closely.* Duties arise from these mobile configurations of space. These duties are very significant principles of tort law.

Thus, humans occupy the surface of the earth in complex patterns of territorial allocation, large and small. This allocation is a necessary part of human orderliness. Study of feudal law leads one to suspect that the nation state itself evolved from these very patterns of territorial connection to land. The origin of the concept of human freedom may have originated in release from a tenure to land. National boundaries place territorial limits on power of a nation to regulate human conduct by law. Lawmaking power is defined by territory. Laws of burglary and trespass and the right of privacy protect us from other members of society. Constitutional provisions regulating search and seizure protect from governmental encroachment. Traffic rules allocate use of highway space. Zoning laws regulate land usage. Real estate laws define rights in land. These congeries of principles find a motive basis in territoriality, and our beliefs about them are firmly etched into our belief systems and mythology. Different cultures resolve territorial need in different ways, but it is always present, and asserts itself as a part of social order.

Territoriality is a facet of the basic need for survival. This discussion of territoriality shows how motives for law involve psychology. Basic needs give rise to both substantive and procedural principles of law. Needs express themselves through psychological and mythological dynamics that we have discussed. We state principles in words and back them with emotion. These principles, when articulated and authenticated, become legal principles.

Evidence of incorporation of territoriality into modern mythos is readily available. Songs about home abound. Deep sentiment attaches to *home.* On a larger scale, there is community. Also consider the well-recognized *home court advantage* in sports. Robert Ardrey pointed out that in nature, the defender of territory usually prevails. Patriotism is an expression of territoriality. We could extend the list of examples of territoriality reflected in mythos, but it is pointless to do so. Territoriality is a strong psychological force, reinforced by mythos. It is one of the motive forces of society, with dramatic impact in the dynamics of law. Territoriality affects modern western society as well as ancient or primitive societies.

Territoriality is obviously a factor in the psychological underpinning of the nation state. The nation state garners forces of patriotism to further its purposes. National boundaries draw on the powerful mythological force of the *horizon*. Internally, our histories serve as myths of origin. They generate strong emotional forces. We cannot overstate the importance of this connection. All of modern legal philosophy concerns itself with the relationship of law to the nation state. We have shown earlier that legal positivists trace law to the *command of the sovereign*. The territorial nation state is the embodiment of the sovereign. Natural law concerns itself with individual rights. It often sees the role of law as protecting individuals from encroachments of government, as reflected in the territorial nation state.

It all relates. Psychological principles that support sociological dynamics are as tightly interwoven as the various functions by which cells cause the human body to operate. A particular mythos springs from a particular population. Territory affects the characteristics of the population. Populations determine genetics, and vice versa. Genetics determine inward structures of psychology. Those structures react to mythos, in turn. It is massive and mind-boggling, an unending labyrinth. It is cyclical and self-perpetuating. Our mythos funds archetypes with identifying experience and taps onto their energy to enforce social organization. It also relates humankind to its larger environment, which includes the entire cosmos. Mythos is a part of the natural system of human ecology, and is due great respect. Law is a part of the social organization resulting from these complex dynamics.

Cultural Relativism

Discussion of territoriality affords a good opportunity to return to the earlier discussion of cultural relativism. If law derives naturally from psychological factors of human nature, and human nature is everywhere the same, why aren't laws everywhere the same? The answer is not difficult. Social needs merely mandate that a group reach *some* form of orderliness. They do not mandate a particular form. The opposite of law is chaos, but chaos has many opposites. As different racial stocks, ethnic differences, and different customs evolved in different ways in different places, so did the patterns of social order. The archetypes can be utilized in differing workable patterns. Pascal stated the problem of cultural relativism as well as it can be stated:

On what shall man found the order of the world which he would govern? Shall it be on the caprice of each individual? What confusion! Shall it be on justice? Man is ignorant of it.

Certainly had he known it, he would not have established this maxim, the most general of all that obtain among men, that each should follow the custom of his own country. The glory of true equity would have brought all nations under subjection, and legislators would not have taken as their model the fancies and caprice of Persians and Germans instead of this unchanging justice. We would have seen it set up in all the States on earth and in all times; whereas we see neither justice nor injustice which does not change its nature with change in climate. Three degrees of latitude reverse all jurisprudence; a meridian decides the truth. Fundamental laws change after a few years of possession; right has its epochs; the entry of Saturn into the Lion marks to us the origin of such and such a crime. A strange justice that is bounded by a river! Truth on this side of the Pyrenees, error on the other side.[137]

Differing geographic territories present differing exigencies of survival. For this discussion, it is not important that law evolved in different forms in different cultures. The significant point is that every culture must come to grips with territoriality and other psychological factors. All human beings exist in relationship to territory, and people of every culture exist in relationship to each other. Natural forces that produce orderliness are the same, whether or not actual measures and methods are the same. This is not a simplistic suggestion that geographic differences explain all differences in cultures. Physical separation alone during periods of social evolution accounts for many differences. Most social problems require only one of any number of possible solutions. Once a particular solution is adopted, it tends to become entrenched.

The entirety of the circuit in which I am judge is territory that Andrew Jackson took from the Creek Indians in the 1830s. Horseshoe Bend National Military Park is a national historic site. There, the Creek Indians made a stand in a large bend in the Tallapoosa River in the spring of 1813. The site is now part of my circuit. My circuit includes many places with Indian names, such as Tuskegee, Tallassee, Wedowee, Calebee, and Tallapoosa. Indians left names everywhere, but there are practically no Indians.

---

[137] Pascal, *Thoughts*, from *The European Philosophers from Descartes to Nietzsche*, p. 125.

Creek Indians had little concept of individual ownership of land. Each shared necessary living space with the tribe. Does this mean that the Indians lacked territoriality? History documents the answer well. White settlers opened the Federal Road from the Georgia line to settlements on the Tombigbee River in west Alabama in 1811. This violation of the Indians' *territory* was a major cause of the ensuing war.[138]

Intrusion into their territory incensed the Indians. They went on the warpath—much to their grief. Despite the superior weapons of the forces of Andrew Jackson and white soldiers, the Creeks thought that they would be safe—invincible—at Horseshoe Bend. They thought it was sacred. There was another battlefield farther downstream actually named *Holy Ground*. Native Americans had worked out their territoriality in a different manner than that of the English common law. They shared territory on a tribal basis, which served their needs very well. They believed the threat to their territory by outsiders was a threat to their survival—as indeed it was.

Other Psychological Forces

Territoriality illustrates how one specific psychological factor gives rise to specific legal principles. Territoriality also demonstrates the relationship among mythology, psychology, and law. I am not saying that we *should* enact laws in response to psychological principles, as objective data. We do it automatically. It is not necessary that we be conscious of territoriality as a concept in order to be affected by it. We are usually unaware of psychological forces at work in the origin of law. In fact, consciousness of psychological forces may undermine the rules they produce. Awareness of our prejudices and psychological leanings often makes us lean in the other direction. Nevertheless, psychological factors are intrinsically and dynamically a part of law. They are motive forces that cause law to happen. Mythos of society molds and supports psychology. Without these psychological forces, there would be no law. Mythology and belief systems mold, shape, preserve and perpetuate the system of social order. Rationality can improve law; but without motive forces I have described, it cannot make law.

Territoriality is only one psychological feature of humanity. Other traits, borne of basic needs, are also important. The needs—to survive, reproduce, achieve maximum potential, fit into the social structure, and relate to the cosmos—all play a part. They produce laws which promote

---

[138] See generally Halbert and Ball, *The Creek War of 1813 and 1814.*

their own satisfaction. Myths—ancient and modern—reflect and encompass them all. Robert Ardrey was careful to point out that we cannot explain all behavior by territoriality. He was right. I have used territoriality as an illustration of the larger principle for which I contend. Many other psychological forces contribute to social order.

Without developing the ramifications of each area of law and psychological principle, let me suggest a few relationships. Public law, municipal law, and corporate law relate directly to the herd instinct—the socialization drive itself. Criminal law arises from survival principles as well as territoriality. Any threat to the individual is a threat to society. The territorial principle undergirds property offenses, as well as property law. Tax law is a sublimated rational expression of the herd instinct. Mythologically, taxes relate to rituals of sacrifice or offering. The medium of exchange receives value by mutual acceptance and faith. We collect it into governmental coffers to promote corporate purpose. We buy security with our tax dollars. All of these psychological forces contribute to collective psychology. Collective psychology transforms them into social forces. The web of motive forces that produce law is vast and complex. This listing is illustrative, not exclusive. The forces exist in a continuum and are one, just as energy for satisfying human needs is one. In fact, the motive forces arise from energy that satisfies basic human needs. Their complexity mirrors the complexity of social existence.

Domestic law finds a basis in reproduction needs, as well as a host of other psychological needs. As we have shown in the chapter on conscience, family is the starting point in the moral formation of the child. Our society instinctively gave the family a preferred place in legal norms. Family was and is the basic building block. This is the way western civilization worked out its solution to a whole group of needs. The family arrangement frees energy for purposes other than reproduction. The family is economical of energy available for satisfying basic needs. Every member of the family has a counterpart among Jung's archetypes.

Once we understand all of this, it is somewhat irrelevant that different cultures accomplish the child-rearing task in different ways. There may be other ways to do it, but the family is extremely important in *our* system. Conscience, nurtured in the traditional family, is the bedrock of our system of social control.

Mythos reinforces and perpetuates solutions to social problems worked out by a particular society. Folk stories, songs, sermons, plays, literature, movies, books, and, ultimately, language itself reinforce norms that work for society. However, mythos of a given society is not fool-proof. Based on their mythos, the Creek Indians thought they were safe at Horseshoe Bend and Holy Ground. Their mythos duly incorporated the territorial principle. They fell victims to an ancient method of dealing with conflicts in mythos. The Nazis did not invent genocide. Ironically, the Old Testament is full of it, and "ethnic cleansing" is resurfacing in current events. It has appeared many times in the course of history. Nevertheless, Creek Indian mythos apparently worked all right before whites appeared. Even then, it alerted them to danger. A different, stronger, conflicting mythos proved their undoing.

Territoriality and Civil Rights

Territoriality plays a strange and obscure role in conflicts between African Americans and their neighbors of European descent. Dr. King, in his most powerful speeches compared his own role to that of Moses. Moses led the children of Israel out of bondage in Egypt, where they were considered, and considered themselves, to be aliens. Later, when the Jewish people were dispersed from their homeland, they "wept by the waters of Babylon." A Negro spiritual, drawing on this Biblical background declares "I am a poor wayfarin' stranger, travelin' in a foreign land," and "I'm a goin' over Jordan, I'm a goin' over *home.*" The lingering feelings of being torn from their homes in Africa, and forced into bondage in a land in which they felt no ownership or control comes through clearly. Their white neighbors often assign to Blacks the sinister archetype of the alien.

One significant law that emanated from the Civil Rights Movement was the Voting Rights Act. The Voting Rights Act and increased participation of Black voters has enabled Blacks to virtually control local governments in some rural Alabama counties, including Macon County. Many Blacks from other areas of the country have moved into Macon County. The historic pattern of Black migration northward is reversing itself. In a very real sense, territoriality is asserting itself in these predominantly Black areas. However, archetypal imagery of the *alien* may be directing all this activity, rather than being eliminated by it. Under the Voting Rights Act, segregation is reasserting itself in a checkerboard pattern that will present very difficult problems in the future. Separate is still not equal. Any system that requires continual classification of citizens according to racial stock, and appends rights to the classification, builds on existing archetypes if not stereotypes, that need to be culturally de-emphasized. For instance, if a man is Black and his wife is white, are their children Black or White? Can we attach rights to any such classification without defining the class? And if we use law to define the class, are we not rediscovering the kinds of laws that caused problems to begin with? Territoriality is a powerful and socially formative force, and great care should be exercised in allowing it to have full blown expression in shaping the future social structure of the South.

5 | Applications and Implications

nless a theory has practical application or effect, it is hardly worth developing. We are now ready to explore the significance of principles discussed up to this point. In this section, we will discuss some practical implications of the motive theory. Because of space limitations I must be selective in discussing applications and implications. The theory leads to many areas of possible discussion. Just to mention a few examples of areas where motive theory of law may have significance: (1) mental health and retardation and the institutional framework that deals with those problems, (2) criminal corrections, which is now in a state of crisis because of prison overcrowding, (3) Church/state relations, (4) educational theory and institutions, (5) juvenile laws, (6) human resource structures, (7) domestic and family law, (8) theory of government, (9) civil rights. The list can be extended to every area and institutional expression of law. I selected the three discussed in this chapter because they help to bring the theory into focus.

First, we discuss practical implications of the connection between *law and psychology*. I have already shown the important role of psychology in the motive for law. In this chapter we explore negative effects for law and social order arising from psychology. A primary concern is the attack on guilt feelings.

Next, we explore the important subject of *conflicts in mythos*. If mythos undergirds law, what happens when there are conflicting belief systems? There are clearly important implications for conflicts in mythos for international law, but they are too vast for me to undertake in this volume. My main concern is to show the effects of mythological conflicts *within* the United States. Legal systems have traditionally existed mainly within nation states. An examination of conflicts in mythological systems within nation states gives good insight into shortcomings of our legal system.

We round out discussion of applications and implications of motive theory of law by discussing *the impact of media*. If the theory I have described is correct, modern media has an enormous impact on formative processes of law. Media is the vehicle of modern mythos. It shapes images and narrates themes by which we live.

| Chapter 5.1 | Dangers of Psychological Dogma |

Psychology has made many positive contributions to the understanding of human nature. I have probably given more attention to more facets of psychology than any other serious student of legal philosophy. My description of motive for law draws heavily on Freud, Piaget, Maslow, Jung, Frankl and other leaders in the field of psychology. Thinkers in the legal field must take a strong look at the relationship between psychology and law. We must give much more attention to this very important area of study.

Psychology Goes to the Essence of Law

The relationship between law and psychology is an *in-depth* relationship. Law begins in psychological forces, as I have shown earlier in this volume. I am not referring to a superficial relationship. Usual topics when we refer to "psychology and law" may be somewhat superficial. The superficial approach usually *applies* psychological principles to *certain aspects* of the legal system. I do not mean to say that these relationships are unimportant by using the word *superficial*. They simply do not go to the essence of law. Psychological principles I described earlier are at the heart of law's force. The superficial approach assumes the existence of law and does not trace the origin of the force of law to psychological phenomena. It fails to see that any workable theory of law must describe law's motive forces, which include both psychological and social forces. The reality of law is not simply the visible, rational, articulated principles of law. Law's reality includes unconscious, instinctive, impulses that give rise to legal principles. The force of law arises from those psychological impulses. Law is not a separate, independent phenomenon that we should study *in light of* psychological knowledge.

Typical topics in the superficial arena include the inherent weakness of eye-witness testimony. We also study the psychological profile of witnesses, jurors, and even judges. Analysis of the mental processes of judges has been a principle thrust of legal realism. Issues of sanity and mental health are part of the interface between law and psychology.

Psychotherapy and therapy for alcohol and drug abuse have legal implications. Marriage counseling and family counseling are important to
courts in resolving marital issues. However, none of these important
matters goes to the essence of law. They are simply matters with which
law deals, or that relate to law in a particular way. Often our legal system
deals with them as matters of *evidence*. They are all very worthwhile,
practical applications of psychology, and deserve continued study.
However, they all *assume* the existence of law as something separate and
apart from psychological impulse. As we have seen, psychology plays a
much more fundamental role in law. Legal philosophy of the twenty-first
century will likely acknowledge a deep indebtedness to advances in
psychology during the nineteenth and twentieth centuries.

We have also seen that the psychological basis of law in individuals
has a counterpart in mythos of society. The two are parts of a single
holistic system. Modern psychology enables us to understand the force
of law. Mythos molds psychological forces into a system of social order.
Unfortunately, most members of the psychological community have not
realized that law arises from psychological impulse. The legal community is also unaware of the significant connection between law and
psychology. Whether the connection between law and psychological
impulse has escaped notice of *all* psychologists and lawyers is unimportant. People who need to know the *importance* of this relationship do not
know it. The results of this oversight are alarming.

The Dark Shadow of Determinism

The most important and dangerous undercurrent of psychology and
social science is the haunting specter of determinism. Determinism is
totally inconsistent with any meaningful concept of law. The whole edi-
fice of law depends upon free agency. If individuals are not morally
responsible for their behavior, law is meaningless. Yet a roll call of leading social scientists of the twentieth century reveals a strange fascination
with determinism. B. F. Skinner attempted to found an entire school
based on determinism. One can only wonder why he bothered with the
matter at all. I suppose he *had* to. If only one social scientist had fallen
into the trap, the infringement onto the philosophical foundation of law
would not have been serious. But many others, including Abraham
Maslow, Carl Rogers, and Sigmund Freud embraced the idea of
determinism.

Interestingly, physical sciences are not nearly as certain of determinism as they were a hundred years ago. Quantum physics and the theory

of relativity cast grave doubts on determinism. One suspects that social scientists bought into the idea of determinism by analogy with elementary principles of physical science from the nineteenth and early twentieth centuries. Today those principles are being questioned by physical scientists, and social scientists must also reconsider their positions. Suffice it to say that it is well beyond the ability of science, conducted by humans, to decide whether human behavior is ruled by determinism. Here, if nowhere else, the fact that the observer and observed are one renders the question unanswerable.

Damage brought about by widespread endorsement of determinism is significant. Determinism says that a person is not responsible for his or her own conduct. Determinism cannot be reconciled with either natural law or legal positivism, since it takes away the possibility of choice. According to determinism, the most atrocious murder is inevitable conduct, as is the reaction to it. Such an approach eliminates all meaning that can be assigned to human existence. Human behavior is nothing more than the end result of biochemical and biophysical reactions. The human behavior we call law is merely a link in an endless chain of cause and effect.

The Attack on Guilt

The psychology that we discussed in earlier chapters clearly sheds a bright new light on jurisprudence. However, the bright light which psychology throws onto jurisprudence has its dark shadow. Jurists have not acknowledged and incorporated psychological forces into their understanding of jurisprudence. Perhaps more significantly, psychologists have not understood the impact of certain practices and operating tenets on law. Each discipline's concern with its own supposedly isolated area has caused it to ignore the impact of its practices on other areas. Therapists have not noticed the negative impact which their dogma has on the effectiveness of law. I refer particularly to the strong attack on guilt.

The problem that concerns me does not lie in the superficial relationship between psychology and law. Matters such as the inherent weakness of eyewitness testimony are not likely to keep law from working. The problem that concerns me goes to the essence of the motivating force of law. Sigmund Freud, you will recall, theorized that civilization can progress only at the expense of an ever-increasing burden of guilt. He questioned whether the advance of civilization is worth the price. I have tried to show that he was wrong. The advantages of organization produced by advanced civilization offset the negative impact of individual guilt.

Freud is at least partly right. Rights arise only when duties arise. The sense of duty arises from processes of moral formation that Freud and others described. Duty and rights are inseparable. Rights arise only when moral formation successfully inculcates into individuals a sense of duty. One person's right is another's duty. The sense of duty, or conscience, therefore lies at the heart of civilization. This is how civilization progresses. The walls, ceiling and floor of civilization are duties. Freedom and rights are in the undefined emptiness of the room. This analogy goes back to an earlier discussion. What is useful about a room? It is the basic question of the Taoist oxymoron, "What is useful about nothingness?" The advance of civilization and the increase of duty—and guilt—go hand in hand.

Farmers who broke the deep sod of the prairies had no idea they were creating a dust bowl. They found good soil and worked hard to accomplish something worthwhile, but they created a dust bowl anyway. In ecology, there are many examples of such well-intended, but disastrous practices. Often, they are done in the name of science and progress. The work of psychology and the social sciences has unwittingly disarmed law to some extent.

Freud understood the necessary relationship between moral formation and civilization. Unfortunately, everyone does not share his deep understanding of the function of guilt. We tend to latch onto his concern about the *dangers* of guilt while ignoring guilt's benefits. We have launched an all-out attack on guilt, completely disregarding implications for civilization. Normative forces of society aggravate and perpetuate the problem, in that we have actually developed a taboo against guilt! To paraphrase FDR, "Our only guilt is guilt itself." Lots of people other than therapists are into the act. I am not sure who is responsible for our attitude about guilt. I only know that the popular mind credits psychology with the anti-guilt dogma. However, the problem is more in the popular domain than in the opinions of real experts. Many, perhaps most, psychotherapists realize that healthy guilt serves a useful function, even though they may not fully understand its role in social order and law.

Guilt: An Endangered Species

Freud and others amply proved the relationship between *guilt* and mental illness. In cases of neurotic guilt, ability to expose the nature of the problem to consciousness, through psychotherapy, helps to solve the problem. If guilt is the cause of problems, then let's put an end to guilt, the reasoning runs. Elimination of neurotic guilt proved effective in liberating patients from their symptoms. This is a valuable clinical approach, and I am not criticizing valid use of psychotherapy.

Unfortunately, we sometimes feel that if a little medicine does a little good, a big dose will do lots of good. Western society has taken just such an approach to elimination of guilt. We have sold this panacea for mental and emotional problems over-the-counter when it should have been by prescription only. As a result, we may have impaired healthy moral formation which causes justified guilt feelings. Healthy guilt is a prerequisite for law. Guilt is an important part of our way of producing social order in western civilization. I have seen many criminals who regretted getting caught, but few who feel real remorse for their crime. Lack of a healthy sense of guilt places on the legal system, including the penal system, an unmanageable burden of imposing compliance with essential elements of social order by force.

Moreover, we have erected a taboo concerning any comment on morals. In modern society, many social scientists and social workers regard themselves as value-free observers. The myth of the unobserved observer affects the fields of psychology and psychotherapy as it does other social sciences. These unobserved, value-free observers remove condemnation from their vocabulary and encourage everyone else to do the same. Popular prejudice forces the anti-guilt dogma on teachers, social workers, government employees, psychologists, sociologists, and everyone employed in the realm of social endeavor. It is difficult to criticize violation of the most basic principles of decency. Often, a *non-judgmental* attitude applies, even in instances of absolute criminality. The value-free approach, unnatural as it is, is the counterpart of the taboo against guilt. It, too, has taken on normative force.

Pop-psychology not only breaks the sod of moral prairies on which healthy herds of social order once grazed; it is destroying rain forests which produce the oxygen law breathes. Erosion of a well-established sense of duty destroys the impulse that causes law. I have already developed the idea of the relationship of law to emotional impulses which arise from moral conscience of the people. That impulse energizes collective psychology that supports law. If I am correct, we should view any assault on the domain of duty and conscience with suspicion. We should approach it as we do the breaking the prairie sod, cutting the rain forests, or destroying the ozone layer. It is waste of a valuable natural resource.

Clergy long since abandoned its role as guardians and protectors of this priceless asset. They worried that we would consider them *intolerant* or *narrow*. Some clergy have even helped quarry this bedrock of civilization, and used it to construct altars for the cult of *reason*.

The fountainhead of the sense of duty, you will recall, is the family. During the very early years, family instills the initial sense of duty that is essential to moral formation. Thus, it is through the family that "justice rolls down like waters. . . ," to quote Dr. M. L. King, Jr., who was referring to Scripture from the Biblical Book of Amos. Unfortunately, the traditional family is, itself, an endangered species. If we are to regenerate the moral base that supports law, we must begin with the family.

The Concept of Sin

A few years ago, psychiatrist G. Carl Menninger wrote a thought provoking book which he entitled, *Whatever Became of Sin?* The title alone relates the book to this chapter. Menninger did a good job of chiding the public, particularly ministers and religious leaders, for not recognizing certain *national* omissions and commissions, as *Sin*. He mentioned briefly moral formation, including development of the super-ego. Nevertheless, he proceeded to draw on a metaphysical source of moral knowledge, presumably of supernatural etiology, and used this knowledge to condemn the matters that *he believed* were wrong in society. When I found his book, I thought I would be able to shower it with praise. However, I fear that Menninger's own sense of guilt may have become clear. He saw that elimination of guilt had bad effects. He became defensive about the role of psychology in guilt's elimination. The answer to the question posed by the title of his book may be that psychological dogma destroyed sin. Even so, we must credit him with seeing problems that have arisen because of loss of the sense of guilt in our society. The book provides good insight into the problem I am describing here.

Clergy must note the importance of their traditional role as guardians of conscience. Menninger was certainly correct in this suggestion. But clergy should resort to its traditional definitions of sin. The concept of sin needs to be revitalized, and we need to feel guilt because of it. Clergy must not allow Menninger and other social scientists to rewrite their book for them. I am not telling religious leaders what they need to say. I am acknowledging their territory.

Overstepping the Role

The problem is not simply one of eliminating the sense of guilt. Psycho-therapists are like the proponents of a new religion. One is reminded of the religion propounded by Auguste Comte, referred to earlier. They have projected their own values and made their own contribution to our modern mythos. Maslow noticed the problem.

> . . . I am afraid that a number of psychologists are also working with erroneous preconceptions and unconscious assumptions about human nature (and about society) which, because they are implicit and unconscious, can maintain and perpetuate themselves beyond the reach of testing for a considerable time to come. Meanwhile they are projected by the psychologist upon his data.[139]

Unfortunately, Maslow himself was not immune to this occupational hazard. He extolled the virtues of his "self-actualized," ideal individuals. By strange coincidence, he had the ability to select the *self-actualized* from a large group. He must have been one of them. Naturally, he found very few of them. He only relaxed the self-sufficiency of these well-balanced, well-nourished heroes long enough for them to be the very best of lovers, forming one ego with the beloved. In these matters, Maslow obviously projected his own values onto his supposed observations.

Psychiatrist Viktor Frankl also expressed deep concern that members of his profession overextend their area of expertise.

> Yet we psychiatrists should refrain from dabbling in fields other than our own. I would say that each issue deserves to be taken up by a specialist. So why not leave something, say, to the sociologists? We psychiatrists simply don't have the answer for each and every question. Least of all do we have a prescription to hand out when it comes to the question of how to cure all the ills and ailments that afflict our society. Let us start humanizing psychiatry—rather than divinizing it—and, to begin with, let us stop ascribing divine attributes to psychiatrists. We psychiatrists are neither omniscient nor omnipotent—we are only omnipresent: we are present at all symposia, and mingling in all discussions. . . .[140]

It's a bit strange that Frankl thought only of *sociologists* and not of religious leaders and the legal community as people to share in the work of curing of social ills.

---

139 Maslow, *Motivation and Personality*, p. 353. Maslow did not choose to include this language in his second edition.
140 Frankl, *The Unconscious God*, pp.140-141.

Therapists themselves, along with everyone else, have a deep-seated, innate faith in law or justice. They see nothing strange about their appeal to *justice*, although they usually have little respect for anything *metaphysical*. In fairness to members of the psychological profession, they probably do not realize that anything they do or say could have profound impact on the building material of law. Justice is as much an article of faith to modern social scientists as it was to Aquinas when he described natural law.

Sigmund Freud may have very properly felt that his views would have little or no impact on law. One doctor was not likely to impact at all on the vast psychosocial forces that produce law. Freud knew that those forces produce law, but did not realize that he was producing dogma that would potentially undermine law. Neither did one sodbuster cause the dust bowl. A belief usually does not become dangerous until everybody starts believing it and acting on it. The "one doctor" became an archetype, and a large segment of the community drew on the wisdom of that "wise old man."

Pop-psychology is now a major influence in our society. The whole theme that I am developing in this chapter was well addressed by William Kirk Kilpatrick in his book, *The Seduction of Psychology*. He discusses problems of elimination of guilt and also the priestly role assumed by therapists in the religion of secular humanism. A religion, like a rose, by any other name is still the same. Our indoctrination to secular humanism is strong. We turn to psychotherapists to deal with problems of suicide. However, the incidence of suicide is much greater among psychotherapists than among the general population. Does this make sense, or are we dealing with images?

Pop-psychology is the idiom in which we discuss behavioral problems today. We seldom resort to the ethical or moral idiom. To condemn a particular activity or viewpoint we call it *irrational*. This is a more serious criticism than to say that it is *immoral* or *sinful*. In fact, moral judgment seems to be considered downright immoral in some quarters.

Psychology as Science

Psychology is still trying to authenticate itself as *science*. Psychological theorists devote many pages to this rather unproductive subject. Who cares if it is a *science*, if it produces useful, workable principles? But psychologists, along with all other scientists and rationalists, feel compelled to make their offering at the altar of reason. The compulsion derives from the need for meaning—for authenticity. It has ritualistic, if not religious, implications, which helps to explain psychology's preoccupation with the *scientific* label. *Rubricizing,* according to Maslow, is preoccupation with labels—the naming of concepts. After devoting many pages to the effort to label psychology a *science,* Maslow spent many additional pages criticizing *rubricizing* in learning!

Actually, the greatest threat to usefulness of psychology may lie in the effort to make it *scientific.* Mechanical theories of chemical and physical reactions have not yet come close to explaining the ultimate mystery of *life.* Psychology is, by its nature, a study of inwardness. It is highly introspective, and must not lose its subjectivity. Psychology is a study of the *observer* as much or more so than a study of the *observed.* The effort to make the study of psychology purely *objective* will fail. In no other science is the effect of the observer on the observed more plain than in psychology. The *observer is the observed.* Remember Maslow in the self-appointed role of selecting self-actualized people, and the point will be clear.

Injection of personal bias in such a study is unavoidable. Therapists understand the importance of imagery and they must come to understand and respect the imagery of their own role. These modern day shamans are highly effective in the area in which they work. Nevertheless, they must realize the relationship of their area of expertise with that of others. They need to remember the legal community and religious community, and respect their own limitations. They must arrive at a full understanding of the impact that their work and their teachings have on the holistic social system. They are part of it, and clearly are not merely detached observers. Their behavior has definite impact on the system. They must disavow determinism, or else admit that they themselves are locked by deterministic forces; and therefore, their ideas are totally meaningless. Their actions belie their words. They not only believe they have escaped determinism, but that they have eluded humanity itself, and observe humanity in detachment.

Psycho-therapists must not use their powerful potions to cast a wicked spell on the people. They may find, to their dismay, that after they cast out the demon of guilt, seven demons will return and occupy the freshly cleaned demoniac. If they silence Poe's "tell-tale heart," murderers will go unpunished. Perhaps when everyone accepts a *value free* ethic, which has already become a normative force in society, no one will really care.

Holism of Society

Throughout our discussions of psychology, we built toward a dynamic, holistic basis for an energizing force for law. We responded to the *why* question by explaining motive forces for activities that we call law. Motive force is essential to the existence of law. First we examined individual conscience which is a somewhat specific but important part of the motive force of law. We then moved on to basic human needs, which enlarged the examination of motivating force. Discussion of archetypes and symbols explained internal mechanisms that fit individuals into society and assign roles. We culminated this progression of psychological ideas with the powerful, encompassing concept of collective psychology.

The group and the individual interact. Interaction produces norms and a system. The system is maintained by beliefs and deeply grounded in mythos. Both individuals and the group expect compliance with the norms. Society is holistic. We find the energy of law in the interaction between individuals and society. Here is the answer to the *why do we do it* question, and it is not a simple answer. Yet the whole process was occurring quite naturally long before we became capable of describing it. Our rationalistic invasions into this arena can prove disastrous. We must maintain a profound respect for natural forces of moral behavior. They are part of the ecology of the human environment, and we must have great respect for them. We must not be quick to reject notions of morality, since they may serve purposes of which we are not fully aware.

Earlier chapters described the origin of law in psychological impulse and social dynamics. We saw that mythos is the storage place for values, mandates and taboos of society. All these factors work together to effect survival for society. I described how law finds its force in impulses of conscience and basic human needs. Energy for law embeds in archetypes. Genetics reproduce archetypes. Experience gives them specific cultural content and meaning. Archetypes condition individuals to a particular society through mythos. Armed with this information, we can understand certain problems, or inadequacies, of law which I raised in the first chapter.

Moral Formation in the Individual

Let's get the basics of moral formation back in mind. The microcosm, the individual's immediate surroundings, have the greatest influence in moral development. Parents and family are the fountainhead of values. Moral development progresses in stages, by internalization of standards of family and immediate surroundings. Genetics precode the maturation process. Moral development relates closely to cognitive or intellectual development. During maturation, values of the peer group loom more and more important, and rationality plays a greater and greater role in moral behavior. Individuals, in turn, expect and demand adherence by others to standards he expects to follow himself. Archetypes cause us to assign roles in the social order and become involved in relations with other people. Certain practices and customs work for a particular group, and enable its members to meet basic needs. Language, ceremony and custom reinforce the inherent values in the system, in what we have labelled *mythos*. Mythos stabilizes values within a group. It is a medium for linguistic transmission of the group values from generation to generation. Mythos produces collective representations. These are shared beliefs and shared ways of perceiving the environment. Mythos provides society's *lateral* support for *lineal* transmission of values and taboos through family. In this manner, a broad general concurrence between law and the values or ideals embedded in the mythos of a particular culture occurs. It is a holistic system that operates subtly and often in processes that are unconscious. This is, no doubt, what Aquinas identified as the *moral order*. Through these mechanisms the moral order forms the basis for law. Aquinas, of course, was not aware of the psychological nature of moral formation. He was content that God created the moral order. No further explanation was necessary in the world-view of his times.

Differing Mythological Systems

Archetypes build and energize mythos. They are basically the same for all humanity, but there are variations in the mythical systems of various cultures. Different cultures fund archetypes in different ways. For instance, territoriality can manifest itself in several different ways, depending on the culture. The hero differs from one culture to another. Nevertheless, there is a basic similarity. The differences are superficial, but definitely not inconsequential, while similarities lie at a deeper level. There can be conflicts in mythos, or belief systems. These conflicts pit groups against each other and cause groups to reject members of other groups.

Differences give rise to conflicts between and among the mythological systems of cultures and subcultures wherever they exist alongside each other. Since mythological systems provide raw material for the value systems of individuals, these conflicts are quite important. The cultural differences between Japan and the United States, separated by the Pacific Ocean, are open and obvious. Such cultural differences have important results in the views held by the two peoples as to basic values. Difference can also exist within a particular culture and nation. Pirsig referred to these differences in the passage from his book that we quoted earlier as we developed the idea of mythos. The possibility of sharp differences obviously exists in a heterogeneous society that has subcultures.

Based on dynamics described earlier, these mythological differences can have significant impact on effectiveness of the legal system. This observation applies to all societies in which there are subcultures. The possibility of mythological differences between subcultures gives insight into causes for the breakdown of law. Problems of differences in mythos are difficult to resolve. Origin and perpetuation of law involves mythos. Conflicts in mythos bring about law's toughest problems. Law itself is often inadequate to cope with these problems, because of its very nature.

Law has difficulty effectively resolving conflicts in the forces that gave rise to law in the first place.

These mythological differences in subcultures are everywhere evident. Religious differences between Protestants and Catholics in Ireland; religious differences in the Middle East; and conflict between Pakistan and India are all examples. There are many others. Reunification of Germany perhaps demonstrates the opposite force of cohesiveness, when there are no real mythological differences. Reassertion of ethnic identities in the Soviet Union after they had been subdued for many years is also directly in point. The total collapse of the Soviet Union vividly portrays the point. When the communist regime failed to provide a system for meeting basic needs, old territorial, ethnic loyalties began to reassert themselves. Dramatic changes in Communist China in the near future are predictable, based on this analysis.

These types of differences are also significant within the United States, where there is a potpourri of cultures. Significant weaknesses in social order occur at interfaces between these differing cultures. Chicago's Westside, Miami's Cuban population, China town in San Francisco, and many other such areas have a reputation for unrest that law has difficulty controlling. America is not a "melting pot," as was suggested in my junior high civics book. Mythological differences do not just disappear.

Differences in Black and White Mythos

The Civil Rights Movement centered on relations between Blacks and whites in the South. I have been deeply affected by the conflicts, and have tried to understand its underlying causes. I have intentionally tried to overcome vestiges of prejudice. I have particularly concentrated on the work of Dr. Martin Luther King, Jr., and have tried to understand his message. The Civil Rights Movement, and the interface between Black and white subcultures in the South provide an excellent case study for the present discussion.

My immediate social environment, the South, reflects differences in mythos or culture between Blacks and whites. I believe that these observations apply in any geographical area where there is a heterogeneous mixture of groups. By *heterogeneous*, I mean identifiable groups within a society that have racial, ethnic, cultural, linguistic, or religious differences. There are probably few who doubt that such differences impact on the usefulness of law for social control. Nevertheless, I am not aware of any theory or working hypothesis as to *why* there is such an impact.

Those caught up in the conflict tend to think that members of the *other group* are lawless. The general assumption among those not directly involved is that problems arise because of unmitigated prejudice and ignorance, or class economic conflict, but such is not necessarily the case. More likely the problems arise from unresolved, age-old mythological differences or differences in belief systems. Archetypes are continually funded with different contents from the culture of the differing groups, giving rise to differing perceptions of social reality.

All human beings are basically the same. There is no reason why a rational and just legal system will not work equally well for everyone. That is the problem, however. Our purely rationalistic approach to legal philosophy does not include or even consider the motives that make law happen. Nor does it consider elements of collective psychology that are necessary parts of the motive for law. There can be conflict among the very motives that cause law to happen, if there are different belief systems. If the system doesn't work equally well for everyone, we assume that it is because the system is either not rational enough or is lacking in justice. These assumptions are not always true. More likely, we are not dealing with all the motive facts.

Cultural Differences

There are broad cultural distinctions between white culture and Black culture in my area. Integration did not end these differences. There are broad differences between family structures, attitudes toward marriage, attitudes about sex, about children and child support, and the like. Of course, there are many exceptions to this generalization. Broadly speaking, the white subculture is patriarchal while the Black subculture tends to be more matriarchal. The Negro spiritual *Wayfarin' Stranger* contains the intriguing line "I'm going there to see my *Mother*." The matriarchal reference is unusual in traditional religious music, and possibly symbolizes a feminine godhead. Again there are many black families in which the father is the head of the house. You will recall that Jung identified a father archetype and a mother archetype, with remarkably different characteristics. Freud gave particular emphasis in conscience formation to commands of the *father*. One would therefore expect a different pattern of development, depending on which archetype is paramount.

I have no idea whether anthropology can trace the roots of these differences to mythos of Blacks in Africa and whites in Europe. Clearly the roots of the legal system are European. The violent social trauma of slavery and the effects of segregation make the effort to trace these differences difficult. One would suspect, however, that value systems transmitted through parents are extremely durable. The mysterious ways of mythos have likely preserved some of the values of Black culture from African origins. The available evidence suggests that mythos from Africa did indeed survive in America. Legends surrounding the hare, for instance, discovered in Africa have continued in America.[141] The hare is one archetype of the *trickster*, and relates to the hero archetype.

No doubt, however, the impact of slavery and segregation has also had lasting effect on both Black and white subcultures and their mythic structures. The problem shown by all of this is simple. Whatever the cause, there is no adequate unifying mythos. There is no belief system which causes all people to have compatible expectations of the legal system. There is no generalized belief that the system is adequate to meet everyone's basic needs. We still are rejecting non-members.

These observations shed light on beliefs of legal realists. While there are few threads unifying their beliefs, all legal realists call for *realism*. Apparently they believe that there is such a thing as *reality*, and that it is the same for everyone. While considering cultural biases of judges, realists have given no consideration to the fact that *notions of reality are culturally posited, and there is more than one culture*. They focus attention on psychology and values that affect decision's of judges, without realizing that a more significant fracture of reality is in society itself. They attempt to advocate the good life as a basis for decision, without solving the problem of what is universally good. In the absence of a common belief system, people who play key roles in the legal system take on different images in the eyes of the beholder, depending on the beholder's cultural and mythological vantage point. One person's *hero* is another's *trickster*. This explains Harry Truman's caustic remarks and J. Edgar Hoover's suspicion of Dr. M. L. King, Jr.

Linguistic Differences

There is a distinction between the language commonly used by Blacks and the language commonly used by whites in my area. A Black person can usually tell whether the voice on a telephone is that of a white person or a Black person, and so can a white person. Use of language varies much more widely between individual whites or individual Blacks than between whites and Blacks in general. Even though we may

---

[141] Lankford, *Native American Legends*, pp. 222-224.

not believe the difference is important, we *experience it as a difference*. These linguistic characteristics of both Blacks and whites is not universal. In other places, there is no noticeable difference, and the difference is disappearing in the South, but is likely to remain to some extent for many years. Its disappearance will be an important step toward eliminating mythological differences. It is seized upon to accentuate racial differences—and as a means of identification and differentiation.

Among poorly educated Blacks and whites in the South, the linguistic difference is quite noticeable. The term dialect applies to both groups, and the two dialects are quite different. Although these differences obviously result at least in part from educational deficiency for both races, the difference is real. The difference is not purely an education difference. The difference is certainly not that the white dialect is *superior* to the Black dialect, even though, by definition, it may correspond more completely to the dominant culture. The difference is often as real between an educated Black person and an uneducated white with obviously poorer linguistic skills as in the opposite case. The difference is less obvious to a person who is not a part of either subculture than to anyone who is a part of either. Linguistic differences are evidence of even deeper cultural and mythological differences.

Persistence of Differences in Mythos

Differing mythologies in Black culture and white culture are very predictable. Historical facts help to explain the differences. Until the 1960s, Blacks had little or no voice in government in the State of Alabama. Mythology tends to define and assign only the roles that are available. Now, Alabama has more Black officeholders than any state in the nation other than Mississippi. This surface evidence belies continued existence of a sharply dichotomized culture. The dichotomy is clear, despite successful integration of most public facilities such as restaurants, parks, restrooms, and public schools.

Mythos is very lethargic concerning change. Its primary vehicle of enforcement is custom and habit, not reason. Mythos is usually the mother of law, not the child. Lethargy is not a simple matter of whites "dragging their feet" about change. Lethargy exists on both sides of the racial line. It is the condescending mistake of many social programs that Blacks want to assimilate into white culture. Blacks have legitimate concerns about preserving their own culture.

Solidarity in Mythos

Politics of the day excluded Blacks from government for many generations. The basic drive for survival dictated that Blacks *avoid* white dominated governmental and legal systems. *Brothers* stuck together and didn't squeal on brothers. This message was and is a part of Black mythos. The best tactic was absolute unity, with no exceptions. Solidarity is a source of strength and security. In dealing with each other, Blacks found means of social control other than law. The approach is reminiscent of Jesus' advice to his followers that they avoid the courts of law. This is always an option for a people who have no real input into the system. But once this ethic is established, it is difficult to change.

To maintain solidarity, and avoid courts, alternative means of social control must be found. One such device, still popular, is to take law into one's own hands. Black-on-Black crime is a predictable outcome of the situation just described. Infliction of the death penalty or corporal punishment occurs far more frequently in self-help social control than it does in our legal system. Law can guarantee participation by Blacks in governmental function, but it cannot immediately instill appropriate motive and respect for law in the population. It cannot cause a common perception of law and justice in all persons. Tension will subside only when full participation coupled with a feeling of participation and security actually occur. Only the mythos can accomplish this delicate task.

We cannot end the mythologically supported principle of absolute solidarity merely by electing even a significant number of Blacks to public office. Tradition is too ingrained in fundamental belief systems of the people. Similar cohesiveness exists among whites in their effort to maintain control of government and law. Racial cohesiveness is a natural product of the dynamic forces that I have described and exists for all racial and ethnic groups to some extent. It is part of the residue of myths of horizon and the wasteland beyond. The wasteland is peopled, remember, by less-than-human strangers or enemies. Our history, which is our cultural mythology, has us descended ultimately from Europe, not Africa. America is an extension of Europe. The legal system, for instance, is distinctly English. Africa is not part of it. All of this, of course, is more a state of mind than of fact. Nevertheless, our history shows pervasive effects of undissolved remains of territorial attitudes. Earlier, while discussing territoriality, I pointed out paradoxical results that the Voting Rights Act can sometimes create. The present discussion adds further understanding of the paradox of the Voting Rights Act, by pointing to additional psychological points of division between Blacks and whites that the Voting Rights Act tends to perpetuate. The political system is being built on the differences that really need to be discouraged.

White cohesiveness was the reason for major civil rights legislation. Civil rights legislation dealt with clear-cut issues of *white resistance* in the 1960s. Problems of the 1990s are more subtle. We can deal with them effectively only if we can come to grips with the forces I have been discussing. Despite a basic equality of all people, differences in mythos are real. Only by acknowledging those differences can we hope to find solutions to baffling problems. For instance, we must approach overcrowding of prisons, with a disproportionate Black prison population, with these principles in mind. One reason for overcrowding is nonparticipation of blacks from the mainstream of social control, and the exercise of self-help remedies in Black culture. In my judgment, the church must play a vital role in this process of reconciliation. This is a central thought in the later chapter on religion and faith.

Differences in Religious Ritual

Forms of worship in black and white churches differ dramatically. I have had many opportunities to observe both, because of my involvement in politics and in the United Methodist Church. Black churches and Black ministers involve themselves far more deeply in politics than do their white counterparts in Alabama. More importantly, spiritual life itself is markedly different. Sermons are on a different wave length. Songs are distinctively different. Even when churches use the same songs they sing them differently. Blacks are far more *spiritual* or *intimate* in their worship. There is much more *feeling* or *warmth* and audience participation in the service. The attitude toward *giving* is also very different. The congregations raise money for Church purposes very differently in white churches than in Black churches. Funeral rites and customs are markedly different between the two subcultures.

Typical of thematic differences in emphasis in Black churches are the strong themes of *deliverance;* of *overcoming adversity;* of *perseverance,* and the *ultimate victory of righteousness.* Current white church themes might include *spiritual formation, missional outreach,* and *concerns of the church family* such as illness and death of church members. The differences, understand, are in emphasis. All these themes are present in both Black and white churches, but the differences in emphasis are significant. Once, when I spoke in a Black church, the minister told me at the end of the service, "We have our ways." He was referring to a ritual of greetings and celebration then in progress, that has no counterpart in customary worship services in white churches. The church was a United Methodist Church: my own denomination!

Differences in Collective Representations

Collective representations arise in mythos and can occur along racial lines. Since Blacks did not participate in government in the South until the past few years, punishment for crimes against society were not a function of their collectivity. It was not necessary or even desirable that Blacks develop strong collective representations in this area of concern. Whites would attend to punishment—often without any great precision in justice for Blacks. Black offenders close to the white establishment received more lenient treatment.

The collective response of Blacks to criminal convictions was often more akin to grief than to moral indignation about the offense. Collective representations are persistent. Those that developed during slavery and segregation did not prepare Blacks for certain roles that are necessarily theirs in an integrated system. The sympathy, or grief response, continues in effect, in instances when moral indignation would be more appropriate. For the defendant, it gives rise to the moral defense, "They are picking on me because I am Black," which often finds a receptive audience.

In all of this, the effect of collective representations forming along racial lines is readily apparent. The legal establishment needs the emotional support of strong Black organizations such as the NAACP. We need to be intentionally inclusive in the selection of judges. We need capable Black judges who will give Blacks a participatory interest in the system both in image and in fact. The needs of Blacks extend to routine cases—not just civil rights. It is entirely possible, even likely, that the legal system prosecutes more Black officials for corruption than whites. Likewise, it is somewhat easier for Blacks to invoke collective representations of *discrimination* in prosecution. *Nevertheless, if we are to survive as a people and government, we must be willing to prosecute all corrupt officials regardless of race. We must condemn their corruption with one voice.* The same is true of all crime.

So what am I getting at? Difference in language, difference in family structure, difference in perception of government, difference in the spiritual realm. These areas where there are significant differences are foundation stones for the legal system. They are the sources of motive forces that make law happen. No wonder the legal system is not delivering solutions to social problems. Even the *words* used in a court proceeding have significantly different impact and meaning, depending on the cultural background of the listener. Perhaps I am part of the tradition of legal realism after all, but pursuing a new and different aspect of reality. The reality I advocate involves a universalizing morality, but recognizes that at present there are many different perceptions of reality. Legal realists were quick to see that cultural background impacts on judicial behavior in decision-making. Why have we not seen that cultural background—mythos—also impacts on the behavior of everyone else, and brings about differing expectations of law?

Only a common faith, a kind of religious unity, can overcome these mythological differences and create a moral base shared by all. Secular agencies dominated by the "value-free" approach cannot solve the problems. Unfortunately, churches are not providing necessary solutions. Collective representations are a necessary, but not a sufficient, condition for morality. They form the emotional and intellectual basis for ideals toward which a people aspire. However, they are not foolproof guarantors of survival. As conditions for survival become more complex, our collective representations must provide a more workable perception of reality that is more widely shared, if they are to be successful.

Practical Implications of the Conflict

Differences in mythos I have described have practical impact at every turn. At the basic level of moral formation, different mythological systems condition conscience in different directions. Taboos in Black society and white society are quite different.

The current legal system is obviously the recipient of the heritage of the older, white dominated legal system. There is also a background of "law of the land" concepts of constitutional and civil rights law. Those of us in the legal system express all of this in the formal linguistic code of a white civilization. The prevailing Black linguistic code is different. Moral training and moral development for Black culture often does not translate into the white legal system. Often, the rationalistic white oriented legal base extends far beyond the moral base of whites or Blacks. It often extends beyond the limits of linguistic abilities of average people. I understand customs of Japanese Samurai better than many criminal *defendants* understand our court proceedings. While this lack of understanding includes both white and Black defendants, differences in mythos accentuate the lack of understanding. Barriers to understanding are greater for Black defendants. Inability to understand runs both ways. Moral sentiments that enforce black solidarity that will protect violators of the law in today's world are inscrutable to me. The mutual lack of understanding which I am describing has nothing to do with innate worth or innate ability of individuals. It is a product of cultural forces that I have described. Without understanding these forces and coming to grips with them, we cannot expect to resolve complex issues confronting society and the legal system. Attempting to ignore them does no good.

Reinventing "Common Law"

Only by inventing a *common law*— a value system to which all persons subscribe—can we find solutions to these problems. Law emerges from shared values, so we must have a common value system, and it cannot be an amoral, value-free system. We must capture it in appropriate collective representations in a mutually compatible mythological system. A common value system will only come when we fund archetypes of the several subcultures with compatible mythological features. Media will play an important role.

E. D. Hirsch, Jr., cogently argues there is certain basic information which every literate member of society must have to be a fully functioning member.[142] The argument is compelling. It is the Tower of Babel argument, and Hirsch refers specifically to that Biblical story. Humanity's ability to achieve—to advance civilization—depends on its ability to communicate. Ability to communicate complex thoughts on which a complex society depends requires a common base of knowledge. I suggest that the dynamics underlying Hirsch's argument are those that I have set forth about mythos. The problem with which he is contending starts in conflicts in mythos. I agree with Hirsch's major premise. We need a common cultural base of knowledge for our culture to function. I don't necessarily agree with his conclusion about the specific knowledge that is necessary. I suspect that the knowledge that is necessary is very much alive and constantly changing. It is not separate from belief. I doubt that anyone can ever describe it in a definitive list. In addition to commonly held knowledge there must also be commonly held and emotionally supported values if society is to function.

Unfortunately, we base our *political* systems on the very mythological differences that make the *legal* system ineffective. It is easier in politics to deal with blocks of votes than it is to deal with individual voters. Pluralism may require that we defer to groups of people, such as families, churches, schools, labor unions, corporations and the

---

[142] Hirsch, *Cultural Literacy.*

like. But deference to naturally occurring groups can allow the archetype of the alien to cause exclusion. The motive force of racial unity is a very convenient political tool. Politicians know the symbolism of mythos. Political leaders, Black and white, have a vested interest in mythos staying as divided as it is now. Often, their interest is financial. Racial groups function in a pluralistic fashion, just as other naturally forming groups do, whether or not such functioning, which depends on racial identity, is desirable.

On both sides of the racial line, the way political leaders earn their livelihood depends on continuation of the present polarity. These leaders are not about to give up their political power bases. Thus, they will continue to wave flags and symbols of racial differences. They will try to generate ever new racial issues for as long as they can beguile the people with such antics. In doing so, they are invoking the force of very powerful collective representations. They invoke the sinister archetype of the alien or enemy. The technique is extremely effective. Leaders on both sides of the racial line do this in the same breath that they decry racism or give lip service to interracial unity. As was mentioned earlier, the Voting Rights Act itself has the ironic potential for producing territorial segregation.

Only a resonating voice of unifying mythos, calling us to a much broader unity, will silence the voices of discord. This was Dr. King's *mountaintop vision*. This was the promised land that he saw, that included *all God's children*. Black political bosses misconstrue Dr. King as much and as often as white rednecks do. In this chapter, I have discussed the impact of differing mythological systems as the basis of racial conflict in the South. These differences go to the heart of the enforcement power of law. As I mentioned earlier, the same considerations probably apply wherever there are heterogeneous mixes of race, religion, and linguistic groups in a population.

A Basis for Hope

Differences in mythos present knotty, seemingly insoluble problems. At a different level, they form a basis of great hope. The richness of experience involved in an appreciation of the values of more than one culture is profound. One can escape the confines of a limiting and poorly funded mythos and see the values of differing systems. Cultural richness lies in preserving the variety of all our cultures, but developing a commonality and unity in essential values.

Julian Jaynes has suggested that consciousness itself resulted from the confluence of differing cultural systems.[143] Potential for a higher level of consciousness lies in the solution to the social problem of conflicts in mythos. Breadth of experience enables one to develop and activate a wealth of archetypes. This allows individuals to react more appropriately in a variety of situations. Cultural poverty leaves archetypes undeveloped, which leads to inappropriate responses, and inability to cope in modern society. In an enriched cultural milieu, broad, adequate collective representations can emerge to forge a new, more adequate morality.

There can be assimilation of values and production of a common value system. It is a natural process. When I was about eight years old, playing in the front yard one day, I saw a mocking bird trying to build a nest. She placed twigs and bits of grass in the crotch of a limb in a crepe myrtle tree. The twigs and limbs would fall off. She was having a hard time. I got some strings and scissors and cut some short pieces and draped them across the limb. The bird ignored them. I lost interest. Late that fall, the leaves fell from the crepe myrtle, and I found the nest and remembered the strings. She had placed them in the heart of the nest, where the eggs had been, and little birds had hatched.

All of my life, converging mythologies have been placing "strings" before me, and I only hope that I can find how they fit. Rational and non-rational can converge. This is how we will resolve the problem of differing mythological systems. When the world hears *Dixie* with a touch of blues, the solutions to racial problems in the South will not be distant.

---

[143] Jaynes, *The Origin of Consciousness in the Breakdown of the Bicameral Mind.*

Impact of Mass Media

In preceding pages, we described dynamics involved in formation of law. New means of mass communication have arisen in modern times, especially in the nineteenth and twentieth centuries, that have a significant impact on the processes that make law happen. Processes of moral formation before that time occurred in close-knit families, close-knit communities, and the Church. Today, media has a strong potential for interaction with archetypes and collective representations of law. The influence of the Church in funding archetypes with experience was much greater in the past than it is today.

Rapid expansion in ability to produce written words sprang from invention of the printing press. This laid the base for the Age of Reason. The scientific revolution and modern nation state itself could not have come about without invention of printing. Writing continued to be the sole means of sharing information on a widespread basis until well into this century, and its importance continues even now. Writing is particularly important in technical areas. It is our most convenient means for sharing and storing large volumes of information.

There have been advances in the twentieth century in production of the written word. Computers have again revolutionized the means of producing the written page. Nevertheless, the written page may be diminishing in importance, eclipsed by other means of sharing information. Radio, television, telephones and computers are entirely new and different means of sharing and storing information on a widespread basis, and they are definitely having an impact on law. One author has devoted an entire volume to the impact of electronic media on law.[144]

We have used the Civil Rights Movement as a point of reference for many ideas expressed in this volume. Modern media played a major role in the Civil Rights Movement. Dr. King and his fellow workers were keenly aware of the importance of media to their cause and consciously sought media coverage. Images of snarling dogs and powerful fire hoses

---

[144] Katsh, *The Electronic Media and the Transformation of Law.*

in Birmingham flashed across the nation via television. In this way a broader moral base was brought to bear on the issues. Without media, it is safe to say that there would have been no Civil Rights Movement. The role of media in transformation of law deserves careful attention.

Reading Dependency

First, let's consider some practical effects of our past dependency on reading and writing. We place a large premium on the ability to read and write well, because of the societal importance of writing. For hundreds of years, reading and writing have been the primary way of sharing and storing technical data, scientific principles, religious values, humor, and all other aspects of culture. There was no other means of sharing such ideas on a massive basis before the twentieth century. It is not surprising that we have assigned such a premium to the ability to read and write. Law, too, was stored and passed on in this medium.

A large percentage of persons incarcerated for crimes are illiterate. Understandably, this has been a cause of much concern, but our concern may be misplaced. The same thing that causes persons to be unable to read may be at the root of their difficulty with law. I am all for literacy, but it is not the solution to the problem of crime. A mere hundred years ago, it was no disgrace to be unable to read. But utilitarianism, which is the most widely argued justification for law in the theory of positivism, was certain to discover that persons who cannot read are less useful. The problem is built into the system. Reading and writing have been the sole means of the ability to share—to participate in the larger community of humankind. Persons without this ability suffer a severe handicap. They are less useful. Perhaps we should call the period from 1500 to 1900 the age of *print* rather than other, more abstract designations such as the Age of Reason.

Total dependence on this one means of communication until well into the twentieth century, caused reading and writing skill to become strongly identified with *intelligence* itself. No other expression or exhibition of intelligence *had any means of massive expression*. In this century radio, telephone, television and computers became available. Previously, intellect not reflected in the ability to read and write had no *mass* means of expression. Far-flung society could not recognize intelligence that one could not express in writing. Reading was the only means of getting significant information about the world. This is a part of the basis of the assertion of cultural bias in intelligence testing by Blacks and other ethnic groups. The argument has validity.

I am convinced that individuals invest their psychic energy—their capacity for coping—in structures and values that appear most profitable in meeting needs, including the need for self-esteem. Self-esteem in a subgroup can be acquired by eschewing values of the larger group, which can create a major challenge to education as a tool for social progress. I have known many world-wise, street savvy persons who did not hold education in high esteem. Often, these individuals appeared to know things that the most gifted psychologist might have difficulty comprehending. For instance, the persons who formulate the tests might have great difficulty "scoring" in some of the night clubs frequented by my worldly wise acquaintances.

There is another side of that argument, however. Reading and writing have been and still are critical means of coping in society as it actually exists. Talents of some other order, that one cannot share, cannot further the satisfaction of basic human needs as well. Although real, these talents are of less general practical importance than ability to read and write. Standardized tests may be defective as measures of absolute ability. Yet they are reasonably accurate and very useful in a relative, practical sense. They measure skills useful for coping in society as it is. Indeed, advanced means of communication are themselves dependent on a command of the language and knowledge of the culture. E. D. Hirsch writes:

> Why is literacy so important in the modern world? Some of the reasons, like the need to fill out forms or get a good job, are so obvious that they needn't be discussed. But the chief reason is broader. The complex undertakings of modern life depend on the cooperation of many people with different specialties in different places. Where communications fail, so do the undertakings. (That is the moral of the story of the Tower of Babel.) The function of national literacy is to foster effective nationwide communications. Our chief instrument of communication over time and space is the standard national language, which is sustained by national literacy. Mature literacy alone enables the tower to be built, the business to be well managed, and the airplane to fly without crashing. All nationwide communications, whether by telephone, radio, TV, or writing are fundamentally dependent upon literacy, for the essence of literacy is not simply reading and writing but also the effective use of the standard literate language. In Spain and most of Latin America the literate language is standard written Spanish. In Japan it is standard written Japanese. In our country it is standard written English.
>
> The recently rediscovered insight that literacy is more than a skill is based upon knowledge that all of us unconsciously have about language. We

know instinctively that to understand what somebody is saying, we must understand more than the surface meanings of words; we have to understand the context as well. The need for background information applies all the more to reading and writing. To grasp the words on a page we have to know a lot of information that isn't set down on the page.[145]

To paraphrase in our own idiom, one must participate in mythos if ability to read and write are to be effective. There are other details in the external world that we could observe but don't because we are reading. We must recognize that investment of coping energy into reading, writing, and any other modern means of communication is accompanied by a loss of attention to other observable details, a fact which anthropology has documented.[146]

Modern Developments

In the twentieth century, there have been significant changes in mass media. Radio, motion pictures, television, telephone, and computers and other electronic devices have made massive inroads. Society still depends on writing for bottom line information, but we convey public opinions, political images, political propaganda, and ideas that shape national policies and the moral base largely through media other than writing. This shift from written to non-written mass communication, once technology became available, is not surprising.

Ability to communicate well in writing, and ability to read well are special abilities. Humankind passed through thousands of years of evolutionary development before reading and writing became widespread. They raised food, hunted, traded and did a thousand other activities to survive. They observed and knew details that are lost in our generation. During the relatively short period of the last five hundred years, there has been a great change. The primary means of survival has come to be ability to read and write. It is a strange activity. We decipher meaning from various shapes or symbols (known as letters) impressed on very thin material (paper) and arranged sequentially. Imagine a video tape of the development of humankind over the last 100,000 years. *Fast forward* it so we see each 50 years in one minute. The last 10 minutes appear very strange, with all the leaders poring over books! Small wonder that, given opportunity, we utilize media that operates on visual images and oral communication.

---

145 Hirsch, *Cultural Literacy*, pp. 2-3.
146 See Levi-Strauss, *The Savage Mind*, 1962.

Literacy Not the Only Bridge

Radio, motion pictures, telephone, television and computers have made a big change in media. There will no longer be the strange compaction of human intellect into one means of communication. Archetypes described by Jung now receive a major part of their experiential funding through these media. These new media define imagery much more clearly. They expose us to lifestyles that differ dramatically from lifestyles of our ancestors. Potential effect on processes of moral formation which we have discussed are obvious and significant.

The shift from a written linguistic means of storage and transmission of the moral base to a means that involves visual imagery is important. Let me illustrate by an example. When television adapts a book, it does not use as many words. The words themselves are transmitted orally rather than by means of writing. Only a small percentage of the words that appear in the book will appear in a television production. However, the visual imagery usually more than makes up the difference. For most people, the combination of pictures and words is much more understandable and powerful than written words alone.

The shift to a new means of mass communication makes *concepts* less important in communication. Modern means of communication may have contributed to the trend. Expression in written words requires that the thought pass through the conscious minds of both the writer and the reader. Television and motion pictures, however, deal more directly with images and symbols. In order for society to progress for the last 500 years, individuals had to walk the tightrope of literacy. The tightrope was the only means of spanning the chasm between individual and a civilization that extends far beyond the immediate community. Modern media opens vastly expanded opportunities for communication and transmission of images. No doubt, ideas presented in this volume can be presented much more clearly with the use of audio-visual aids.

Suddenly, we find that several large bridges, not only safe for walking, but for riding in large buses, have spanned the chasm between individual and society. Visual media opens new vistas, and presents wonderful opportunities in moral formation as well as many other areas of cultural enrichment. However, there are also many risks. Not everyone can pass over those bridges as a *sender* of messages, but all can receive the messages. The same type of individuals who walked tightropes of literacy will not make deliveries via bridges of visual communications. Media may significantly redefine the cultural literacy for which Mr. Hirsch argues. Energy will take the path of least resistance.

Visual, oral means of communication will replace more difficult written means in many important areas of knowledge. Media faces massive ethical issues.

Left Brain/Right Brain

The shift from linguistic to visual media involves more than a shift from one organ of sensory perception to another. It involves a shift in the mental processing of the information involved. Linguistic function is primarily a left brain function. The left brain processes both oral and written linguistic communication. The right brain deals in visual and spatial images. Of course, the division of labor is not complete. Moral formation involves both hemispheres. However, the right brain is more decisive. The right brain has capacity for assimilating the big picture.[147]

You will recall the discussion of the parallel between phases of development of language and development of law. Development of both law and language proceeded historically in the following order: (1) oral tradition; (2) writing; (3) paper; (4) printing; and (5) modern technological means.

The two hemispheres of the brain process different kinds of information. The two sides function somewhat independently. The left brain processes words in sequential files. It organizes sentences and paragraphs. It never tires of the organizational task. The right brain assimilates large amounts of data and forms a composite judgment. For example, the left brain enables one to understand principles of physics, which deal with the *center of gravity*. By contrast, the right brain intuitively instructs a child in stacking blocks. Stacking blocks is, of course, dependent on principles of physics that deal with center of gravity. However, the right brain takes a short-cut.

Both hemispheres must function on an integrated basis for an individual to cope with the world. The sense of duty is an integrated function of both hemispheres. It has no known situs in the brain, and probably consists of a large variety of mental functions, but this is not the point of the present discussion. The point is that the new media is likely to affect processes that fund the sense of duty with specific contents.

If we follow the parallel development of language and law outlined above, there is a very interesting observation. Until the second half of the twentieth century, from the time that law expanded beyond the family, it

---

[147] See Blakeslee, *The Right Brain*, and Jaynes, *The Origin of Consciousness in the Breakdown of the Bicameral Mind*.

has followed in the very footsteps of language. Development of both language and law has been in ever-increasing patterns of complexity of left brain activity—linguistic activity. *However, this is not true of the second half of the twentieth century.* Television has quickly become a predominant means of mass communication. We have reverted to pictures—*a right brain function.* Body language communication can occur on an unprecedented scale through visual media. Body language, with accompanying *affective* behavior, is the media of choice for the masses.

Writing may have been beyond the ken of the masses for complex social and legal issues. The picture tube has now largely replaced writing with regard to such issues. Television involves the masses more deeply than ever before in dynamics that produce law. It communicates symbols directly rather than through the abstract medium of written words. Television bombards us with symbols at an unprecedented rate. Advertising is particularly pregnant with symbolism.

Can there be any question that the impact of modern media upon moral formation is massive? Can there be any question that we are in the midst of a revolution in moral formation? The very port of entry into our minds of vital information for moral formation is different as a result of television. Visual symbols speak directly to deep centers of energy within the individual. Words themselves enter through the ears rather than the eyes, as in reading. Here is an unspeakably large development that psychology and sociology can help us deal with. Here is an opportunity for renewal of moral formation.

Media, (meaning the technical means of communication—not the people in charge of it) is morally neutral. The question is what we will do with the opportunity. The difficulty is that everyone wants to at least *appear* value-free. Introduction of values—often non-traditional values—is intentionally subtle. Visual media supports a consumer morality of waste, by promoting economic interests of advertisers. Advertisers provide the economic support of visual media.

Imagery

We need to understand fully the role of imagery in all of this. Television and motion pictures deal in images and symbols. Dr. C. G. Jung, you will recall, postulated the existence of *archetypal images* in the universal unconscious. These images included the hero, the father, the mother, the self, the wise old man, the anima and animus, and others. These images reside in the unconscious, and have great psychic energy. They have significant impact on individual and social behavior. Their nature and identity indicate that they are mechanisms for relating individuals to groups.

Culture provides specific content for those images through mythos. Mythology, both in its oral phase and its written phases deals in these same images. One theory holds that durability and widespread consistency of mythological themes exist because they are projections of humanity's inward nature. These images and symbols are, in turn, highly effective motivating forces.

Imagery of visual media does not differ in kind from images that have historically been powerful in mythology and psychology. A 1991 beer commercial included a flag, an eagle, heraldic symbols, a mountain range, and a dozen or more other powerful symbols—all in thirty seconds. There is no reason to doubt that television images will be powerful determinants of the creative mythos of the twenty-first century. We have dismantled the tightrope of written media, where only the chosen few could perform effectively. We are in the midst of revolution in moral formation of immense proportions. Ethical considerations for those involved in media are equally immense.

Jung's archetypes relate closely to Durkheim's concept of collective representations. Durkheim theorized that these common elements basic to thought patterns are functions of society, internalized by individuals for their own use. He did not rely on a genetic base. If he is right, then the potential for alteration of thought patterns by mass media is much greater than if Jung's theories, which involve genetically transmitted archetypes, are right. Archetypes and collective representations present the same picture from different angles.

Intervening in the Cycle of Poverty and Ignorance

A full discussion of the moral revolution brought on by media is, of course, beyond the scope of this chapter. I can suggest only a few practical implications. Some are positive and some are negative. Visual media presents an interesting chance to intervene in the under-age-five population. It can help to break the cycle of poverty and ignorance. The *Head Start* program, a federal educational program for pre-schoolers, was an effort to intervene. However, the need is so vast and resources for such a program so limited that the program could not possibly be a great success.

Television, present in many homes even of poverty level, presents several new possibilities. Children of tender years can gain a more adequate linguistic base. Television can standardize language, and can help end crippling educational and moral effects of limited and self-perpetuating dialects. Often, such dialects prevent admission to the mainstream of society. This can be done without sacrificing cultural richness of differing dialects. In short, television may be the greatest hope for overcoming conflicts in mythos.

Images, Not Words

Television can help us to visualize and appropriate more effective modes of conduct. The adage "spare the rod and spoil the child," voiced by loving parents, with appropriate affective behavior towards their children, is okay. In the hands of a sadistic, uncaring, detached tyrant, it is the rationalization and justification for criminal abuse. In coffee shop conversations, the loving parent can talk at length with the tyrant about child rearing, using the time-honored phrase. Both leave thinking they agree and have communicated. The same communication breakdown is avoided when television's visual images accompany the words.

Television allows images, as well as words, to penetrate to the center of the home. It dispels some of the ambiguity of mere words. It can communicate images of moral behavior much more effectively than mere words. Television does not just bring the message to the hearths of the American home. It has *replaced* the hearth as center of the American home.

Many people have expressed deep concern about the sex and violence that is prevalent on television. Some interesting conclusions result from the analysis that I have set forth here. It probably is not so much the large, objective tendencies of television as the subtle, subliminal tendencies that should concern us. What material is funding archetypes of the universal unconscious with experience? What experience is conditioning the conscience? Will those archetypes ultimately (through television ratings) project themselves and reproduce themselves in themes that are successful? Can someone manipulate them? To what extent should we deliberately resort to content of tried and true mythology in selecting television themes?

In children's programming there is probably a much higher *unintentional* resort to classic mythological themes, images and symbols than we realize. Once we know what we are looking for, it is not difficult to recognize ancient myths and archetypes. They are present in the most far-out science fiction space adventure as well as in kiddy cartoons.

Unworkable Social Paradigms

Can media distort our images and symbols into unworkable paradigms, either intentionally or unintentionally? Can it lead civilization to destruction? Interestingly, this theme itself is not missing in mythology. It is the theme of the *Pied Piper of Hamlin*. That folk story gives a painfully poignant answer to the question that I am now raising. The alluring enchantment that rids us of rats can also take our children— our future. We pay the piper one way or the other. Daily, advertisers resort to powerful imagery to promote their particular product. Coca-cola is the *real* thing. Beer drinkers are slim and enjoy the *good life*. Soap and perfume create sex appeal. The list could go on and on. Advertisements are only a small part of the imagery. Perhaps we are on guard anyway, when we know that it is advertising.

Television drama usually portrays churchgoers as narrow and bigoted. Swingers assume the hero role. They are successful and happy—and usually free of any family ties of any importance. There is a certain richness in the funding of archetypes with a broad range of experiences. However, there is danger that an unworkable social paradigm will emerge as the prevailing value system. If Jung is right in his theory of archetypes, individuals will probably provide resistance necessary to avoid tragedy. However, if Durkheim's theory of social origin of collective representations is correct, the danger is much greater. We can become tolerant of acts of immorality that threaten survival. Paradoxically, tolerance itself is a good example. It is not always a virtue, but media portrays it as such. Too much tolerance leads us to be indecisive on critical moral issues.

Control of Media

Ben H. Bagdikian, in his powerful book, *The Media Monopoly*, says there is great cause for concern. He systematically shows the monopolistic tendencies in ownership of media in the United States. Less than fifty corporations controlled a majority of the mass media at the time his book was published. Corporate power, he insists, asserts itself not only in advertising, but in editorial and program content. Dynamics that I have described in this book have not escaped the attention of power brokers. Bagdikian writes:

> Every culture has its official folklore. In ancient times medicine men transformed tribal legends to enhance their own status. The twentieth century is no different, but the high priests who communicate mythic dogmas now do

so through great centralized machines of communication—newspaper chains, broadcast networks, magazine groups, conglomerate book publishers, and movie studios. Operators of these systems disseminate their own version of the world. And of all the legends they generate, none are so heroic as the myths they propagate about themselves.[148]

Bagdikian forcefully argues that the corporate world impacts significantly on content of information coming from media. The dangers that he sees may or may not be real. However, the potential for control that he describes is frightening. He was afraid of conservative, corporate republicans. The prospects of control by liberal democrats, or simply garden variety crooks, is equally real and frightening. His book is an important one for anyone who wishes to understand the perils of media which face us.

Misdirection of Energy

Mass media can cause a deflection of energy which individuals naturally contribute for society's purposes. Media can affect the natural ecology of human emotion. I previously developed at some length the mechanisms which cause individuals to energize norms of society. By pinpointing a specific event, media can bring a very disproportionate amount of energy to bear on a particular situation. What happens when media spends millions of dollars to publicize an attempt to relieve the plight of two or three whales stranded in ice? Other more critical issues go unattended.

Riveted to television, we allow people to suffer in our own community. More directly in point, media often focuses on certain legal events which are no more and no less significant than similar activities elsewhere. Glued to television screens, we condemn or approve of alleged crimes or moral failings in cities a thousand miles away. We are oblivious to suffering around us. Spectators rarely appear in my court. However certain television portrayals of court activities receive much attention. I suspect that for public trials to be effective, the public needs to be present. Instead, the public is content with a media account.

Media diverts attention from the problems and importance of events in local communities. It siphons off societal energy required for secure local government and law enforcement. Considering Bagdikian's book, we must ask ourselves whether the diversion of attention is accidental or deliberate. The diverted energy is the energy for law.

---

[148] Bagdikian, *The Media Monopoly*, p. 68.

Archetypes and Symbols

Bagdikian describes how advertising companies test subjects to determine their psychological and sociological responses to commercials. They obviously intend to affect *motive*. Their actions belie their denials. Bagdikian brings the point home.

> When parent groups and others complain to broadcasters about the impact of sex and violence on the young, broadcasters traditionally answer that sex and violence on television do not change human behavior. That answer has been contradicted by extensive studies and surveys by the Surgeon General of the United States. But each year broadcasters sell more than $10 billion worth of commercial time whose only purpose is to change human behavior. Presumably, the most sophisticated corporations would not continue spending billions of dollars if they thought they were not altering human behavior in their favor.[149]

Ads intended to perpetuate our materialistic view of the good life have drawn on every conceivable symbol. Bagdikian makes the following telling observation concerning television and its use of and impact on symbols.

> The reclothing of ads in ever-new symbols has contributed to the devastating attrition in the lifespan of symbols in modern culture. Advertising is not the only cause of this attrition. All modern communications has a hand in it. Two hundred years ago the common symbols of society were those of rulers and the church, their flags and icons displayed individually and seen solely by live audiences. Mechanical printing and other mass communications changed that. Contemporary society is filled with images, some in a constant state of change like television, or in continuously altered states, as in radio. Printing reproduces words and illustrations in multiples of billions and can be absorbed by millions. Through electronic devices and modern printing processes, flags, crosses, and other emotionally laden symbols can be mass-produced for huge audiences. But no single force has equaled the merchandising process in its use of all the sacred and semisacred symbols to create a culture of material consumption. Advertising is a source of symbol manipulation unknown to earlier generations. The advertising industry spends $1,000 per household in order to break through the resistance of human senses and sometimes of human intelligence. Selling symbols are in continuous flood for six and a half hours of television a day. Printed images are seen on countless billions of magazine pages every week and the four billion newspaper pages printed every day. As viewers and readers get used to the massively displayed symbols, the symbols change to the latest idea or

---

[149] Ibid., p. 186.

personality or national emotion until it, too, in days or weeks, becomes
meaningless, part of the continuous and deliberate slag heap of mass
communications.[150]

Advertisers use sex, beauty, mountains, valleys, springtime, crosses,
heroes, heroines, great personalities, and an endless list of symbols. They
spend billions on television advertising, and obviously expect to impact
on human behavior. How can anyone argue that television programming
itself does not impact on behavior?

We must not assume that the points that I am making about the basis
of human behavior have escaped the attention of the world of materialism. The media world carefully guards these points as secrets, because
they are profitable. The secrets are safe, for the time being. A degree of
sophistication is necessary to understand them. The danger is that in the
meantime, damage to the moral base is occurring. Those in charge of
media may have no understanding of this undesirable side effect of their
practices. The immense amounts of money involved discourage deeper
understanding or concern.

Media as an Estate to Itself

Having direct access to mythos and its immense power, media is an
estate unto itself. Control of media is concentrated in the hands of a
relatively small number of individuals. We do not elect these individuals,
and they are not answerable to the people in any way other than through
marketing polls. Any attempt to regulate is fraught with First
Amendment free speech problems. Yet those who actually control media
have an almost unfettered right to select and control the content of
programs. In a real sense, modern media, controlled by an unelected few,
is as much a means of censorship as a means of free expression. This
problem is probably one of the weightiest problems for the twenty-first
century. Regulatory policies can provide and require far greater competition and make a wider range of choice available to the public. This may
be at least a partial solution.

At the beginning of the modern era, secular government wrested
control of governing power of mythos from the Church. Media now has
direct access to that power. Media shapes myths that shape us. Mass
news media, controlled by the unelected, wields great power. The
question is whether an extra-governmental power has arisen that
actually competes with government for control. There is probably a

---

[150] Ibid., p. 187.

delicate balance at the present time. Most of us feel better that a non-governmental power exercises a *watchdog* function over government. However, there is a haunting question as to who is really in charge. If the framers of the Constitution reconvened today, would they be more concerned with Church/State relations or with Media/State relations? The power of media and the forces on which it draws, are now the equivalent of the power of the Church in an earlier day.

Media impacts on formative forces of law which I discussed in earlier chapters. Media has powerful means of oral and written communication, with highly affective propensities. It is reshaping the moral base. The moral base, whatever its contents, will undergird law, for better or worse. Obviously, the themes of modern mythos which we discussed earlier dominate television programming. Themes of individuality, sexuality and rationality promote sales. But will they also fund motive powers that lead to social order necessary for our survival?

6 | Faith

In the first five sections, I developed, step by step, an image of the dynamic, holistic system that causes law to happen. First, I questioned why people do the things that amount to law. Point by point I answered that question. I explained individual psychological factors of motive, beginning with conscience. Then I moved on to basic human needs, and showed that they are the key to motive. I described how individuals give energy to group norms. Thinkers such as Jung and Durkheim, our mentors in the search for law's dynamics, led us to examine mythos. In mythos, we found the storehouse of values expressed in law. Mythos converts impulses into language. It contains images and ideals by which we authenticate law. We subscribe to rationalism, so the rituals that authenticate *our* law are rationalistic. The group psychology that shapes the shared perception of reality has its basis in mythos. Mythos is the source and substance of norms.

Moreover, mythos is the mechanism by which society shapes individuals to its standards. Myths include emotional as well as rational content, and they give meaning to experience. They convey values from generation to generation. They address the unconscious mind as well as consciousness. They lie at the heart of our belief systems, or faith. Law depends on faith. There is a close association between myth and religion. This connection helps to explain how myths include and convey emotional content, according to Mircea Eliade and Emile Durkheim.

Language arises from mythos. The connection between mythos and language is intricate and extensive. Mythos, with its belief systems, authenticates law. We placed law into a geographic context by exploring territoriality. Territoriality also shows very explicitly the close connection between law and psychology. We have seen that the motive theory of law has important implications, in such areas as conflicts in mythos, the impact of psychological dogma, and mass media.

In this section, I show that faith lays the foundation for law. I make some important distinctions between myth, religion, belief, and faith. Religious faith is clearly not mere myth. There are qualitative differences in myths, and not all myths are of equal value. Systems of myth reinforce faith, but faith is a precursor of mythological systems themselves.

I have repeatedly referred to *faith in reason* and *faith in justice*. In this section, I argue that our attachment to reason is an expression of faith. Chapter 6.2 explores *justice* and traces its origins to psychological and social dynamics. I show that justice is an article of faith, and explore some specific ingredients of our faith in justice. Our reliance on justice is a ready example of the importance of adequate systems for development of faith.

For many, including most of the scientific community, the suggestion that religion *has* a role in law may sound strange. The suggestion is not in keeping with the mentality of our times. Nevertheless, religion and faith are important. The contribution of organized religion to social order is not a matter of indifference in questions we are discussing. I distinguish between religion and faith. Not all of us are *religious* in the usual sense of the word. Nevertheless, all of us have *faith*. Religious practices engender a *particular kind* of faith. Faith—what we believe— engenders a particular kind of behavior.

Social order results from belief systems. We readily understand that systems of belief determine social order in cultures other than our own. Nevertheless, we feel that our own social order results from ideals that are *real*. We believe that rational thinking reveals these ideals to us. Actually, our certainty is typical of belief systems which form the basis for all social orders. George Lankford, delving into beliefs of American Indians, writes:

> For human beings, survival demands an awareness of the way the world works. No matter how we look at the world around us, it is endlessly complex. In order to reduce that complexity, every human society posits a relatively small number of principles that seem to explain and predict the dynamic forces of the non-human natural order. This lore is crystallized into patterns called belief systems, and those patterns find expression in all areas of social life, from the verbal, aural, and visual arts to organization, customs, and economics. All together, the belief systems and their expressions comprise our "culture," the thought and behavior that make us part of one society and not another.[151]

Despite the universal nature of those words, we apply them to Native Americans, but not to ourselves. Such faith or belief systems must be present for law to exist. Our social order, like all other social orders,

---

[151] Lankford, *Native American Legends*, p. 54.

arises from *our* belief systems. We examined belief systems and how they operate in earlier chapters. Belief systems obviously result from *faith*. Now we look at faith itself.

All Religion Included

In discussing the *Church* or *religion*, I do not intend only some branch or denomination of the Christian religion. I am not limiting the term to the Christian religion. As used here, the term *Church* may refer to *organized religion*, including Judaism, Islam, and the oriental religions, in addition to Christianity. I use the word *Church* for two reasons. First, in western civilization, the word stands, in a general way, for the historic institutional representative of religious tradition. The Church was the institutional competitor of the state during the Middle Ages. Today, we say that the U.S. Constitution provides for separation of *Church* and State. I use the term in this broadest possible sense.

Secondly, I am an active member of a particular Church. As I have pointed out several times in earlier chapters, there are no neutral observers; and I am no exception to that rule. I am a member of the United Methodist Church. I know more about my own denomination and religious faith than I do about others. This is my frame of reference. I am active in the Church. If not, I would not know anything about it, firsthand. The frame of reference affects my presentation. I do not mean to say, of course, that I agree with every social principle of the United Methodist Church. Moreover, the thoughts expressed in this book may not be typical of United Methodists.

I see the role of the Church in a quite positive light. Nevertheless, this chapter contains many suggestions as to what the Church *ought to be* rather than what it *is*. Failings of the Church are Church problems, not State problems. While there are some areas in which the State should perhaps exercise more restraint, separation of Church and State is a sound legal principle. It is not usually considered a characteristic of religion. As a legal principle, it protects various institutional representations of religion, as well as preventing any one religious community from acquiring control of the machinery of government. These two functions are provided in separate clauses of the U. S. Constitution, the *establishment* clause and the *free expression* clause. "Congress shall make no law respecting an *establishment* of religion, or prohibiting the *free exercise* thereof. . . ."[152] We should not look to the State to deal with problems that the Church should solve.

Moral fiber which results from activity of the Church is a necessary condition for law and government. It is not the other way around. The Church's concerns should include the hearts, minds, and souls of the people first. Its contribution to law is a secondary, indirect result of its activity. Values in which people really believe are the moral substance of law.

The Abandoned Role

In suggesting reaffirmation of the role of the Church in society, I join distinguished company. In his seminal book, *Whatever Became of Sin?*, to which I referred earlier, Dr. G. Carl Menninger deplored the diminished role of the Church in society. He also expressed concern about the diminished role of clergy in the resolution of societal problems. Earlier, I expressed concern that Dr. Menninger did not acknowledge the extent to which psychotherapists and psychologists have usurped the role of the Church and ministers. Pop-psychology makes cultivation of a healthy sense of guilt unfashionable. Dr. Menninger is on target, however, when he urges ministers to become more active and influential in the moral conduct of society.

The Church has traditionally played a role in moral formation. Yet, although moral formation is legitimately within the non-exclusive province of religion, I am not suggesting that moral formation is the primary purpose of religion. Moral formation is an indirect result of religious experience; it is not the central purpose of the experience. Hence, I am not suggesting that the Church is a mere vehicle of social work. Indeed, when such concerns become the primary focus of the Church, the Church falters.

The prominence which I give to the importance of moral formation as a function of the Church may be misleading. It is not a plea for social activism in the Church, and moral formation is not the purpose of the Church. When the Church pursues its religious function as a primary goal, it causes moral formation as an indirect result. Even survival of society is not the primary purpose of the Church. Viktor Frankl argues:

> However, survival cannot be the supreme value. Unless life points to something beyond itself, survival is pointless and meaningless. It is not even possible. This is the very lesson I learned in three years spent in Auschwitz

---

[152] U.S. Const. Amend. I.

and Dachau, and in the meantime it has been confirmed by psychiatrists in prisoner-of-war camps: Only those who were oriented toward the future, toward a goal in the future, toward a meaning to fulfill in the future, were likely to survive.[153]

The quest of religious experience is for meaning. The greatest people who have ever lived have been religious leaders. They have given more to civilization than anyone else. Their values have reinforced survival prospects for society. Yet in their enlightenment, Jesus, Buddha, Muhammad, and all other great religious leaders rejected *the world. They found meaning by turning Maslow's hierarchy of needs upside down.* They rejected material goods that satisfy immediate physical needs for spiritual values that provide meaning. Unfortunately, this visionary role is often missing in the Church today.

Even the reduction of the purpose of the Church to a *quest for meaning* is misleading. As William James pointed out, reading the menu is not the same as eating the meal. James writes:

> A bill of fare with one real raisin on it instead of the word "raisin," with one real egg instead of the word "egg," might be an inadequate meal, but it would at least be a commencement of reality.[154]

To understand the physical and chemical properties of water will neither satisfy one's thirst nor substitute for baptism. The role of the Church is not merely to state or even to understand its purpose. Its rituals, its teachings, its traditions, and its community, must inspire and support *faith* that is necessary for meaning. The Church is the vehicle of faith. When organized religion accomplishes its purposes by giving meaning to life, moral formation also occurs. We cannot get the same results by direct, intentional methods.

Let me give an example. John Wesley, the founder of Methodism, did his evangelistic work in eighteenth century England. Social conditions were deplorable, and he did what he could to help. Nevertheless, his primary concern was with the spread of *scriptural holiness.* He preached his gospel messages in the fields and gained a large following. He organized *classes* for further study. He reached the masses with his message—people who would never have associated with the Church of England. Wesley never withdrew from the Church of England. Some historians credit Wesley with preventing a bloody revolution in England

---

[153] Frankl, *The Unconscious God*, p. 139.
[154] James, *The Varieties of Religious Experience*, p. 490.

similar to the one that occurred in France. As in Wesley's case, the role of the Church in moral formation often supports government. However, the role of the Church is not merely or even incidentally to support or defend organized government.

Throughout history, organized religion has been the bearer of sacred myths. By using the word *myth*, I am not implying that the message of the Church is false or less than factual. Those are not issues for discussion here. The point is that the culture of the West evolved in the matrix of Judeo-Christian values. The Judeo-Christian heritage is, in large measure, the source of our very concepts of *good* and *evil*. As mentioned earlier, even a thinker of Nietzsche's stature cannot take us *Beyond Good and Evil* as the title of his book implies. Judeo-Christian concepts of right and wrong are important parts of our mythos. Within this cultural framework, motive force for law evolves.

My thesis, then, is that the Church should continue in its historic role of spiritual formation. But it need not apologize for its interest in morals. Its mission is broad. James Fowler suggests that persons in the highest stages of faith commit themselves to some "image or images of a faithful ultimate environment." They shape "their lives in the human community so as to live in complementarity with it."[155] The role of the Church is to sponsor development of such faith. Not everyone can reach that level of faith. Not everyone needs that level of faith. However, each of us has a role to play in life, and we must have faith enough to support the role.

The role of the Church is to *sponsor* faith at the highest level that individuals can accomplish. The religious instinct—the need for meaning—is one of the basic human needs. A sound theological approach to life, which finds meaning that transcends mere human existence, is an essential feature for real happiness and fulfillment.

The Church should therefore carefully protect its historically recognized role from the ill-defined, *valueless* values of secular social sciences. This is not, of course, to eschew the value of counseling and therapy by experts in treatment of mental illness. However, the cause of many of the "stress problems" and other disorders in our society is lack of meaning. Dogmas of social science are inadequate to fill the need. We have difficulty realizing there actually *are* dogmas of social sciences, so strong is their hold on the modern mind.

---

[155] Fowler, *Stages of Faith*, pp. 292-293.

Concern with Morals

Along with its concern for spiritual values, the Church has a historically affirmed concern with moral values. In this area, infighting between
the Church and social sciences is intense. The sad truth is that the Church
leaders seldom realize that the Church's role is under attack. Often secular values closely correspond to traditional values of the Church. The
similarity is not accidental since secular values arose from mythos
permeated by the Church. Humanism is not necessarily bad.
Nevertheless, the attack on the Church is very real, and the Church
should respond to the challenge. Secular social sciences seek truth
through the logic of science and adopt a detached viewpoint to do so. As
the quest for detached *objectivity* permeates social sciences, it increasingly becomes a normative force in society. We all try to become
detached observers, free of the biases of involvement. These processes
normalize an uncaring position, and undermine traditional moral values
that are the motive force of law. We need inward meaning, but we seek
outward objectivity.

We cannot all sit around, unobserved, observing each other. Nothing
good would happen if we did. We need to involve ourselves in active
concern about problems confronting us. We need to actually care about
others and their problems. Too widespread, the dogma of detachment
interferes with the very dynamics of moral formation. Sterile, disinter-
ested intellectualism with no survival potential replaces basic moral
values, that are essential to the legal system. *Knowing* and *caring* are
excellent companions, and should seldom be separated. Faith in reason
dominates the world as the highest *source* of values, rather than the mere
arbiter of values.

Rationalism easily finds fault with the Church. Unfortunately,
evidence supports the charges of abuse on the part of certain "Church"
practices. Unscrupulous ministers use the appeal of religion for personal
enrichment. Without question there has been extreme moral failure on
the part of some pretenders to religious faith. However, my experience
shows there is more to the story. There are fewer criminal acts, fewer
marital difficulties, and fewer problems with alcohol and drugs among
churchgoers, than among their secular counterparts. A mean, mal-
adjusted person can easily hide behind religious faith to express his true
nature. This does not mean that all religion is phony. When psychotherapists take sexual liberties with their clients, we do not conclude that all
psychotherapy is phony. The attraction of religion, which can be abused

like any other powerful force, merely marks its power. It does not prove its falsity.

Dr. Martin Luther King, Jr., was, above all else, a man of faith. His life would not have been as effective from any other approach. The dry, barren reservoirs of our faith long for words that have the ring of ultimate truth. His words did. We long for words that will relate us to our ultimate environment. Our ultimate environment includes our relationships with each other.

Sins of Omission

The problem with religion and the Church today is not so much what it does, as what it fails to do. When I sentence a convicted individual, mainline religions are not usually there. When I dissolve marriages and deal with other family problems that inflict emotional trauma to the very soul, mainline denominations are not usually there. When time comes to consider probation and alternative sentences, the Church is not usually there.

Churches sit in suburbia and cater to the middle class. Few are the John Wesleys, setting up Sunday school classes in housing projects— especially across racial lines. This is not a plea to promote a strong program of racial integration in Churches, nor to plan a social agenda for the Church. It is merely a common sense suggestion that Churches need to minister where people are hurting. If the Church does not include everyone in its gang, other gangs will form, and will be governed by radically different values.

The Church needs to deliver its powerful message to those who need it. Only in this way will there ever be the resulting by-product of integrated *values*. This is the way to achieve a common value system that will support an effective legal system. Division of labor in a corporate economy divides the population into specialties, each with its own loyalties and its specialized morality. Common faith that produces a moral system shared by everyone is essential to our survival.

Approaching the Ultimate Environment

Religion is no more than myths, the modern day skeptic says. An opiate for the masses, chime in proponents of communist dogma. Even as I compose this work, communism seems to be massively failing all around the world. Jung, Durkheim, and Campbell have shown us that myths—all myths—are important. Mark Twain said, "Let me make the superstitions of a nation, and I care not who makes its laws or its songs, either." We must not discount myths too quickly. Religion is still here, but communism appears to be on its way out. Myths are a way of explaining life; of giving meaning. They address unconscious mental life. They touch parts of our mental life where rational, cognitive processes cannot go. They activate the realm of faith.

Durkheim has shown us the important normative social function of myths—indeed their involvement in evolution of our very patterns of thinking. Seen in this light, rational thinking—science itself—is a product of mythos. It is itself a part of our modern mythology. We *believe* in science. Truth that we cannot scientifically prove is suspect, because of this dogma. However, we obviously cannot even know, let alone prove, many truths concerning our very existence. Neither can we prove the truths about intricate workings of society. Yet, these unverified, unverifiable truths are critically important to our continuing existence. We can approach these matters only through *faith*. Rationalism falls short. The faith approach involves the whole person, not just intellect.

The *ultimate environment*, which we approach through faith, includes our perception of the cosmos. Mythos has always concerned itself with cosmology. It hypothesizes the scheme of nature. The hypothesis forms the basis of collective representations as it gains in acceptance. Regardless of imperfections in any hypothesis, collective representations provide us with *concepts* for sharing it. Indeed, concepts enable society to operate. Society has no basis for expanding knowledge until a new hypothesis appears. These thoughts apply equally to the theory of relativity and to the most esoteric point of religious faith. Intuition—the hypothesis—always provides the basis for cognitive expansion.

The Mystery of Intuition

Without hypotheses, there could be no science. Without intuition, there could be no hypotheses. Intuition is the growing edge of knowledge. It participates in creation. Durkheim possibly dismissed ultimate truth—the existence of God—as unimportant. He may have felt that his social explanations of the origin of religion were the last word. He probably felt that we could penetrate the mystery no further. However, social progress depends on intuition, which he did not explain.

Did whole Australian clans as described by Durkheim come into being, with each member believing himself to be an ostrich? More likely, one person *intuitively* reached this conclusion and convinced others. Intuition and hypothesis expand human knowledge and start new myths. Science has not and cannot explain intuition. Like any other faith system, science is the product of intuition, and relies on intuition. Science, too, is a matter of faith. It is part of our system for interpreting the total environment.

William James concluded that religious experience starts in the subconscious or subliminal mind. It irrupts into consciousness and affects the world of which we are aware. We might add that the hypotheses that advance science appear to irrupt in precisely the same manner from precisely the same source. This is where Durkheim's lizard men and ostrich men got their ideas and their identity. Jung has intimated the vastness of the unconscious realm, including the universal unconscious. Our mental apparatus creates or recreates the external world of cause and effect. We are not likely to see God breaking into this external chain of cause and effect. We exclude Him in the very way we envision the external world. In the inwardness that we cannot explain, where intuition starts, we cannot exclude Him.

Our inwardness—the world of faith—is where consciousness and rationality themselves arise. There our own powers of observation fall short. There is where myths arise. There we cannot ignore the possibility of a creating, living God. Hypotheses irrupt into consciousness from the unconscious, but we can approach their origin only through faith. The source of the unconscious is as uncertain as that of consciousness. The hypotheses so produced become the subject of faith. Religious systems preserve them. The hypotheses, in turn, deeply affect social reality.

Does this leave us without means of discernment as to matters of faith? Does it mean that *content* makes no difference, as long as faith is personally meaningful? The faith of the Creek Indians in Alabama at Horseshoe Bend and Holy Ground did not preserve them, despite assurances from their *medicine men*. The cosmos supported by the faith of the Middle Ages gave way to superior metaphors of science. The relatively short lived tenets of communism appear to be giving way to some as yet unidentified new faith system. There is something quite creative here, and it has to do with the evolutionary nature of systems of thought and behavior. Survival chooses truth, in a sense. Evolution proceeds through an unbroken line of survivors. But what makes progress itself possible? The possibility of progress, which is a cornerstone of our belief system, is the reason that we cannot exclude creativity.

Changing Perceptions of Cosmos

The Age of Reason ushered in a new perception of the cosmos. The flat earth to which the Church clung fell by the wayside. Along with everything else, the *moral order*, disappeared as an article of collective faith. Aquinas' natural law theory lost its foundation and has reeled in uncertainty ever since.

Homologous space and time, with counterparts in unlimited extension and unlimited duration were the building blocks for the *rational* perception of the cosmos. Undeviating cause and effect were cornerstones of that perception. The Cartesian system is the psychological model from which the system operated. In the Cartesian system, the observer and his mental processes are discretely separate from the *external world*. An important normative ideal has been progress in our dominion *over* nature, rather than defining our role *in* nature.

The idea of rationality is built into the system of thought in operation since the beginning of the Age of Reason. It evolved along with the system. Rationality is built into the way we interpret the universe—it is a mental element. We cannot be sure that it exists in the world outside our minds. We do not know whether we observe rational connections in the world outside our minds, or whether our minds are imposing them on the outside world.

Francis Bacon and other proponents of utopian worlds proposed social organizations based on their new perceptions of the cosmos. They created images that now shape our lives. These early thinkers in the Age of Reason created images of nations ruled by reason. These are images that shape our world-view. Their images, laid the foundation for legal positivism. By the time Bentham arrived, it was easy to say, "Law is the command of the sovereign." We continue to reap the benefits of the mighty dreams and visions of thinkers who first interpreted the Age of Reason. Their world-view remains a part of our belief system.

However, we now face a new perception of the cosmos with very different foundations. Our picture of the universe builds upon that of the Age of Reason, but goes further. The aura of mystery has returned. Time, space and motion relate to each other. Each is a function of the others in Einstein's famous theory. Matter and energy are also relative. Parallel lines actually meet. Straight lines return. The distinction between observer and observed is indistinct. Our scientific metaphors are inadequate for the very large and the very small. Unconscious mental processes are as important as conscious rationality. Evolution introduces *creativity* into nature's scheme. All this is quite different from the basic perceptions of the Age of Reason. *A new world-view is emerging.* Just as the emerging world-view builds on but surpasses the Age of Reason, our moral structure must build upon and surpass earlier moral structures.

Residual Morality

Science did not completely displace moral norms of the Church. The residue of the Church's moral order has been adopted and adapted into principles of humanism. That residue of morality continues to be a leading motive for law. However, the moral base which undergirds the law is failing. Division in beliefs and loyalties splinters the moral energy of society. The division interferes with formation of adequate, enforceable norms.

We described conflicts in mythos earlier. Those conflicts are one source of division, but there are others. In the work force, loyalty attaches to the subgroup, and is not universal. Lawyers look after lawyers. Doctors look after doctors. The list goes on and on. No one is tending to the big picture. Our images of morality are too small. Each group adopts its "ethics," which often serve the purpose of protecting economic interest of members of the group. The divisions rob energy from morals that we should all share, and the force of law consequently fails.

The only common denominator in our world of values is money. The predominant modern myths which we considered earlier—individuality, sexuality, and rationality—lose touch with the *ultimate environment*. They are convenient to a specialized materialistic world built on advertising symbols and themes. However, they will not stand the test of time. When we consider the evolving perception of the cosmos and social reality, our modern myths are clearly inadequate. They are incapable of providing an adequate source of meaning. We cannot leave moral formation to government, corporations, media, and social programs that are not even in the business of moral formation. Schools cannot completely fill the need. The *prayer in schools* issue is a non-issue. If the Church does its job effectively elsewhere, it will not want to assign this sacred function to secular officers. Instead of promoting religion through laws and political programs, the Church should shoulder its own historic responsibility and jealously guard it. It is not that I take issue with repetition of a simple prayer in school. It can do little harm, and its prohibition was far from the minds of our nation's founders. However, the Church should protect its own prerogative in the important matter of moral formation. It should not pass that duty on to the State. The City of Jerusalem and the City of Babylon, as described by Augustine, will always be distinct even though many profess citizenship in both. Even the value of money is dependent upon our faith in government and financial institutions. Justification of that faith reintroduces the necessity of our entire cultural system of morality. Morality is a prerequisite to our economic system.

Government is not the parent of morality, but morality of government. We must *believe* in the commandment "Thou shalt not steal" before there can be an economy.

Faith

As we proceeded through this chapter, our focus has centered on *faith*. Religion promotes a particular kind of faith. I have shown how faith is the fountainhead of myths that sustain us and give us meaning. Now we will explore meanings that others have assigned to the word *faith*. Faith is not always religious. Countless volumes have been written on the subject, and I must be selective.

James W. Fowler's book, *Stages of Faith* has been most helpful to me. Fowler outlined stages of faith that correspond to Kohlberg's stages of moral development. This approach, which might be called a developmental theory of faith, links faith to psychosocial theories of moral development. This linkage between faith and moral development shows the significance of faith in the motive forces of law. We act on our beliefs. Fowler argued, as I do, that moral formation closely relates to spiritual formation. He drew on works of Piaget, Kohlberg, and Erikson. He recognized the importance of the stages of moral development outlined by Kohlberg. Nevertheless, he also recognized the involvement of the emotions. Fowler writes:

> From the beginning I knew that I could not follow Piaget and Kohlberg in identifying the structural features of faith with the formal, logical structures of reason Piaget had identified. Nor could I afford to accept the Piaget-Kohlberg assertion that cognition and the affections, though intertwining in behavior and choice, must be analytically separated in cognitive-structural research. Faith, I knew, involves rationality and passionality; it involves knowing, valuing and committing.[156]

Kohlberg advanced the cognitive developmental theory of moral formation, extending the work of Jean Piaget. Fowler sensed the inadequacy of the purely cognitive theories of Kolberg and Piaget, and insisted that psychosocial factors play a part in the individual's development. Fowler rightfully refused to exclude the emotional side of our being from his stages of faith. His developmental theory of faith, which draws deeply on psychological components, is highly significant for the motive theory of law that I am describing. Developing faith draws on both internal

---

[156] Fowler, *Stages of Faith*, p. 272.

psychological development and environment. Fowler's writing shows the place of faith in nature's scheme.

Fowler's approach should have appeal in our analytical world. He does not debate the specific contents of faith. However, he shows the role and importance of faith as a human function in the real world in which we live. I am indebted to Fowler for the term *ultimate environment* to which we relate in faith. The stages outlined by Fowler illustrate the unfolding nature of faith during the process of human development.

Fowler begins with a *pre-stage*, in which the child establishes basic relationships of trust with parents, or parent substitutes. This is the period from birth to emergence of thought and language. Stage one he calls the *intuitive-projective*. In it, he says, "(T)he child can be powerfully and permanently influenced by examples, moods, actions and stories of the visible faith of primally related adults."

The second stage is the *mythic-literal*. "The new capacity" of this stage, according to Fowler, "is the rise of narrative and the emergence of story, drama and myth as ways of finding and giving coherence to experience." This is the stage at which the individual internalizes the stories, beliefs, and practices of his community of faith. The idea expressed here describes one of the functions of myth which I have discussed in earlier chapters.

Next comes the *synthetic-conventional*. This third stage of faith is the one in which the individual comes to grips with the world beyond the family, which again parallels my theory. Here, Fowler says, "Faith must synthesize values and information; it must provide a basis for identity and outlook." At this stage, associated with adolescence, the individual forms his own myth, "the myth of one's own becoming in identity and faith." The personal myth incorporates "one's past and anticipated future in an image of the ultimate environment unified by characteristics of personality."

The fourth stage Fowler calls the *individuative-reflective*. Here, "(T)he late adolescent or adult must begin to take seriously the burden of responsibility for his or her own commitments, lifestyle, beliefs and attitudes." The individual attains an identity independent of roles assigned by others. Fowler says, "To sustain that new identity (the self) composes a meaning frame conscious of its own boundaries and inner connections and aware of itself as a 'world view.'"

Fifth is the *conjunctive* stage. At this stage, "Symbolic power is reunited with conceptual meanings." The stage "Involves a critical recognition of one's social unconscious—the myths, ideal images and prejudices built deeply into the self-esteem by virtue of one's nurture within a particular social class, religious tradition, ethnic group or the like." This stage is unusual before mid-life. Fowler states, "The new strength of this stage comes in the rise of the ironic imagination—a capacity to see and be in one's or one's group's most powerful meanings, while simultaneously recognizing that they are relative, partial and inevitably distorting apprehensions of transcendent reality."

The final stage of faith is one that is seldom attained. Fowler calls it *universalizing faith.*

> *Heedless of the threats to self, to primary groups, and to the institutional arrangements of the present order that are involved, Stage 6 becomes a disciplined, activist incarnation*—a making real and tangible—of the imperatives of absolute love and justice of which Stage 5 has partial apprehensions. The self at Stage 6 engages in spending and being spent for the transformation of present reality in the direction of a transcendent actuality.
>
> Persons best described by Stage 6 typically exhibit qualities that shake our usual criteria of normalcy. Their *heedlessness to self-preservation* and the vividness of their taste and feel for transcendent moral and religious actuality give their actions and words an extraordinary and often unpredictable quality. *In their devotion to universalizing compassion they may offend our parochial perceptions of justice. In their penetration through the obsession with survival, security, and significance they threaten our measured standards of righteousness and goodness and prudence.* Their enlarged visions of universal community disclose the partialness of our tribes and pseudo-species. And their leadership initiatives, often involving strategies of nonviolent suffering and ultimate respect for being, constitute affronts to our usual notions of relevance. It is little wonder that persons best described by Stage 6 so frequently become martyrs for the visions they incarnate.(emphasis added)[157]

Regardless of the contents of faith, these are the stages of its development. The description of stage six brings to mind Dr. Martin Luther King, Jr., to whom we have referred so often. Not everyone proceeds through all these stages. Nevertheless, these are the lines along which faith develops. Fowler's suggestions blend soundly with the findings of developmental psychology. We see in the higher stages of faith the potential for origin and importance of myth. In the more common stages, we see a basis for maintaining moral order. The faith system integrates

---

[157] Fowler, *Stages of Faith*, p. 200.

processes of moral formation and cognitive development into a workable frame.

Implicit in Fowler's theory is the obvious truth that all of humanity lives by faith. William James quotes Leo Tolstoy on this point:

"Since mankind has existed, wherever life has been, there also has been the faith that gave the possibility of living. Faith is the sense of life, that sense by virtue of which man does not destroy himself, but continues to live on. It is the force whereby we live. If Man did not believe that he must live for something, he would not live at all. The idea of an infinite God, of the divinity of the soul, of the union of men's actions with God—these are ideas elaborated in the infinite secret depths of human thought. They are ideas without which there would be no life, without which I myself," said Tolstoy, "would not exist. I began to see that I had no right to rely on my individual reasoning and neglect these answers given by faith, for they are the only answers to the question."[158]

James himself had this to say about faith:

[W]e have seen how this emotion overcomes temperamental melancholy and imparts endurance to the Subject, or a zest, or a meaning, or an enchantment and glory to the common objects of life. The name of "faith-state,". . . is a good one. It is a biological as well as a psychological condition, and Tolstoy is absolutely accurate in classing faith among the forces *by which men live*. The total absence of it, anhedonia, means collapse.[159]

Fowler pointed out that "(f)aith is not always religious in its content or context,"[160] and defined faith as follows:

Faith is a person's or group's way of moving into the force field of life. It is our way of finding coherence in and giving meaning to the multiple forces and relations that make up our lives. Faith is a person's way of seeing him- or herself in relation to others against a background of shared meaning and purpose.[161]

Fowler differentiated faith from such related terms as *religion* and *belief*. Faith clearly plays a role in relating humankind to the *total* environment, which is a role that rationality can only partially play. There are other active mental elements involved in faith, including emotions, and

---

[158] James, *The Varieties of Religious Experience*, p. 181.
[159] Ibid., p. 495.
[160] Fowler, *Stages of Faith*, p. 4.
[161] Ibid., p. 4.

they are an important part of the way that we relate to each other and to the total environment.

We all have faith, and our faith deeply affects our behavior. St. James argued, "Faith without works is dead," and he is right. Real faith—what we really believe—affects and motivates our actions. In the Sermon on the Mount, Jesus himself said, "Ye shall know them by their fruits," which implicitly carries the same message. Faith is recognized by the activity and behavior it produces. St. James is referring, at least in part, to works of Old Testament law. But at every turn it is clear that what we do reflects what we really believe. Scientists have faith in the dogmas of science. Businessmen have faith in the profit motive. We all have faith in our work—our job or profession. Faith is a part of the developmental process. Environment, especially the social environment, shapes its contents. What we must ask ourselves is whether our faith is adequate for the exigencies of the ultimate environment as we now perceive it. An adequate faith system must incorporate all that we *know* and integrate it comfortably with our intuitions about *ultimate mysteries* that exist beyond our range of provable knowledge.

Value of Religious Freedom

The United States Constitution admits the importance of the role of the Church. Freedom of religion is a constitutional guarantee. No doubt, the nation's founders protected religious freedom because of its value and their great respect for religion. It was not because of animosity towards religion, which sometimes seems to be the modern interpretation. Even though the *establishment* clause seems to receive much more attention than the *free exercise* clause, government is the beneficiary of a healthy moral base which results from religious freedom. The moral base that results from religious freedom is the basis of law.

Separation of Church and State is as essential now as it ever was. The role of the Church is to develop the inward witness. The inward witness is both the basis of law and the source of sound criticism of government. The Church fares better as the accused than as the accuser. It thrives as the persecuted, not as the persecutor. It gathers strength from adversity. It must now rise to the challenge. Its role is not to *demythologize* its message, but to *mythologize* the world—with transcendent truths of its myths. Its role is to quicken the world to the powerful symbols of its true messages. It must provide the foundation of faith, built on living history, that anticipates and includes the unfolding perception of the total environment.

Considerable tolerance has always been a strong feature of deep religious faith. In a world of subjectivity, there is room for pluralism. That does not mean that the inward witness should cease. It simply means that although immorality is an appropriate subject of religious taboo, sincere difference of opinion is not. The fact that others believe differently is no reason for an inadequate faith.

The Ultimate Need

Viktor Frankl, in *Man's Search for Meaning* says it better than I can. He is a psychiatrist who survived the rigors of concentration camp. His book deals with survival issues of life in a concentration camp. The best tool for survival, he said, was the quest for meaning. It is a story of survival because of purpose, or motive.

Values. . . do not drive a man; they do not *push* him, but rather *pull* him.

Man is never driven to moral behavior; in each instance he decides to behave morally. Man does not do so in order to satisfy a moral drive and to have a good conscience; he does so for the sake of a cause to which he commits himself, or for a person whom he loves, or for the sake of his God. If he actually did it for the sake of having a good conscience, he would become a Pharisee and cease to be a truly moral person.[162]

His concluding paragraph capsulizes what I am saying about the inadequacy of reason alone, or even conscience, as the transcendent source of values:

Our generation is realistic, for we have come to know man as he really is. After all, man is that being who has invented the gas chambers of Auschwitz; however, he is also that being who has entered those gas chambers upright, with the Lord's Prayer or the *Shema Yisrael* on his lips.[163]

As I mentioned in the foreword, faith is a cornerstone of law. Belief systems preserve the values that sustain law. The internalized values fire the furnaces of motive both for obeying and enforcing law. They form conscience. They tell us how to relate to each other. They fulfill our most basic needs, including the need for meaning. In the next chapter, we will look at some of the contents of those facets of our faith that sustain the legal system, as we explore justice.

---

162 Frankl, *Man's Search for Meaning*, pp. 157-158.
163 Ibid., p. 213.

Chapter 6.2   Justice and Faith

Our faith in justice knows no bounds. Dr. Martin Luther King, Jr., had absolute confidence in justice when he wrote from the Birmingham Jail. Lawrence Kohlberg, who wrote extensively about moral formation, frequently referred to justice, as did Abraham Maslow and Dr. G. Carl Menninger. James Fowler's writing, quoted in the previous chapter, often referred to justice. We could expand the list indefinitely, and it would include names of many other distinguished persons.

Faith in justice is the basis for our confidence in law. If we did not believe that justice really exists, we could not possibly be motivated to construct a legal system. We really believe that right and wrong exist. We believe that we can find the difference between them. We believe that order is better than chaos, and that there are just principles for establishing social order. I am not certain that we always know what justice is. Nevertheless, we *believe* it exists. Our faith in justice is implicit and unquestioning. We seldom even ask what justice is. We think that we know. For us, justice is as real as the air we breathe and ground we walk on.

This faith in justice shows the importance of faith and adequate faith systems, which we discussed in the preceding chapter. Our faith in justice is the foundational belief that supports law. We not only believe in justice, we believe that we can, at least sometimes, capture it in our legal system. Our faith—what we really believe—is the immediate source of justice. Without our composite faith system, justice could not exist. Justice will exist as long as we have faith in it.

We come into this world, as Wordsworth pointed out, with intimations of immortality. Our finiteness and imperfection lead inexorably to the conclusion that perfection exists. Our incompleteness causes us to sense completeness. Unless there is completeness, there is no incompleteness; unless there is perfection, there is no imperfection. In our incompleteness, we reach out for completion, and this is the basis for religious impulse. This is the arena in which faith operates. It is the need to achieve the infinite; to find meaning; to relate to the ultimate environment. The impossibility of achieving perfection is irrelevant. We are discussing *motive* forces. The cow can try to jump over the moon, even while scoffing little dogs laugh. Justice is the perennial hope and aspiration for our imperfect, incomplete legal system. It is the attractive force that directs our motive power.

Justice truly is a dinosaur in the Age of Reason. It is quite metaphysical. It is a *universal*, like those decimated at the outset of the Age of Reason. William of Ockham's penetrating analysis, sometimes called Ockham's razor, carved away the basis of many universals which had dominated the thinking of the Middle Ages. This helped to pave the way for the empirical scientific method. Today, many people say the word *justice*. However, when pressed for a definition, few can give one that is satisfactory.

The Reality of Justice

What is the nature of justice? It certainly is not tangible. We do not contact it with the five senses. Does it exist independently in the cosmos, or is it merely a creation of human reason? If the legal system condemns someone without giving him a hearing, we call it *unjust*. Likewise, when two people convicted under the same set of facts receive grossly unequal punishment, we label it *unjust*. If a jury finds a person not guilty, and then police file new charges arising out of the same factual circumstances, we again yell *unjust*. Precisely what do all three of these examples have in common? Go ahead and try to word an answer. Then check your answer to see if it is *objective*.

Trying to answer this question generates such terms as *equality, due process, fundamental fairness, notice requirements*, or others. The only term that applies to all three examples is *fairness*, which is a synonym for justice. It adds nothing to our understanding. The three examples have as little in common with each other as members of Durkheim's lizard clan had with lizards. Placing these examples in a class or category with the name *unjust* is quite arbitrary. There is no common element which makes them all members of a single class.

Nevertheless, we all agree that each of these three actions is *unjust*. Maybe we could argue that justice has different attributes such as *equality, due process* and *finality*. However, this provides no rational element— no intrinsic, qualitative similarity—that forms a basis for definition. Perhaps we could argue that each of these examples violates our *sense of justice*. It does, but now the word *justice* has crept back into the definition, along with an emotional tone. As with *law* in Auden's poem, quoted at length earlier, justice is *justice*. We can find no other word that really adds clarity to its meaning.

When we discussed authentication, we referred to *authenticating* principles. These are rules by which we make or confirm other rules. If the legislature tried to legalize any of the three examples given above, we would label those very laws *unjust*. Some people have tried to define justice as exact and uniform enforcement of law. This was a tenet of Kant's system. It was also an Old Testament approach to justice. Old Testament righteousness involved faithful adherence to law. Sin was any departure from the law. The Old Testament did not seem to make any distinction between morals and law, which reinforces the impression that our distinction between law and morality is an abstraction of the Church/state dichotomy. However, defining justice as exact compliance with law obviously will not work. As Dr. King pointed out, there can be laws that are unjust, although properly enacted by a power majority. We might add that a power majority can occur in a fully representative legislative body.

Perhaps, as someone said about pornography, we don't know how to define justice, but we recognize it when we see it. However, despite the inherent difficulty of definition, justice is quite important, and commands a tremendous emotional basis of support. Imminent researchers, including Kohlberg, Maslow, Piaget, Menninger, and other proponents of objectivity, appeal to the word *justice* as the foundation of their theories. Their appeal does not negate its completely subjective quality. The word *justice* also crops up, undefined, in writings of legal philosophers. Do they all have the same meaning in mind? How can we know whether they do or not?

Church literature is full of it: *peace with justice, social justice, racial justice*. Was the justice that Amos wanted to roll down like waters the same as our justice? What in the world do you suppose we're talking about? Do we know? Suffice it to say that justice is a very important article of our collective faith. Its origins transcend our rationality. However, again as Auden said of law, we know that justice "is, and that all know this." Without our collective certainty of the existence of justice, it would not exist in human society.

Kohlberg points out that Socrates (according to Plato) held that *justice is one*. However, such an assertion is more a matter of faith than of knowledge. Justice is of like kind with truth or beauty or other similar terms. We could subject those terms to the same jarring analysis to which we subjected justice. After all, what do roses really have in common with the *Mona Lisa* or a scenic mountain range? We are dealing with the similarities between lizards and lizard clans again. However, like beauty and truth, justice exists. I believe it. We all do, and this is what they have in common. In a very real sense, they exist because we believe, but the result nevertheless proves very useful in promoting survival.

Justice and Reason

Possibly the preceding discussion will not convince you that justice is a matter of faith rather than a matter of reason. I have asserted several times earlier that reason itself has become an article of our faith. Reason comports with our perception of the cosmos. We formulate theories based on principles that we believe clear and obvious. We check our experience using those principles and arrive at other principles. The system extends itself to what we consider a basis for all phenomena. If we don't understand something, our faith in rationality tells us that we simply have not deduced the correct explanation yet. We still think the answer is somewhere in the system. This, of course, is purely a matter of faith. I am not suggesting that it is an improper exercise of faith. It appears to work well.

Nevertheless, we do not know where insights come from that allow us to expand the rational system. If we had no faith in the system of rational thought, we would have no faith in its expansions. If we did not believe that solutions exist, we wouldn't look for them. The usefulness of the rational system is an evolving process. Intuition is the cutting edge of social evolution. It is not the nature of the external world that has rapidly expanded and changed over the past several hundred years. The evolution is in our own thought processes. It is in our *perception* of the external world. Growth depends on faith.

Even in the most basic principles that provide starting points for our rational system, there are important assumptions. We assume that the observer is distinct from the observed phenomena. Moreover, we believe that the process of observing neither adds nor detracts from the matter observed. Such is not the case. If we see a vehicle moving along a roadway, what actually happens is that the senses send the brain certain impulses. The brain transforms those impulses and records them as a series of impressions or images. *Concepts,* such as motion, force, time, and space result from the mind's effort to organize the material. The mind *adds* concepts and organization. Matters derived from the mind are articles of faith or belief, not observation. We can't see *force,* for instance.

We see only material objects that appear to change or move. We theorize force.

We have faith in the consistent behavior of matter and energy. We subject a chemical to certain conditions, and it behaves a certain way. It will behave the same way again if we repeat those conditions. Pure water freezes at 32 degrees Fahrenheit every time. Scientific proof depends on the ability of others to repeat an experiment with the same results. The scientific method depends on our ability to mutually *verify* our shared reality. Seen in this light, science is merely a formalization or toughening of the process by which we precipitate a picture of reality from shared beliefs. Obviously, our faith is appropriate, but it is faith nevertheless. It doesn't work because we believe it; we believe it because it works and we can share it. This does not make faith unimportant. Faith is part of the way we share reality. This observed consistency works well in the *physical sciences,* at least at an elementary level. But Durkheim points out:

> It may be objected that science is often the antagonist of opinion, whose errors it combats and rectifies. But it cannot succeed in this task if it does not have sufficient authority, and it can obtain this authority only from opinion itself. *If a people did not have faith in science, all the scientific demonstrations in the world would be without any influence* whatsoever over their minds. Even to-day, if science happened to resist a very strong current of public opinion, it would risk losing its credit there. (Emphasis added)[164]

The matter becomes even more problematical when we try to apply scientific principles of observation to the social sciences. Here the observer and the observed are one. Humans are interpreting humans. The impact of the observer's mental processes is much more pronounced than in the physical sciences. Whether we believe it because it works, or it works because we believe it, becomes a much more difficult problem in the social sciences. The observer cannot possibly detach himself from the observed phenomena.

When we try to derive justice logically, appeal to nature is of little avail. In nature, there are food chains and predatory habits enough to dispel any notion of an *observed* state of justice in nature. Among some of our relatives in the animal kingdom, we see parents caring for young and for each other, and protecting territory. We even see groups that cooperate for security. But even in these examples, which clearly relate to social order, the word justice will not fit. Big fish actually eat little fish. We may

---

164 Durkheim, *The Elementary Forms of the Religious Life,* p. 239.

be at the threshold of applying our concept of justice to other animals, given the current interest in animal rights. However, it does not occur to us to *expect* justice of non-human beings. Just because we treat rats more humanely does not mean they will reciprocate. They will likely go on acting like rats. Some may say I have chosen an example with a bad image for this bit of satire. However, snail darters and whales won't reciprocate justice, either. Let me hasten to add, though, that if we chop down the rain forests and kill all its animals, we won't be able to breathe. There is good reason for us to respect nature. Failure to do so can give rise to justice issues. Thus even if justice is an eternal verity, a metaphysical universal, it is nevertheless a human quality. It arrives on the social scene *via* humans. As with principles of science, we believe in justice because it works, and we can share a perception of it. The fact that it works is a sufficient basis for its reality, just as is the case with the principles of science. Because of its human quality, however, justice clearly is an article of faith, and it works because we believe in it.

Justice: The Basis of Rationality

Existence of justice is a basic assumption of law. It is an article of our faith. Appeal to justice is the basis for rationality in law, by the religious and the irreligious alike. Like all rational systems, we begin with an *assumption*. The impulse to law, and the dynamic processes that cause law to happen do not happen because of reason. They have already asserted themselves before reason takes hold. Reason rightly asserts itself as a tool of adaptation in articulating, formally authenticating and enforcing law. It asserts itself in the medium of language, but it fades away again as we aspire to absolute justice. Justice is the transcendent basis of reason in matters legal. It is a matter of faith: the substance of things hoped for. Reason acts on that substance to produce law.

Justice itself appears to transcend individual mental processes. Earlier, in the discussion of language, we showed that all abstract terms for which there is shared meaning transcend individuals, in that they exist socially. This gives abstractions of a culture a life of their own, independent of individuals. It makes them almost completely external to the individual, in a sense, because they exist independently of each individual, in other individuals. The appearance of externality is important, and in the case of law, contributes to coercive power.

Justice transcends our finiteness and we only know it as it transcends *into* our field of knowledge. Recall the earlier discussions of Durkheim's idea that collective representations shared by a large group transcend individuals and exist and can be perpetuated in society. They are projected as an external reality, and have an existence of their own, independently of any particular individual. We sense that justice has meaning even more profound than the externality created by the collective belief system. We can only intimate such further aspects. We cannot express them. They appear to arise beyond the dimension of duality which gives rise to expressible human knowledge. The Biblical, "peace which passeth all understanding," is much more than just a trite saying. The author of that statement, no doubt, believed there is essence that transcends all words and all rationality. It is like the bell in a steeple. We don't see it. The rope dangles (transcends) through a hole in the ceiling. We know the bell is there, because it rings when we pull the rope. Peace is one of the many characteristic traits, or goals, of justice. Like peace, there is also justice which "passeth all understanding." In the words of St. Paul, we see "through a glass darkly." We cannot escape Plato's cave to inspect justice in the bright sunshine of reality.

We find a middle ground between ourselves and medieval universals by examining unconscious mental processes described by Freud and Jung and social development of *concepts* and conceptual thinking described by Durkheim. After all, that is where moral formation occurs. The universals of metaphysics may be psychological projections of and from the realm of the unconscious into the social arena.

Collective Representations

My references in this chapter to lizards and lizard clans have not been accidental. Emile Durkheim taught us that when members of the lizard clan came to believe they were one with the lizard, they founded a useful category. It was a beginning point for the conception of categories as such, and therefore, the origin of logical thinking. It provided the basis for sharing a reality—the *ultimate environment*, in Fowler's terminology. It provided a basis for identity. We understand errors of the ways of the people of the lizard clan, and probably have a better grasp of reality. However, they were sharing their reality to the limits of their understanding. It is in this realm of shared reality that we do our conceptual thinking. Thus, the group is necessary for there to be conceptual thinking, as we have demonstrated earlier.

The primitive totemism of the lizard clan and all other clans provided a means of social conformity. Their confidence in the reality of what they believed vested that "reality" with enough emotional strength to enforce moral norms of the group. Lizards, after all, were supposed to do things a certain way. It was expected. The high school athletic teams in my hometown are Tallassee Tigers. Tigers are supposed to behave in a particular way. Christians are supposed to behave a certain way, because of their identity as Christians.

Myths of the clan generated a system of beliefs, you will recall. Durkheim identified those commonly shared beliefs as *collective representations*. We have shown that they may be supported by Jung's *archetypes*. Merely because faith creates and sustains beliefs does not make *shared beliefs* unreal. After all, our faith in reason does not make reason unreal. As we believe in reason, the lizard clan believed what they believed, because it worked for them. It produced order. It helped them satisfy basic human needs. It may not have brought rains, as they believed, but it brought order, which was valuable. The assumptions on which we base our rational system are simply more obscure than beliefs of the lizard clan. They have no more reality, beyond the fact that they are shared and useful. The mere fact that a belief is shared gives it a certain type of reality and power, especially in matters of behavior.

In our own social reality, collective representations continue to be important. They continue to bring order to our lives. Moreover, they are still matters of faith. *Justice and law are collective representations.* We construct them from other collective representations: *equality, finality, due process,* and others. You will recall that collective representations are synthesized from, and perpetuated in, myths, narratives, themes, songs, and all the other forms of expression that we included in the concept of mythos. Belief is not discretionary or a matter of indifference. Since order promotes human survival, *we must believe in our collective representations if we are to survive. Other people* are real and are a part of our environment. Justice lets us live together. Like the lizard clan, we have no higher perception. These beliefs are a part of our ultimate environment. We may generate them ourselves, with the support of archetypes embedded in psychic structure, but that does not detract from their reality, even though we may have a more accurate perception tomorrow. This analysis does not exclude transcendency, since we do not yet know the origin of thoughts. Indeed, belief in an ultimate reality, of which our expressed beliefs are mere shadows, is an essential part of the motive power of faith.

Mystery shrouds our very existence. Therefore, an immediate human origin of beliefs does not exclude an Author of law and justice beyond our own finite being. After all, as we saw in the preceding chapter, our faith systems must explain our ultimate environment. It includes much more than justice and law, and even individual thought processes. Despite our inner world in which we actually live, none of us is prepared to say "I'm all there is to it." Who would we say it to? Have we added anything by saying "We're all there is to it," as we begin to understand the power of our collective beliefs? No, our collective beliefs are sustained by faith that they are not mere beliefs, but participate in a transcendent reality.

Perceptions of Justice

We have our perceptions of justice which call us, inexorably, to law. We respond to these perceptions with highly energized archetypes, funded with specific content by our culture. Justice, in the modern world-view, always includes consistency, uniformity, due process, finality and equality. These concepts surface in stories that give them meaning. Justice will not involve undue delays, but will be timely and final. It will be fair. The remedy will be commensurate with the wrong. It will promote survival, and even happiness. There is symmetry about it. Our beliefs about justice include all of this. We can all think of hundreds of stories to illustrate each of these categories. That is exactly what the case method does. We believe the stories told in cases; and by them, we authenticate our beliefs about law. Our collective representations, or collective images of justice, support our beliefs about justice. Indeed, the beliefs are collective representations. To some extent, our perceptions of justice may be projections of aspirations and hopes, rather than recognition of hard reality. Abraham Maslow observed:

> Finally, I must point out that we shall have to prepare ourselves in principle for the shocking consequences of giving up the alibi of social injustice. The more we continue to reduce social injustice, the more we shall find this replaced by biological injustice, by the fact that babies are born into the world with different genetic potentials. If we get to the point of giving full opportunity to every baby's good potentials, then this means accepting poor potentials as well. Whom shall we blame when a baby is born with a bad heart, or weak kidneys, or with neurological defects? If only nature is there to blame, what will this mean for the self-esteem of the individual "unfairly" treated by nature itself?[165]

When we articulate outward, observable manifestations of justice, we are projecting our deepest inward intuitions of justice. We are participating in collective representations. As we saw in territoriality, different

---

[165] Maslow, *Motivation and Personality*, p. xviii.

cultures fund these inner images differently. In coming to grips with justice, we engage in a complex and inescapable interaction with culture. Underlying it all and very imperceptible is the practical consideration of cultural survival; of meeting basic human needs. The existence of different *perceptions* of justice in different cultures only reflects our finite, incomplete natures. This is true, even though the perceptions may be contradictory and even antagonistic. Our imperfect perceptions of justice imply the perfect and complete concept. This is the essence of transcendency, and the transcendent nature of justice.

Justice and Religion

Our perceptions of justice thus consist of a group of collective representations which mythos of culture assigns specific contents. However, archetypes deeply embedded in human nature itself are nature's way of assuring our response. The response is as certain, and as nonrational as sex. Justice is not merely a free-floating, external metaphysical phenomenon. Constant interactions between deep psychological forces of individuals and mythos of society maintain its images. The process is necessary and natural. The clear truths of the justice of western civilization are *clear* only because they are a part of the mythos of the West. Most of them have roots in the Judeo-Christian heritage.

These perceptions of justice and law are a part of a workable system based on universal archetypes shared by all humankind. Therefore, they are a valid approach to truth. Moreover, since archetypes are of primordial and unknown etiology, there is no suggestion in any of this discussion that contradicts traditional beliefs. In fact, the explanation just given provides a strong argument *for* the true role of religion in culture in dealing with transcendent truth.

Justice, like Moses' pillar of fire, pulls us onward to our destiny. It directs us toward our highest ideals and aspirations—our promised land. It enables us to deal with our ultimate environment. It engages our faith. Because of our faith, we continually try to secure justice in human affairs. Our faith brings about our actions.

The question is whether we will place our faith in reason, or in some other source, for law. The answer is clear. Reason alone is a mere tool of adaptation. It is devoid of meaning. It is neither the source of justice, nor the source of law. We must look to other aspects of human nature for the immediate source of law. We are condemned to faith. Will our faith be big enough to encompass civilization, yet founded on a reality that may be inarticulable? Can we place our faith in a reality that we know only intuitively and by analogy? Yes, we can. Our faith at present includes belief in a transcendent justice of infinite proportions which we believe that we can capture in finite articulable laws. This faith is essential to the existence of law. Justice is not just a rational solution to a problem.

What I have just said is a very dangerous truth to reveal to an Age of Reason. The faith that sustains the legal system is an unquestioning, *supposed knowledge*. If the masses were to realize that it is *merely faith* that supports the legal system, then civilization could collapse like a house of cards. The force that undergirds law could disappear. The same could be said, however, of the monetary system and our faith in the dollar. And at this juncture, I should point out that faith is not something we can turn on and off like a faucet. Also, faith can be misguided—we can believe the wrong things. For the masses, belief in law as an external reality may be a condition for law's existence. Law's reality is at least *partly* external, since for any individual, it emanates primarily from *other* people in the social system. But we cannot trust solely in our reasoning capacity. In other aspects of our environment, our rationality has led us into grave danger. Our rational activities threaten the system of ecology that exists in nature. Let's not make the same kinds of mistakes about forces that undergird law.

Faith Can Be Simple

This section is a complex expression of my faith. My faith is helpful and satisfying to me. My friend, the late Fannye Harris, served as president of the Tuskegee Civic Association, a pioneer civil rights organization in Macon County. She often said, "Judge Segrest, there is a God in Heaven, and He is in charge of what happens here." Coming from her, during an election when my job was at stake, the words were very comforting.

The Bible says, "The fool hath said in his heart, there is no God."[166] My theory is not inconsistent with the existence of God, nor with the divine origin of law. I do not suggest that the theory *proves* God's existence or the divine origin of law. For believers, I hope that my theory suggests the infinitely complex nature of God's creativity. As J. B. Phillips suggested, our image—in fact any image of God—is too small. Proofs are for rationalists. God is the ground of our being; not we of His. Justice shines into our lives in the *inward* dimensions of our being, and our faith in it is sound. The bid for survival affects many matters, includ-

---

[166] Psalms 14:1

ing human motive for law. Survival is not the source of meaning: meaning causes survival. Our quest is for meaning, not merely for survival. The quest for meaning *causes* us to survive. Justice gives meaning to law.

7 | The Paradox

efore I admit the crowning paradox of this entire effort, let me present an analogy, which portrays law's paradoxical nature.

The Analogy of a Stream

In Chapter 1.1, I mentioned the Taoist oxymoron, "What is useful about a spoon?" It suggested the usefulness of nothingness. Later, I raised the same question about the usefulness of a house. In both of these instances, I developed the same theme. It is the *nothingness*, surrounded by the material structure, that is actually useful. It is not the roof, walls, or even the floor of a room that is useful. Space enclosed between the roof, walls and floor makes the house useful.

Law is essentially negative. Civilization is the house which it forms. Law restricts. It does not *provide* freedom, but perhaps the *protected area* enclosed within the restrictions of law *allows* freedom. As civilization progresses, the allowed freedoms (and rights) grow with the growth of law (and duty). Perhaps this is what is useful about law. Law and freedom each seem to be a condition for the existence of the other.

A Taoist might ask, "What is useful about the banks of a stream?" Of course, in this instance, there is at least one answer. Banks keep streams from overflowing; banks keep the stream on course. But if there were no water, what would be useful about the banks of the stream? If there were no social life, what would be useful about law?

As a stream courses its way downhill toward the sea, it cuts it own path. Joining other streams, it has more and more force as it proceeds. It picks up bits of soil here and there and deposits them elsewhere, forming its own bed as it goes. This is similar to the way law works. Life itself and human nature create motive for law, like the stream creates its own banks. Banks are not the ends for which the stream exists. Although they direct the stream along its course, the stream itself creates the banks.

Individuals are both the recipient of a genetic predisposition to orderliness and the beneficiary of mythos that shapes culture. Interaction between individuals and society is the fountainhead of law—the origin of the stream. Family and significant others—the microcosm—are exchange points of critical values that flow into law. Small tributaries of opinion unite to form larger streams, with more force. Psychological force of individual opinions coalesces into a mighty moving current of law. All streams find their way to the sea. In our analogy, neither the fountainhead nor the sea is the law. The force is the moving current as it courses downward.

Neither is law the ends, but a means. Law is the hollow, well-travelled course, created by the vital force of life in society. In society, many individual impulses join to form the collective force that creates law, like streams come together to produce larger streams. From time to time, the location of the bed of the stream moves. It is the force of the stream that changes it, like the force of life changes law.

If we assume that law is like the banks of a stream, then in and of itself, law is useless. If there were no water, the banks would be nothingness. Without living forces, law is nothingness. However, there can be no stream without banks, and there can be no life of a society without law. The freedom of the stream is relative. Banks restrict it, although it creates the banks with its own flow. Streams differ: no two are alike. Law varies from culture to culture also. There are forces which create the dynamics of streams, and there are forces that create the dynamics of law.

I have said that streams create their own banks. Am I saying that people create their own laws? The answer, in a sense, is *yes*. The immediate cause of law arises in human motive force in the manner that we have described. However, this is not the end of the matter. Does the water itself create banks of the stream? No, it is actually the force of gravity pulling the water ever downward that creates the banks, isn't it? No, the force of the sun picks up the water and brings it back to the source. Perhaps it is the two opposing forces. If it is actually these forces, which are the same everywhere, then why do streams differ? Is it the resistance of the soil? Is it all of these?

The immediate cause of law may be human nature, augmented by mythological and psychological mechanisms that I have described. However, final causes are like these external forces that affect droplets of water in a stream. The droplets obviously do not fully contain all the forces that are at work. We are in the same position as a drop of water, concerning ultimate forces. After all, where did the archetypes that we have discussed come from? Where does intuition come from? Where does justice arise?

Law is very similar to the banks of the stream. It restricts. It directs. It keeps the stream on course. It organizes. Nevertheless, we do not understand a stream simply by analyzing its banks. Likewise, it is pointless to look for the meaning of law in the banks or the bottom of the river of life. The banks of the stream are the counterpart of law. The dynamics of law arise from the river of life itself. Any amount of sifting the soil of the banks and bottom will not reveal the true nature and purpose of law. It will not add to our understanding of law's meaning. This is what we do with the case method.

We may put a dam here and there on a river. We may build levies or dikes to keep it from overflowing the countryside, but forces well beyond our control determine the course of great rivers. It is the same with law.

After the Church bombing deaths of four children in Birmingham, Alabama, at the height of the Civil Rights struggle, Dr. Martin Luther King, Jr., spoke out. "We will not be satisfied until justice rolls down like waters and righteousness like a mighty stream," he proclaimed, paraphrasing Amos 5:24. Law is merely the banks of the stream, formed by justice and giving direction to justice. Dr. King's eloquence resulted in many new laws and decisions that brought about greater justice. He struck the resonating chord. Mythos was there. While his appeal was imminently reasonable, his appeal was not to reason. Justice is the *basis* of law's reasonableness. It reflects in our mythos and is part of our being. Reason is not the basis of justice.

The Paradox

So there you have it. I have unburdened myself of my thoughts about what makes law work. More than anyone, I realize that the processes involved are much larger than I can capture in a single volume. I read somewhere that a written linguistic description of the known biological and physiological processes of the human body would occupy more than 200 volumes. In a sense, those 200 volumes are a starting point for the much more complicated processes of motive that produce law. Here, we *start* with living human beings, so we already have 200 volumes worth of information with which to wrestle.

I have said that the origin of law is non-rational. I have made it clear that motive for law arises from unconscious processes. Normative processes that produce law cannot prosper in the withering light of reason. They partake of affective behavior with a full measure of love, affection, concern, guilt, anger, shame, indignation, humiliation, and lots of other words that we use to describe various emotions. I have thoroughly disparaged reason as the origin or motive force for law.

I will not await some future Albert Camus to explain again the Myth of Sisyphus for my benefit. This book is, itself, an exercise in analytical reason. The medium is the printed word. The words purport to discuss and analyze dynamic processes, some of which are usually unconscious processes. The words try to apply reason. In his biting essay, Camus showed that all irrationalists ultimately face this paradox.

> It is futile to be amazed by the apparent paradox that leads thought to its own negation by the opposite paths of humiliated reason and triumphal reason. From the abstract god of Husserl to the dazzling god of Kierkegaard the distance is not so great. Reason and the irrational lead to the same preaching. In truth the way matters but little; the will to arrive suffices.[167]

I am, therefore, banished to a position similar to that of psychologists earlier in this century who reportedly decided that communication is impossible and who actually tried to argue the point! Or perhaps I can be compared to those who argue for absolute determinism as if their argument made a difference. Contrary to my argument, I have used reason. I hope I got Sisyphus' rock somewhere near the top of the hill before it rolled back to crush me.

We may not be able to penetrate the unconscious. Nevertheless, the unconscious and its progeny of taboos, mandates, prohibitions, symbols and archetypes is a useful logical construct. We can deal with it within the realm of reason. This does not make the origin of these motive forces *rational*. To point at the ocean is not to describe it and identify everything in it. The unconscious and its forces are as vast and mysterious as the ocean, and to name it is not to control it. Comparison of the unconscious to the ocean is not accidental. The sense of cosmic significance is sometimes described as *oceanic*. Freud and Jung argued that water often symbolically represents the unconscious. The Apocryphal Book of Second Esdras describes a parable in which the sea and the forest each formed a plan to take over territory of the other. The forest was

---

[167] Camus, *The Myth of Sisyphus*, p. 35.

destroyed by fire, and the sea held back by sand. Conscious and unconscious each have their valuable roles to play, but they do not displace each other. Students of the psyche found that discovery of the *existence* of the unconscious is helpful in understanding individuals. Likewise, it will be helpful for us to recognize the role of unconscious processes in the motive force that creates law.

Unfortunately, the unconscious and the non-existent have much in common. We are unaware of both. It would be a major intellectual accomplishment for this age if we learned to distinguish between the two. The line dividing them is *not* at the edge of scientific proof. Sigmund Freud created an awareness of the unconscious processes of the individual. However, we have not begun to explore the vast implications of those unconscious processes in the social arena. It is in that great, unexplored abyss that the motive for law arises.

If this book is a start toward an understanding of what makes law happen, I have attained my goal. Thinkers more qualified than I can develop and amplify the ideas.

Bibliography

Ardrey, Robert. *The Territorial Imperative*. Atheneum, 1967.

Argyle, Michael. *Social Interaction*. Chicago: Aldine, 1969.

Auden, W. H. *Selected Poems*, edited by Edward Mendelson. New York: Vintage, 1979.

Bagdikian, Ben H. *The Media Monopoly*. Beacon Press, 1983.

Bettelheim, Bruno. *The Uses of Enchantment*. New York: Random House, 1977.

Blackstone, Sir William. *Commentaries on the Laws of England*, First Edition 1803. New York: Reprinted, Rothman Reprints, Inc., edited by St. George Tucker, in five volumes, 1969.

Blakeslee, Thomas R. *The Right Brain*. Anchor Press, 1980.

Bolen, Jean Shinoda. *The Tao of Psychology*. San Francisco: Harper, 1982.

Buber, Martin. *I and Thou*.

Bultman, Rudolf. *New Testament and Mythology and Other Basic Writings*, selected, edited and translated by Schubert M. Ogelen. Philadelphia: Fortress Press, 1984.

Campbell, Joseph. *Creative Mythology*. New York: Penguin, 1968.

———. *Myths to Live By*. New York: Viking/Penguin, 1972.

———. *Occidental Mythology*. New York: Penguin, 1968.

———. *Oriental Mythology*. New York: Penguin, 1968.

———. *Primitive Mythology*. New York: Penguin, 1968.

———. *The Hero With a Thousand Faces*. Princeton: Princeton University Press, 1949.

Camus, Albert. *The Myth Sisyphus*. New York: Vintage, 1955.

Capra, Fritjof. *The Tao of Physics*. Boston: New Science Library, 1985.

Carson, Rachel. *Silent Spring*. Boston: Houghton Mifflin, 1962.

Cary, M. and Scullard, H. H. *History of Rome*, third edition. New York: St. Martin's Press, 1975.

Cicero. *Laws Book II: The Great Legal Philosophers*, edited by Clarence Morris. University of Pennsylvania Press, 1959.

———. *The Nature of the Gods*. New York: Penguin, 1972.

Cohen, Felix S. *Ethical Systems and Legal Ideals*. Cornell University Press, 1959.

Coon, Dennis. *Introduction to Psychology*, fourth edition. St. Paul: West, 1986.

Copleston, Frederick J. *A History of Philosophy, Vol. I*. New York: Newman, 1946.

Durkheim, Emile. *Sociology and Philosophy*, translated by D. F. Pocock. New York: The Free Press, 1953.

———. *The Elementary Forms of the Religious Life*. New York: Free Press, 1915.

Eliade, Mircea. *The Sacred and the Profane*. New York: Harcourt, 1957.

Fast, Julius. *Body Language*. New York: Pocket, 1971.

Fowler, James W. *Stages of Faith*. New York: Harper, 1981.

Frank, Jerome. *Law and the Modern Mind*. New York: Coward-McCann, 1930.

Frankl, Viktor E. *Man's Search for Meaning*. New York: Pocket Books, 1959.

———. *The Unconscious God*. New York: Simon and Schuster, 1975.

Frazer, James G. *The Golden Bough*. New York: MacMillan, 1972.

Freud, Anna. *Psycho-Analysis for Teachers and Parents*. New York: Emerson, 1935.

Freud, Sigmund. *Civilization and Its Discontents*, translated by James Strachey. New York: Norton, 1961.

———. *New Introductory Lectures on Psychoanalysis*. New York: Norton, 1933.

Fuller, L. Lon. *Anatomy of the Law*. New York: Praeger, 1968.

Garrow, David J. *Bearing the Cross*. New York: Random House, 1986.

Halbert, H. S. and Ball, T. H. *The Creek Indian War of 1813 and 1814*. Tuscaloosa: University of Alabama Press, 1969.

Hall, Calvin S. and Nordby, Vernon J. *A Primer of Jungian Psychology*. New York: Penguin, 1973.

Haugen, E. "Dialect, Language, Nation," in *American Anthropologist*, Vol. 68, 1966.

Hirsch, E. D., Jr. *Cultural Literacy*. Boston: Houghton, 1987.

Hobbes, Thomas. *Leviathan*. New York: Collier/Macmillan, 1962 (First published in 1651).

Hopcke, Robert H. *A Guided Tour of the Collected Works of C. G. Jung*. Boston: Shambhala, 1989.

James, William. *The Varieties of Religious Experience*. New York: The Modern Library, 1936.

Jaynes, Julian. *The Origin of Consciousness in the Breakdown of the Bicameral Mind*. New York: Houghton, 1982.

Johnson, Robert A. *We*. New York: Harper, 1983.

Jung, C. G. *Psychological Types*. Princeton: Princeton University Press, 1971.

Katsh, Ethan M. *The Electronic Media and the Transformation of Law*. Oxford: Oxford University Press, 1989.

Katan, Anny. "Some Thoughts About the Role of Verbalization in Early Childhood," in *The Psychoanalytic Study of the Child, Vol. XVI*.

Kant, Immanuel. *Critique of Pure Reason*, from *The European Philosophers from Descartes to Nietzsche*, edited by Monroe C. Beardsley. New York: Random House, 1960.

Kilpatrick, William Kirk. *The Seduction of Psychology*. Thomas Nelson, 1983.

Lankford, George E. *Native American Legends*. Little Rock: August House, 1987.

Leshan, Lawrence and Margenau, Henry. *Einstein's Space and Van Gogh's Sky*. New York: Macmillan, 1982.

Levi-Strauss, Claude. *The Savage Mind*. Chicago: University of Chicago Press, 1966.

Mackay, Charles. *Extraordinary Popular Delusions and the Madness of Crowds*. New York: Page, 1932 (First published in London in 1841).

Malinowski, Bronislaw. *Crime and Custom in Savage Society*.

Maslow, Abraham H. *Motivation and Personality*. New York: Harper, 1954

———. *Motivation and Personality, Second Edition*. New York: Harper, 1970.

Menninger, G. Carl. *Whatever Became of Sin?* New York: Hawthorn, 1973.

Mill, John Stuart. *On Liberty*. New York: The Legal Classics Library, 1992.

Moore, A. B. *History of Alabama*. Nashville: Benson, 1934.

Morris, Clarence. *The Justification of the Law*. University of Pennsylvania Press, 1971.

Newcomb, Theodore M. *Social Psychology*. New York: Holt, Rinehart and Winston, 1960.

Nietzche, Frederich. *Beyond Good and Evil*, translated and edited by Walter Kaufman in *Basic Writings of Nietzsche*. New York: Random House, 1966.

———. *The Will to Power*, translated by Walter Kaufman and H. J. Hollingdale; edited by Walter Kaufman. New York: Random House, 1967.

———. *Thus Spoke Zarathustra*, translated and edited by Walter Kaufman. New York: Viking, 1954.

Nonet, Philippe and Selznick, Philip. *Law and Society in Transition: Toward Responsive Law*, Octagon, 1978.

Norrell, Robert J., II. *Reaping the Whirlwind*. New York: Knopf, 1985.

Orwell, George, *1984*.

Parks, Joseph Howard and Moore, Robert Edgar. *The Story of Alabama, A State History*. Atlanta: Turner, 1952.

Pascal, Blaise. *Thoughts*, from *The European Philosophers from Descartes to Nietzsche*, edited by Monroe C. Beardsley. New York: Random House, 1960.

Piaget, Jean and Inhelder, Barbel. *The Psychology of the Child*. New York: Basic, 1969.

Pirsig, Robert M. *Zen and the Art of Motorcycle Maintenance*. New York: Bantam, 1984.

Pound, Roscoe. *An Introduction to the Philosophy of Law*. New Haven: Yale University Press, 1922.

Robson, W. A. *Civilisation and the Growth of Law*. New York: MacMillan, 1935.

Rosengarten, Theodore. *All God's Dangers*. New York: Knopf, 1974.

Ruch, Floyd L. *Psychology and·Life, Fifth Edition*. Chicago: Foresman, 1958.

Shopenhauer, Arthur. *The World as Will and Idea*, from *The European Philosophers from Descartes to Nietzsche*, edited by Monroe C. Beardsley. New York: Random House, 1960.

Stumpf, Samuel Enoch. *Morality and the Law*. Nashville: Vanderbilt University Press, 1966.

Tompkins, Sylvan. *Affect-Imagery-Consciousness*. Springer, 1963.

Vickery, John B. *The Literary Impact of the Golden Bough*. Princeton: Princeton University Press, 1973.

Wilson, James Q., and Hernstein, Richard J. *Crime and Human Nature*. Simon & Schuster, 1985.

Emile Durkheim on Morality and Society, an anthology edited by Robert N. Bellach. Chicago: The University of Chicago Press, 1973.

European Philosophers from Descartes to Nietzche, edited with an Introduction by Monroe Beardsley. New York: The Modern Library, 1960.

The Basic Writings of Sigmund Freud, edited and with Introduction by A. A. Brill. New York: Random House, 1938.

The Great Legal Philosophers. Edited by Clarence Morris. University of Pennsylvania Press, 1959.

The Holy Bible. KJV.

The Wisdom of Laotse. New York: Random House, 1948.